Video Game Design

Fairchild Books
An imprint of Bloomsbury Publishing Plc

Imprint previously known as AVA Publishing

50 Bedford Square   1385 Broadway
London   New York
WC1B 3DP   NY 10018
UK   USA

www.bloomsbury.com

**FAIRCHILD BOOKS, BLOOMSBURY and the Diana logo are
trademarks of Bloomsbury Publishing Plc**

British Library Cataloguing-in-Publication Data
A catalogue record for this book is available from the British Library.

ISBN:
PB: 978-1-4725-6748-2
ePDF: 978-1-4725-6749-9

Library of Congress Cataloging-in-Publication Data
A catalog record for this book is available from the Library of Congress.

Library of Congress Control Number: 2015954101

Typeset by Roger Fawcett-Tang
Printed and bound in China

Video Game Design
Principles and Practices from the Ground Up

Michael Salmond

Fairchild Books
An imprint of Bloomsbury Publishing Plc

B L O O M S B U R Y
LONDON · OXFORD · NEW YORK · NEW DELHI · SYDNEY

CONTENTS

PART 3: SYSTEMS AND DESIGNING WORLDS

INTRODUCTION

WHAT IS THIS BOOK, AND WHO IS IT FOR?

Teaching video game design is an incredible privilege; it is as much fun to teach making games as it is to play them. Over the years I have been able to communicate some very important rules to my students about how we should all approach making better games. This book has evolved over time out of those classes. This book introduces some of the concepts and principles of video game design and goes on to apply them when making a video game for whatever platform or genre. This is because ultimately the first rule of game design is, if you want to make games, go make games. Make games, make mistakes, and learn from them. It is much better to make five bad games and learn something important from each of them than spend years trying to make a perfect game. Rule two is, to make better games, you need to be informed about the discipline and process of making video games, whether that is as an independent, maker-as-owner small team, or as part of a larger team working for a big developer.

This book covers the fundamentals and principles of video game concepts and production. This is the book for you to use as a starting point from which to think about video games and to then make them. This book has evolved from my own experiences making art video games for exhibitions as well as from the video game design courses I have taught over the years. It is further informed by the students I have taught who have gone on to work at large video game design companies, as well as those who have created their own successful independent games. It is by design that the interviews and case studies in this book are focused towards independent game production because

that is far more achievable for students. Although there are insights from the 'AAA' (big video game titles) industry and from academics like myself, who study the industry and its output, there is deliberate focus on smaller, more achievable games. Small teams working on small titles are the heart and soul of the new video game industry; it is where the student becomes the designer and where ideas can be played out without the risk of losing millions of dollars. The examples and interviews examine the passion and drive of individuals who make small games that become best-sellers because that is what I hope my students will achieve.

TIP

JUMP AROUND!

This book is not a novel, and you may read the chapters out of order if that best serves your needs. The chapters and their content do follow a logical progression, but video game design is a multi-threaded and complex process, and you may find it helpful to flip back and forth between chapters as you work on designing your game(s). Feel free!

The first two chapters are the only ones that follow a set progressive pattern because they introduce conceptualizing and analysis of games, which you will need to better understand the medium.

Once underway, jump around to areas and content that interest you and take what you need as you need it. My hope is that this book will serve as an introduction to the complex, frustrating, and rewarding process of making your first video game. There is also additional information on the book's website: **www.bloomsbury.com/Salmond-Video-Game**

As a game designer you must find your own path and create the game you want to make. There is no substitute for experience, but this book is focused on getting you from nowhere to starting earnestly creating your first game. The subject matter of this book cannot be applied wholesale to every genre or medium of video games. The book has been designed so that you can take the knowledge you need and work with it towards the process of creating a game. It offers guidance, theory, and subject matter that enable you to think of video games more deeply and to begin to understand the medium conceptually as a designer rather than as a player.

0.1

0.1
As with this perilous move in *Mirror's Edge*™ (DICE), all creative activities require a leap of faith. If you want to make video games you have to start now. Make that jump from someone who thinks about maybe one day making a game, to someone who is making a game. (image is from Mirror's Edge)

TIP | **UNDERSTANDING THE EXAMPLES IN THIS BOOK**

The examples scattered throughout this book are focused for the most part on Role Playing Games (RPGs), Action games and First Person Shooter (FPS) style games. Other genres are mentioned of course, but in order to streamline the content and make it relevant I am focusing on these popular genres/mechanics. As a game designer, it is important to understand that these principles and building blocks can be applied to a variety of video game formats and platforms. A level design for an FPS game could be modified to work just as well in an RPG game, and so on. It is the same for the platforms the games will be published to—it is not within the scope of this book to delve into the specific nuances of developing for mobile versus console, or PC to web-based platforms. The principles and practices can be adapted to any game in any genre or for any platform once they have been understood.

PART 1: CULTURE, PLAY, AND GAMES

CHAPTER ONE
SO YOU WANT TO BE A VIDEO GAME DESIGNER?

Chapter Objectives:

- Understand the nature of play.

- Define the basic terms of game, play, culture, game cultures, and game rhetorics.

- Begin the quest.

1.1
Characters from *LittleBigPlanet* and
LittleBigPlanet 2, developed by Media Molecule.

RULES AND FORMULAS

Designers, like the games they make, work within rules. The rules may be constantly evolving and may even be different from person to person or studio to studio. Yet there are rules, and most of the rules come from knowing your medium and knowing yourself. This knowledge is critical to any creative pursuit. Passion and persistence will carry you a lot further than you might think, but the video game world is becoming a crowded place; video games are released on a daily basis, some with enormous budgets and some with no budget at all. The focus of this book is not simply to help you make a game, but to help you then make a *better* game. This chapter sets you on your journey towards becoming a better game designer, and that journey begins with listening, observing, and researching.

There is no one formula for creating a successful video game. If there were, more people would do it. Being informed about the industry and the important steps that go into the process can help you devise your own strategy for creating a viable game. There is no one example—no one tutorial—that will show you how to make your game (my students try to find it every semester and so far they still have not). Instead, you need to draw from multiple sources and multiple points of interest: from psychology to art, from programming to traveling, from dreaming to sketching. Video games are often the personification of their creator; that is what makes them unique and interesting. They are the culmination of everything that person has learned and experienced, no matter what their age.

RULES AND
FORMULAS

DEFINING
GAMES

GAMES HAVE
ALWAYS BEEN
WITH US

GAME
CULTURE

INTERVIEW:
ADAM
SALTSMAN

CHAPTER
SUMMARY AND
DISCUSSION
POINTS

1.2

Aesthetics					Art	Coding
Ae					Ar	Co
Fun					Interface	Strategy
Fu					In	St
Character	Addiction	Story	Mechanic	Genre	Reward	Planning
Cr	Ad	St	Me	Ge	Rw	Pl
Levels	Audio	Originality	Feel	Pacing	Feedback	Testing
Lv	Au	Or	Fe	Pa	Fe	Te

1.2
The formula for the killer video game! Sadly, this does not exist; there is no formula that will create the "greatest video game ever." Instead, like every creative process, designing games requires hard work, inspiration, and perspiration.

DEFINING GAMES

To better understand the medium of video games, we need to explore how games and video games are defined. This is a fundamental step towards a deeper understanding of the medium. When we think about defining video games as an entertainment or expressive medium, the first question to ask is: What do we actually mean when we use the word "game"? The words "game" and "play" are much misunderstood and, in some ways, maligned words. This part of the chapter begins the exploration of what games are, how we play, why we play, and how we study games. It sets up some of the fundamental thinking within game design and explores how that informs the development of games for entertainment, learning, and simulation.

Games have been defined in many ways. The definition I will use in this book is provided by game theorist Jesper Juul in his paper, "The Game, the Player, the World: Looking for a Heart of Gameness" (2003): "A game is a rule-based formal system with a variable and quantifiable outcome, where different outcomes are assigned different values, the player exerts effort in order to influence the outcome, the player feels attached to the outcome, and the consequences of the activity are optional and negotiable."

A game is defined as different from normal life because games have agreed upon rules, goals, and defined outcomes. As an overview this works well, but there are nuances that can be extrapolated from this definition, based on the experience of playing the game.

A game's outcomes can change depending on the rules.

There may be levels of "winning" and "losing."

The player must play for there to be a game (this is known as *agency*).

The player wants to achieve the outcome or goal.

Games have consequences (win, lose, sociability, alteration of viewpoints).

1.3–1.4
WipEout HD (2008, developed by Psygnosis) and *Viva Piñata* (developed by Rare) are two very different games. What they share is what defines them as games: outcomes, goals, consequences, and player agency.

1.3

1.4

RULES AND
FORMULAS

DEFINING
GAMES

GAMES HAVE
ALWAYS BEEN
WITH US

GAME
CULTURE

INTERVIEW:
ADAM
SALTSMAN

CHAPTER
SUMMARY AND
DISCUSSION
POINTS

The games children play form the basis for the games that adults play. Many schoolyard games are nuanced and very complex, and they share elements with those we play as we grow up. Players want to feel involved and engaged with the game, and there is a desirable outcome. That may not always be to "win" or to "beat the game"; it may be just to be a part of the experience or to be with friends doing something that's fun. What all games share with one another is rules. In video games, rules can also be thought of as the game's "mechanic" (we explore rules in Chapter 2). So, for example, the mechanic of a first person shooter (FPS) game is shooting things. The action of the game is defined by the mechanic of damage, aiming, running, jumping, hiding, and so on. The game mechanic is also informed by the rules of the world, what you can and cannot shoot, how much damage you can inflict or sustain, and so on.

Rules in games such as tag are simple: Run around and try not to get caught. If you get caught, you are "it." Once you are "it," you must try to make someone else "it" by chasing them and touching them. Part of understanding video games is in the exploration and evolution of rules and mechanics. The focus is always on what makes the game engaging and interesting to play. So the game of tag has a mechanic: running and touching in an open space (often a constrained space, but not always) and then the rules of passing on the "it" from one player to another by physical proximity. There is also a layered rule-set because both players must agree that the "tag" was successful—the impact must be felt for the "it" status to be passed over.

1.5

1.5
In many ways, the *Call of Duty* franchise has defined the FPS genre, in terms of setting a standard for level design, aesthetic, and narrative.

Minor additions to the rules, such as time limits, proximity, or agreements of fairness, in a simple game speak to the discipline of game design because not all first person shooter or action games are alike. From a "core" game such as tag emerge variants such as "stick in the mud," which is the same game but with the twist that tagged players are stuck and another "free" player must tag them to liberate them from the imagined "mud." The goal of the "it" player here is to entrap all of the active players in order to "win." From variations on a core mechanic, more games evolve. This is a phenomenon that is common to game design; many FPS games have a core mechanic, but you would not say that *BioShock* (Irrational Games, 2007) and *Call of Duty Modern Warfare 3* (Infinity Ward, 2007) are the same game.

GAMES HAVE ALWAYS
BEEN WITH US

The advantage children have when playing schoolyard games is that the players can create their own rules (often on the fly) and bend or break the rules in seemingly infinite ways as long as the core gameplay (or mechanic) is maintained. In defining what a game is, there must be an understanding of what play is. As with many aspects of the human condition, we know play when we see or experience it, but we find it hard to linguistically and conceptually define what play is.

Many people have written books and academic papers on the subject of "play," and from this wealth of theory the discipline of ludology, the study of play, has formed. To better understand play, we start by looking at the history of games and play. It is not that surprising to find that we have been playing for almost as long as we have existed. In 3100 BCE, the Egyptians played the board game Senet, a game with clearly defined rules, outcomes, and behavior. *Tomb Raider: The Last Revelation* (Eidos, 1999) alludes to the long history of gaming when its character Lara Croft plays Senet as part of an in-game puzzle to open up a further level.

Many games played on consoles go further back than we may imagine. For example, a multiplayer FPS is essentially a version of the "war" game young boys (mostly, but not exclusively) play in schoolyards. Usually played across two teams, the setup is team X versus team Y. Each team pretends to shoot at the other; once "dead," a player must wait a preordained amount of time before returning to the fray. Or consider board games such as chess or Risk (Hasbro); these are the precursors to real-time strategy games (RTSs). They lack the graphics and some complexity because of the physical constraints of space (how many figures or markers can fit onto a standard sized board), but essentially, the rules of play and outcomes are the same.

TIP | **LUDOLOGY**

Ludology is the academic, critical study of games, game design, players, and their cultural roles. Ludology as a modern theoretical area of study has been based on the works of Johan Huizinga and Roger Caillois. Huizinga is a cultural historian and Caillois is a sociologist; both academics have focused on the theory that play is a cultural entity and one that creates culture. For ludologists, games are very important. They reflect our societies and offer deeper insights into who we are. Modern video games are culturally and historically connected to games that go back decades—if not thousands of years. What's changed is the delivery or the technology (screens, interfaces, artificial intelligence, and so on), the culture (video games transcend their medium into other media and are now part of popular culture), and the location (video games tend to be played inside and involve less movement than schoolyard games). The essence of play—to learn, to be entertained, and to socialize—has not changed at all.

RULES AND
FORMULAS

DEFINING
GAMES

**GAMES HAVE
ALWAYS BEEN
WITH US**

GAME
CULTURE

INTERVIEW:
ADAM
SALTSMAN

CHAPTER
SUMMARY AND
DISCUSSION
POINTS

1.6

1.6
Multiplayer online games, such as *Halo
2 Multiplayer* (Bungie Inc., 2004), are a
sophisticated technological version of many
schoolyard "war" games.

Thus, we have been playing games for eons, and though we have adapted games over time to run on new technologies, they retain much of the essence of games from thousands of years of human history. We turn now to two further questions: How do we define play as different from non-play activities? Why do we do it?

In the 1955 (13) edition of his book *Homo Ludens*, Johan Huizinga defines play as:

• A free activity standing quite consciously outside "ordinary" life.

• "Not serious," but at the same time absorbing the player intensely and utterly.

• An activity connected with no material interest, and no profit can be gained by it.

• Proceeding within its own proper boundaries of time and space according to fixed rules and in an orderly manner.

• Promoting the formation of social groupings, which tend to surround themselves with secrecy and to stress their difference from the common world by disguise or other means.

Or to put it in a slightly different way: Play is free; play is not ordinary and does not have to reflect any reality. Play does not make money (as a goal or outcome). Play, unlike real life, can take place anywhere and for any amount of time. Play is controlled and excludes those not playing the game. Play is essentially a reward unto itself.

So why do we do it? One theory is that play is an important part of our development and learning process as children. We do learn from lessons and tutorials at school and from peers as children, but play is a more fun and creative approach. Play is learning without knowing you are learning, and we use it on conscious and subconscious levels to understand the world around us.

This continues well into adulthood. For example, we may not think of our social media as a game, and yet it is. We collect friends, we post updates (almost like leaderboards), we indulge in fantasy, and we compete with others (Who has the cutest posts? Who is doing the most interesting things?). Our lives have become more and more like games, yet we do not always make these connections. This is because play and playing are so integral to our lives that we ignore elements of play in our everyday patterns of existence—but it is still there. We just tend to call it something else: for example, winning a bid on eBay or beating the odds in a checkout line and getting served first. These are all games to us. Play is so important to our development and everyday lives that psychologists and cognitive scientists study it and have created several different theories about it.

RULES AND
FORMULAS

DEFINING
GAMES

GAMES HAVE
ALWAYS BEEN
WITH US

GAME
CULTURE

INTERVIEW:
ADAM
SALTSMAN

CHAPTER
SUMMARY AND
DISCUSSION
POINTS

Game Rhetorics

Brian Sutton-Smith, in his 1997 book *The Ambiguity of Play*, defined the human condition of play using "rhetorics." This term is used to underline the conscious or unconscious persuasive nature of play and the narrative of play (as used by players who agree a stick is a sword, and so on). The modern rhetorics are progress, identity, imaginary, and the self. When we play we fulfill one or several of these rhetorics.

Sutton-Smith advocates that almost every positive or negative decision adults make can be thought of as a form of play. This might be deciding where to go on vacation or choosing a career based upon the culture of others in that field and how much interest we have in its topics. It seems we play at life as much as we do consciously within the structures of what we call "games." Video games are consciously "games" to us; we play them to escape our everyday lives or for other reasons. They are understood as games separate from any unconscious games we may play, but they can become important in defining who we are as a person. What and how we play is critical to how we understand ourselves. Play is important, and play is part of our culture—so much so that video games have their own sub-culture.

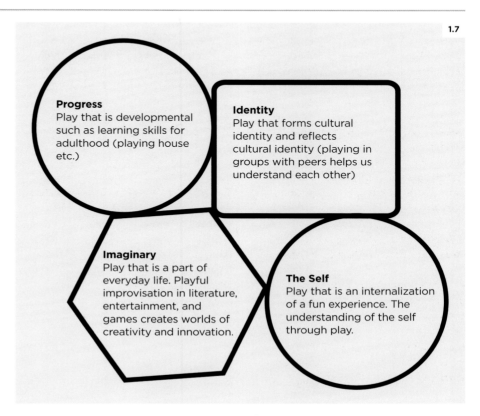

1.7

Progress
Play that is developmental such as learning skills for adulthood (playing house etc.)

Identity
Play that forms cultural identity and reflects cultural identity (playing in groups with peers helps us understand each other)

Imaginary
Play that is a part of everyday life. Playful improvisation in literature, entertainment, and games creates worlds of creativity and innovation.

The Self
Play that is an internalization of a fun experience. The understanding of the self through play.

1.7
The play theorist Brian Sutton-Smith describes the modern rhetorics of play as progress, identity, imaginary, and self.

GAME CULTURE

Game culture—specifically, in this case, video game culture—is very much a part of popular culture. Games have always had cultures surrounding them, which is more obvious when we consider sports as a subset of games. There are distinguishable differences among the cultures of tennis, football, and hockey. From the behavior of the fans to the logos, fields of play, and language used to describe the sports. There are cultures that surround card games, as well, from poker to *Magic: The Gathering* (Richard Garfield, 1993).

Gamer (the moniker often used to refer to video game players) culture is harder to pin down because, unlike defined sports or specific board games, video games are incredibly diverse. When people refer to "game culture" they are often referring to their own particular game's culture. As a rule, cultures are not fixed; they evolve and they are fragmented. Game developers have, over the course of the industry's history, become much more attuned to the cultures that surround their games or franchises. The relationship has become more symbiotic between the culture makers (game developers) and the cultural disseminators (gamers).

Defining Culture

So what is culture? Susanne Schech and Jane Haggis, in their book *Culture and Development: A Critical Introduction* (2000), explain that "culture" is one of the most complicated words in the English language. There is national culture, high culture, low culture, consumer culture, youth culture, and so on . . . and on. *Cultural relativism* is a concept that encourages us to understand cultures on their own terms. Schech and Haggis break down culture into the definitions in Figure 1.9.

1.8
Video games have been around for over 40 years, and the cultures surrounding them permeate all aspects of our larger popular culture.

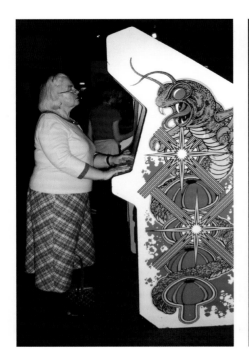

1.8

1.9

Culture

Cultivation of mind, arts, civilization   A process of social development   Meanings, values, ways of life   Practices which produce meaning

1.9
Schech and Haggis (2000) categorize the components of culture, most of which are replicated in videogames.

Games fit these categories well. There are a multitude of games focused on learning (education games) and on developing logic skills (puzzle games). The rise of the "art game" has exploded in the last decade as software and hardware have become more available to artists. Gamers give back to their communities via conventions or charity events (such as Extra Lives and Child's Play). Looked at from a wider cultural perspective, games have been both praised and demonized, with media attention rarely focusing on the more civilized aspects of gaming.

Modern games enable the sharing of experiences, much as other popular cultural activities do (e.g., film, TV, theater); gaming has sharing built into its DNA. Games take culture into the immersive and interactive realm as multiplayer games enable real-time cooperation within an environment with shared goals and intentions. People who have never physically met each other can become friends and have meaningful relationships within and outside of game space.

We play video games because they are fun, because they are immersive and engaging, and because they can unite disparate individuals and groups. Games are a part of our culture as well as a force creating culture. Why do fans of a certain title become vocal advocates for that game? What is it about certain games that makes them so engaging to players? It is that which makes video games a unique medium that we will explore over the course of this book.

1.10
The *Metal Gear Solid* (Konami) franchise borrows heavily from US action film culture and inserts a Japanese perspective as well as offering a commentary on US action films and culture of violence.

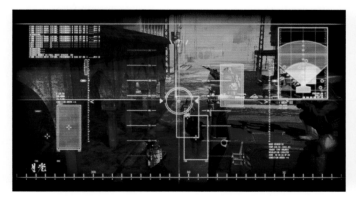

1.10

INTERVIEW

PART 1:
CULTURE, PLAY, AND GAMES

CHAPTER ONE
SO YOU WANT TO BE A
VIDEO GAME DESIGNER?

ADAM SALTSMAN

Game Maker (*Gravity Hook*; 2008, *Canabalt*; 2009)

Adam Saltsman is a game maker best known for two independent games: *Gravity Hook* and *Canabalt*. Both games are available on a variety of platforms.

In this section Adam talks about the process of developing *Canabalt*—from the initial idea to the production of the game on multiple platforms and its inclusion in the permanent collection of the Museum of Modern Art (MoMA) in New York City.

The Game Mechanic

"I wanted the gameplay to be fast and the controls simple. The question in development was how do we tweak the speed versus the jumping so that the player is never too frustrated and feels they can 'win' the game if they get the timing right? To accomplish this we had to balance the width of the screen versus the player's running speed. There's some fairly simple math there that can tell you exactly how much time the player has to react, and when that drops under the limit of possible human reflex time, you know you are starting to have a problem with timing. The math got us started, but during development the timing was mostly 'felt' out during play testing as math can only get you so far when dealing with human reaction times and frustration levels."

1.11
Canabalt is part of the permanent collection of the Museum of Modern Art (MoMA) in New York City.
Canabalt is one of the best examples of a speed-runner game. Many credit Adam Saltsman with the creation of this genre, in which the goal is to get as far as you can for as long as you can.

Game Testing

"A procedural, endless game is much easier to play test than I'd thought. The great thing about procedural games is you can just tell it to run with weird settings for testing purposes. So for example, I could tell *Canabalt* 'Only make buildings with bombs falling' if I was trying to fix the rooftop code in the game. I could see how the reaction times, obstacles, and that one area would play out, then tweak as necessary. It effectively compartmentalized the testing so you didn't have to play for any time to reach 'that point when X happens.' It's perhaps a little weird or different as far as normal game development goes, but ultimately I found it much easier and more interesting. You will often find that you miss some very weird corner case situations, though." (A corner case is an issue that occurs outside of normal operating parameters. For example, a loud speaker may work as intended but suddenly produce bad audio when played at maximum volume with maximum bass in a high-humidity environment.)

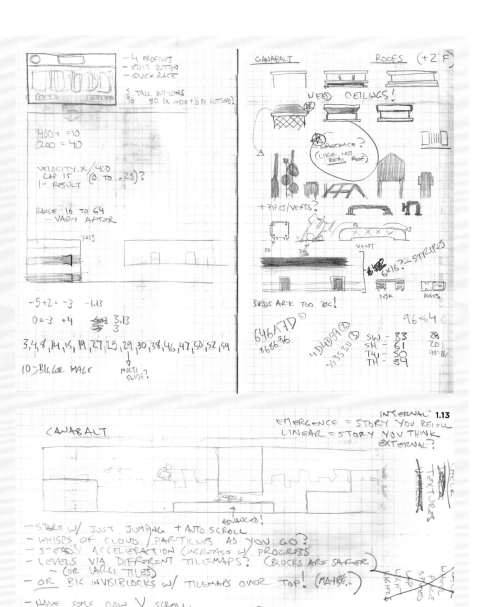

1.12
Pages from Adam's developer notebook. Most developers work out ideas and concepts with sketches before going into any software. In allows for inexpensive ideation and iteration.

1.13
Sketches and notes can ask questions that relate to all aspects of the game. Also, a sketchbook can be mined repeatedly for ideas that may have been abandoned but now make sense.

INTERVIEW

PART 1:
CULTURE, PLAY, AND GAMES

**CHAPTER ONE
SO YOU WANT TO BE A
VIDEO GAME DESIGNER?**

Changing the Game

"The original intention for *Canabalt* was for it to have a finite and absolute end. Before *Canabalt*, I had made another endless game, *Gravity Hook*, and so when I set out to make *Canabalt* I really wanted it to have an ending; that seemed like the evolution of my game development process. As I worked on the game, the ending seemed less and less necessary, and more and more difficult to define. Being flexible is part of the process, and as the game developed it felt like the wrong thing to do so, eventually, the epitaphs, the little death messages, became the game's 'ending,' but the game could go on forever."

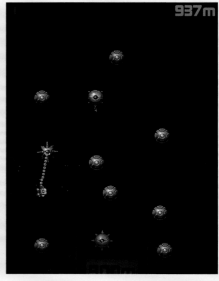

1.14

1.14

Adam's earlier game, *Gravity Hook*, was a precursor to *Canabalt*. It's an endless game with a death state that puts the player back at the beginning of the game. *Gravity Hook* serves as a good example of how video game developers evolve their ideas over time and through experimentation. Although the games are quite different in execution, Adam used *Gravity Hook*'s successes and built on some shortcomings to create *Canabalt*. Making games is the only way to make better games.

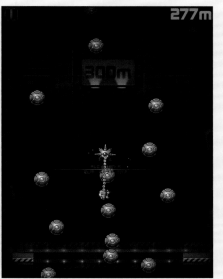

CHAPTER SUMMARY

Games are increasingly being developed with the psychology of the player in mind. Video games have become ever-deeper immersive experiences for players, and developers are looking beyond computer science and art to simply code games and make them look good. Developers now look at optimal experiences for players in order to keep them playing for hours at a time and to create games that are harder and harder to put down.

Play and fun are a big part of what makes us who and what we are. Video games tap into many areas of the human psyche and culture and are deliberately designed to do so. The following chapters in this book explore how the disparate elements of play, culture, engagement, fun, and immersion can be distilled and designed into video games. As a video game designer, you are able to create whole new worlds and whole new fictions for people to play with. This is a huge responsibility and a very exciting undertaking. World building is not just the nuts and bolts of creating a universe. It is understanding what the world is, how it works, who lives in it, and how everything relates to everything else. We now have a better understanding of what games are, who studies them, and who plays them. The next step is to start examining the medium in more depth.

RULES AND FORMULAS

DEFINING GAMES

GAMES HAVE ALWAYS BEEN WITH US

GAME CULTURE

INTERVIEW: ADAM SALTSMAN

CHAPTER SUMMARY AND DISCUSSION POINTS

DISCUSSION POINTS

The following discussion points are designed to help you think critically about the culture, ethics, production, and place of video games in our world. We'll have similar questions at the end of each chapter.

1. How are games best defined? In this chapter we learned about Jesper Juul's definition of "game." Does yours differ? If so, why and how?

2. Rules and mechanics: Take a game—any game—and dissect its game rules and mechanics. Examples could be *Pac-Man* (Namco), *Pong* (Atari), or tic-tac-toe. What do the rules tell you about the game? How do the mechanics support and enhance both the rules and the gameplay?

3. Select a game—any game—and try to define its essence. What experience does it create for the player? How might the game experience change with a simple rule or mechanic alteration (for example, how does the experience of "tag" change when it becomes "stick in the mud")?

References

Huizinga, J. (1955), *Homo Ludens: A Study of the Play-element in Culture*, Boston: Beacon Press.

Juul, J. (2003), "The Game, the Player, the World: Looking for a Heart of Gameness," in M. Copier and J. Raessens (eds), *Level Up: Digital Games Research Conference Proceedings*, 30–45, Utrecht: Utrecht University. Available online: http://www .jesperjuul.net/text/gameplayerworld/

Schech, S. and J. Haggis (2000), *Culture and Development: A Critical Introduction*, Oxford: Blackwell Publishers.

Sutton-Smith, B. (1997), *The Ambiguity of Play*, Cambridge, MA: Harvard University Press.

PART 1: CULTURE, PLAY, AND GAMES

CHAPTER TWO
WORLD BUILDING

Chapter Objectives:

- Explore world building.

- Understand play mechanics, rules, outcomes, and objectives.

- Populate a world with behaviors.

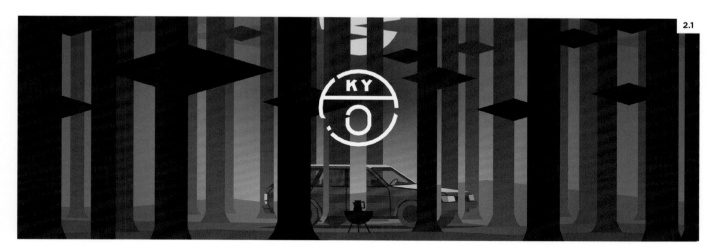

2.1
Kentucky Route Zero, developed by Cardboard
Computer (2013).

WHEN YOU BUILD A GAME,
YOU CONSTRUCT A UNIVERSE

In Chapter 1 we explored why we play, who players are, and some elements of the psychology of play. This chapter begins the process of creating a game world. This is not the technical aspect of modeling, programming, animation, or level design (level design is covered in Chapters 8 and 9); instead, we will explore the idea that to create a video game is to create a unique world. This world may not necessarily correspond to our own. It may have physics unlike our own. It may have different boundaries and interfaces we do not have in our world (when was the last time you hit a green "A" button to pick something up?). It may contain mandates or restrictions that do not make sense in our world (do you run everywhere in real life like characters do in video games?). This is as true for a game of tag as it is for *World of Warcraft* (Blizzard Entertainment, 2004) or *Call of Duty*. Imaginary spaces of play have different rules and different histories.

The term "world building" comes originally from science fiction writers who needed to create a believable space for their characters to inhabit before they knew who their characters would become. They would think about and often map out the geography, ecology, and history of their imagined world. J. R. R. Tolkien was renowned for his fastidiousness in creating the maps, creatures, and back-stories of Middle-earth; even the most insignificant creature or bit of topography was developed and thought out. World building is, of course, a game genre too; examples include the *SimCity* (Maxis/EA, 1989–2014) franchise, *Civilization* (MicroProse, 1991–2014), and *Spore* (Maxis, 2008). These games work from the principles that we examine in this chapter, but the players are given the tools to create their own worlds within the rules and boundaries of the game mechanic.

TIP | **THE VIDEO GAME DOCUMENT**

Before getting too deep into the concepts and principles of game design, it is worth mentioning design documents. A game design document (sometimes known as a GDD) is a "living document": As the game develops and evolves, so too will the document. It may go through many revisions before being fixed. The purpose of the game document is dependent on the size of the team and the production costs. If the game is part of a pitch to a large publisher, it will need to be very detailed with costs, deadlines, market research, and so on. If it is a document for a small independent team, it will be more concerned with keeping everyone focused on the concepts, ideas, and goals of the production, and every member of the team will share in it.

A general document should include:

- An overview of the game's premise: what the game is and what platform it is intended for.

- The story (if there is one).

- Concepts for level designs and environments (which could be mood boards or sketched art).

- Gameplay (What is the mechanic? What are the rules?).

- Art: sketches, mood boards, tone art (What does the world look like?).

- Sound and music (How much will there be? Do specific characters have specific sounds? Does each level require new music?).

- User interface: game controls (which may change once production is underway, but it is useful to know if the game has "conventional" controls and interfaces or if it is bringing something unique or unusual to the genre).

There is more information about game design documents on this book's website at
www.bloomsbury.com/Salmond-Video-Game

WHEN YOU
BUILD A
GAME, YOU
CONSTRUCT
A UNIVERSE

THE FIELD
OF PLAY

THE GAME
MECHANIC

THE RULES
OF PLAY

THE
OUTCOMES
OF PLAY

THE
OBJECTIVES
OF PLAY

PLAYER
RESOURCES
AND
CONFLICT

CASE STUDY:
*KENTUCKY
ROUTE ZERO*

CHAPTER
SUMMARY AND
DISCUSSION
POINTS

Games, Rules, and Mechanics

Games have rules and outcomes as well as the ability to evolve and change dependent on the players. When conceptualizing a game and its world you do not need to be incredibly detailed, but you do need to establish what the world is (alien, real-life, whimsical, or dark), what its rules are (Is there gravity? Are its inhabitants friendly or dangerous? How tall are its structures?), and its behaviors (Does the weather have an effect on the player? Is the world hostile or friendly to the player?). When we talk about world building, we are also talking about the experience we want the player to have in this world. There is a difference between a game a player can get lost in and believe in, and one that is just a series of levels for the player to beat. When starting to think about designing a game world, some questions to ask include:

In what way is my world more interesting than the real world?

Does my world focus on one individual's story or can several stories be told?

How will the player internalize my world?

These questions provide perspective on thinking about the world's relationship to the player. Although simple, these questions are multi-layered; for example, what makes your world more interesting than the real world—is it a sense of wonder you will instill in the player or a sense of power? If there are multiple stories to be told, how are they communicated to the player or players? Will you use non-player character dialogue, in-game audio, or art assets? How players internalize the world is important for the designer; this covers the players' understanding of the mechanics and "feel" of the game world as well as their aesthetic and visceral reactions to it. These three simple questions, once you begin to pull them apart, form the basis for building a game world.

The Building Blocks of Game World Design

The concept of a world can become more concrete as you begin to answer those questions and build out the *formal elements* of the gameplay. It's worth knowing that these formal gameplay elements apply to other game structures as well as video games. These building blocks could apply as easily to *Call of Duty* as to a game of soccer or football. Essentially, the game world is a system, and a system has many parts that make it work. The formal elements, or building blocks, as I prefer to call them, are an aid in describing a deeper understanding of what goes into a game world or game system.

The building blocks of game design are:

- The Field of Play

- The Game Mechanic

- The Rules of Play

- The Outcomes of Play

- The Objectives of Play

- Player Resources and Conflict

THE FIELD OF PLAY

The field of play is the space in which the game takes place, and there are several considerations when designing that space for a game:

- The field of play has to be consistent and work within the mechanics and rules of the game world.

- The design of the interface between the player and the world is also an aspect of the field of play (How does the player navigate through the world and how does the world react to the player or players?).

- The field of play can also be thought of as the game's boundaries, tasks, and outcomes.

- The field of play is defined by the media it is played on. Game worlds can be generated to be infinite or ever-changing, but the rules and mechanic must remain consistent.

- The field of play can constrain and guide the player towards a goal (this is part of level design).

2.2

2.2
Science fiction or fantasy games, such as *Mass Effect*™ *3* (Bioware, 2012), do not have to rely on real-world physics, but an alien environment still requires a consistent mechanic and physics.

WHEN YOU
BUILD A
GAME, YOU
CONSTRUCT
A UNIVERSE

THE FIELD
OF PLAY

THE GAME
MECHANIC

THE RULES
OF PLAY

THE
OUTCOMES
OF PLAY

THE
OBJECTIVES
OF PLAY

PLAYER
RESOURCES
AND
CONFLICT

CASE STUDY:
*KENTUCKY
ROUTE ZERO*

CHAPTER
SUMMARY AND
DISCUSSION
POINTS

TIP | MAGIC CIRCLE

Another often-cited term for the field of play is the Magic Circle. The game scholar Johan Huizinga defines the space in which a game takes place as the "Magic Circle" in a way that is similar to the definition of the field of play. He distinguishes it as a temporary space set aside as different from the rest of the surrounding environment. It is a space of special rules that are understood by the culture that establishes it. Simply put, a magic circle can be anything—a stage or a tennis court, a virtual planet, or a card-table. What is important is that the participants understand this space as set apart, a place where only the rules of the game apply. Thus, spectators stay in the stands and do not walk across the soccer field, the audience does not get up and wander across the stage, and so on.

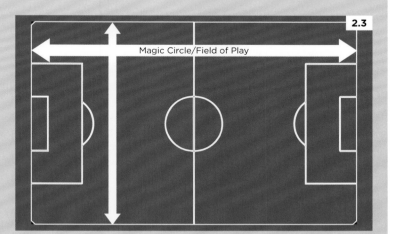

2.3
A soccer field is a form of "sacred ground" where activities take place that would seem nonsensical outside of the game being played. A game world exists within the ordinary world. The player is invited into the "magic circle" to play.

2.4
This is a level from *Call of Duty: Black Ops II*; it is a field of play or magic circle in the same way a physical field is. There are boundaries the player cannot escape; there are rules and mechanics that apply only within this space.

THE GAME MECHANIC

The second building block is the game mechanic. The mechanic of a video game does not just refer to the "nuts and bolts" of the game or just the programming and art assets. Instead, the mechanic is what the game is, how it plays, and how the player interacts with the game. Mechanics explain the gameplay, environment, and physics of the world. They're what a player can and cannot do, as well as how they interact within the game space. The mechanic enables gameplay; it is not the same thing as gameplay. There may be rules and mechanics in place that some players will never see or experience, but they exist for others. Game mechanics are approached from an engineering viewpoint: how the gun will fire, how the damage is taken, and how the world tracks and reacts to this action. Gameplay is a design concept; it covers the experience the player is having as enabled by the mechanic.

THE RULES OF PLAY

In video games, the rules define the potentiality of any space for play and define and restrict an array of possible actions. Rules limit actions; even in open world "sandbox" games, there may be non-player characters that cannot be harmed or spaces that cannot be entered. All rules in some way limit player action within the game.

Because of this, rules must be explicit, unambiguous, and consistent; scoring more goals or points against the opposition always results in a win, but the games' rules represent the conditions of the outcome explicitly. In soccer, the rule is "kick balls into the goal to win"; the more explicit rule is that the player has to kick more balls into the *opponent's* goal to win. Otherwise, players could just put the ball in any goal and win the game.

Rules can become complex quickly, and any ambiguity in the rule set is bad for the player. If a health pack gives back 10% of health one time and then 80% the next time, this result will confuse the player because it seems so random. If there is an obvious and consistent visual distinction—such as small and large health packs in the game *Dead Space* (Visceral Games, 2008)—the player will understand the gameplay and anticipate and plan his or her play around this rule set. Rules have to be fixed and immutable in a game; even if there are "house rules" when playing a board game such as Monopoly, they are consistent throughout the time of play. The game should never give the impression of "cheating" the player by changing rules and outcomes on the fly (for example, if players learn that they must shoot at yellow "damage" points on a boss monster in order to defeat it, they will be frustrated if this suddenly changes for no apparent reason).

WHEN YOU BUILD A GAME, YOU CONSTRUCT A UNIVERSE

THE FIELD OF PLAY

THE GAME MECHANIC

THE RULES OF PLAY

THE OUTCOMES OF PLAY

THE OBJECTIVES OF PLAY

PLAYER RESOURCES AND CONFLICT

CASE STUDY: *KENTUCKY ROUTE ZERO*

CHAPTER SUMMARY AND DISCUSSION POINTS

Video Game Rule Taxonomy

Rules have to be consistent within the game, but they do not have to be consistent across games. Video games are an interactive medium and a complex one, so they can require very complex and nuanced rules. Mechanics and rules add depth to gameplay and establish player experience, experimentation, and exploration. Rules may only apply to one specific game and can be completely different from other games, even within the same genre (for example, not all falls from great heights kill players in FPS games). So there are three main rule types used in the majority of video games:

Objects and Concepts

These are the rules that are placed on elements and objects of the game world. Concepts as rules are inherent to the game and often these concept rules become the archetypes for a new genre's rule set. For example, in *Super Mario Brothers* (Nintendo, 1985) the rule is that if a player collides with a box it will spew out floating coins, which, when collected, will open other levels or produce high scores. This rule-concept has become standard in many other platform-based games. In effect, the concepts and rules of objects in a platform game are a large part of defining that genre, and they build the player's expectations of gameplay.

Similarly, the objects and concepts rules have defined the FPS genre: You shoot at enemies; after taking a certain amount of damage, they die; and the same is true of the player's character. This rule set has not changed since the creation of the first FPS games, *Wolfenstein* 3D (Id Software, 1992) and *Doom* (Id Software, 1993).

2.5

2.5
Gears of War 2 (Epic Games, 2008) sets restrictive actions on the effect (damage) of the weaponry. There are different-powered weapons, and their effects on enemies restrict players; this is also part of game balance. Another restrictive action is in a player having to clear an area of the enemy before moving on to the next level.

Restricting Actions

Restricting what the player can do in a game involves a variety of rationales, which can be planned and controlled within the design process. When designing a game, you may decide to stop a player from entering a room because it's too expensive to build interiors for everything or design a leveling system that means a player cannot defeat a boss until the player has achieved a certain rank. These are examples of restricting actions. All forms of games have restricting actions; turn-based strategy (TBS) games model their rules of combat on games like chess. Each player has to wait for a "turn" before deploying troops/game objects; this is the rule of the game and also a restrictive action. Limiting the field of play can also be a restrictive rule, as a new area is only available when all the enemies are defeated (*Gears of War*, Epic Games, 2006; *Uncharted*, Naughty Dog, 2007; etc.). When designing a game world, it is important to not just consider what the player can do, but also what they cannot do.

2.6

2.6
In *Resident Evil 5* (Capcom, 2009), if your co-op partner dies you cannot continue with the game. This applies pressure to both players to keep their health up or encourages the better player to protect the less proficient player strategically.

WHEN YOU BUILD A GAME, YOU CONSTRUCT A UNIVERSE

THE FIELD OF PLAY

THE GAME MECHANIC

THE RULES OF PLAY

THE OUTCOMES OF PLAY

THE OBJECTIVES OF PLAY

PLAYER RESOURCES AND CONFLICT

CASE STUDY: *KENTUCKY ROUTE ZERO*

CHAPTER SUMMARY AND DISCUSSION POINTS

Circumstantial Effect

Games can have conditions applied to rules that depend on the circumstances of the game. This is a rule set that is designed into the game from the outset, but it can seem as if the game is making "decisions" based on a player's actions. For example, in a game with cooperative play, if one player dies, the other can still continue and beat the level, and then both players can continue, but if both players die, then the game resets to the beginning of the level. However, in the single-player version of the same game, a death state resets the game; the A.I. character does not continue on. These are circumstantial rules and they can vary gameplay a great deal if applied in a consistent manner. Circumstantial rules can also be used as a reward for the player or to get the player back on track within the game. In the *Sonic the Hedgehog* (Sega, 1991) games, collecting rings is an integral part of the gameplay, but rather than have a death state that may frustrate a player when he or she makes a misstep, Sonic loses his collection of rings. If the player does this too many times, Sonic will "die" and the level resets, but only if the player has lost all rings. Circumstantial effects such as these can add tension and nuance to the game.

TIP

EXPLAINING THE RULES

Unlike real-world games, video games do not have "house rules" or negotiations on the rules, so the digital space has to convey fairness and responsiveness to the player. The more complex the rule set, the more the designer is going to have to explain the rules to the player. This does not have to be boring or become an obstacle to a positive experience. (We will look at tutorials in Chapter 10.) Intuitive and rational rules connect the meaningful choices that players make to the outcomes of the game, and they can be implemented over time. For example, a player may take damage in a tutorial level without dying, but will be unsurprised when they die in the "real" game, because they understand the difference between the tutorial level and real level and witness the consequences of that set of rules (get hit too many times = death state). Rules can be taught to the player over time as long as core rules (such as what it takes to create a fail state) are understood quickly. Games that involve combat have a real-world analogue that works as a short cut, but nuances can vary (how much damage the character can absorb before dying, for example).

THE OUTCOMES OF PLAY

Outcomes can be simple "score more points than the other player" or complex challenges where the player may have one ultimate objective (save the world) but to get to that they have to accomplish a myriad of smaller objectives. Outcomes are what guide the player towards the objectives. The player understands that by doing X, they will then be able to advance to point Y (partly due to experience in other games as well as reinforcement through tutorials and what is known as *priming*—more on this in Chapter 8). The outcome of shooting more aliens results in a higher score (*Space Invaders*, Taito, 1978) or the investigation of objects and notes in a house leads to a satisfying, completed narrative (*Gone Home*, The Fulbright Company, 2013). Unlike objectives of play (see below), outcomes do not always have to be explicit and defined for the player. In fact, uncertain outcomes are better at holding the attention of the player than rigidly defined ones. If the game has a strong narrative component and the outcome of every conversation or every decision leads to the same objective, the player is going to become frustrated with that relationship. If the outcomes are unexpected or drive the player's curiosity, the player becomes more engaged.

Outcomes are not the same as objectives. An in-game objective must be clear to the player from the outset (go on a quest, score more points, free yourself from the dungeon) even if the player does not know what the eventual outcome is (save the universe, get the highest score). Outcomes of play are not always about winning or finite states of play. Simulation games (*SimCity*, Maxis Infogames, 1989; *Microsoft Flight Simulator*, Aces Studio, 1982) are more focused on sandbox play and experimentation, so the positive outcome is formed more in the mind of the player and their enjoyment of being able to experiment or learn a new skill. A "serious game" (a video game that may be political, educational, or created by non-profits to raise awareness) may have an outcome of raising awareness for a worthy cause, such as *Darfur is Dying* (directed by Susana Ruiz, 2006), which was created to raise awareness of the refugee situation in that country. The outcomes for these games are not as quantifiable as a high score or achievement point, but each is designed with an outcome in mind.

2.7
Outcomes are not always linked to achievements or kill-counts of enemies. Outcomes can be based on narrative progression (such as filling in back story in *Gone Home*, where there is no voiceover or other character), offering strategy and unexpected surprises for the player.

2.8
Video game designers also mix up objectives to avoid stagnation of gameplay. The racing game *Forza Motorsport 5* (Turn 10 Studios, 2014) also includes an "escape the police" play mechanic.

2.7

2.8

WHEN YOU
BUILD A
GAME, YOU
CONSTRUCT
A UNIVERSE

THE FIELD
OF PLAY

THE GAME
MECHANIC

THE RULES
OF PLAY

THE
OUTCOMES
OF PLAY

THE
OBJECTIVES
OF PLAY

PLAYER
RESOURCES
AND
CONFLICT

CASE STUDY:
*KENTUCKY
ROUTE ZERO*

CHAPTER
SUMMARY AND
DISCUSSION
POINTS

THE OBJECTIVES OF PLAY

Objectives define what the players are trying to accomplish within the game rules; they set not only the challenge, but also the tone of the game. For example, an objective may be to capture or destroy an opponent's forces in a castle defense game. Or the objective could be to spell out more words faster than your opponent. Objectives are often mixed, allowing a game to target multiple audiences. Many games blend objectives within their genre to give the game more depth and to craft a better experience. There are seven common forms of objectives, and they are not immutable. They can be mixed and merged to create more engaging gameplay. For example, a real-time strategy game (RTS) may blend an objective of conquering other lands or countries (territory, deprivation) with a construction mechanic so that the player can construct new buildings or fortifications (building and also possibly hoarding/collecting).

The most common forms of objectives are shown in Figure 2.9.

2.9
The most common game objectives occur across all game genres (a game could be about territory, collecting, and building) and are often the bedrock of a genre (racing games, "god games," puzzle games).

2.9

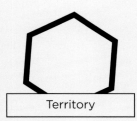

Territory

The player may not be required to completely capture/destroy all other players or game resources but is able to control enough of the game space to win the game.

Hoarding/Collecting

This is a reward system/ objective which may or may not directly affect their game progress. Collecting can form a psychological 'win-state' in games that feed positive gameplay emotions.

Decipher/De-crypt

Games dedicated entirely to puzzles. Or games which include puzzle elements that enable deeper gameplay or that are used to pace the gameplay.

Deprivation

Deprivation of another's goal. This could be taking over another faction's fortress or locking up a character so they cannot play the game.

Racing/Escaping

Racing/Chase car games but this also includes any element of gameplay where the character is running towards or from something.

Building

The objective is to advance resources up to or beyond a given point.

Align/Position

The alignment or positioning of game pieces completes a level or quest.

PLAYER RESOURCES
AND CONFLICT

Managing resources and determining how and when they are available to the player are important parts of the design process. Resources also cover most of the other aspects of this chapter: They are restrictive (e.g., how much health does the player have?). They can be objectives (e.g., the player must get more wood to build a larger boat). They can relate to outcomes (e.g., does the player have the resources needed to explore and experiment in the game world?). Improper balancing of resources can make a game too easy or frustratingly hard. For instance, if you put too many health packs in a shooter game, there is no sense of peril or challenge; too few and the experience becomes exasperating. Resources come in many forms and are part of the rules, mechanics, and aesthetic of the game.

Resources can make the game more challenging or even become a mini-game within the main game. Restricting resources and rewarding resources are common approaches in games to make them more engaging for the player. One example is the use of in-game currency. In Ubisoft Montreal's *Assassin's Creed IV: Black Flag* (2014), the player does not have a lot of money (resources) starting out as a pirate/privateer. The ship the player has is sea-worthy but not great, able to defeat only the lowest level of foes. By completing sea or land missions and by ransacking other ships, the player can upgrade the ship. The world map shows other limited resources, such as building materials, to encourage the player to explore and get deeper into the game.

TIP | CONFLICT (as Resource)

Limited resources can create the basis for conflict in a game: Players vie against opponents to survive or thrive in, for example, *DayZ* (Bohemia Interactive, 2013) or *Don't Starve* (Klie Entertainment, 2013). Conflict does not have to be as explicit as it is in a fighting game or in a combat-based shooter. Players can internalize conflicts based on moral or ethical decisions they must make within the game. Do you give the limited resources to the starving family or keep them for yourself? Do you help a fellow survivor or kill him and loot his body?

2.10

2.10
Action games and RPGs may have resource scarcity built into the inventory system. In *Resident Evil 4* (Capcom, 2005), the main character (Leon) has limited slots in his inventory, which encourages players to think tactically about what resources to buy or carry.

WHEN YOU
BUILD A
GAME, YOU
CONSTRUCT
A UNIVERSE

THE FIELD
OF PLAY

THE GAME
MECHANIC

THE RULES
OF PLAY

THE
OUTCOMES
OF PLAY

THE
OBJECTIVES
OF PLAY

PLAYER
RESOURCES
AND
CONFLICT

CASE STUDY:
*KENTUCKY
ROUTE ZERO*

CHAPTER
SUMMARY AND
DISCUSSION
POINTS

A designer must balance resources because if they are unevenly applied, the game feels formulaic. In the game *Final Fantasy XII* (Square Enix, 2006), defeated monsters drop items that players can trade for spells and money so that they can unlock other areas in the game and additional items. Unfortunately, it became very easy to "game" the system by knowing where monsters with good loot would spawn and then repeatedly defeating them and selling the items. Once getting money and supposedly scarce items became easy, a large part of the game began to feel pointless (although it was a conscious choice of the player to do this). When designing your game, consider resources carefully because they come in many forms. The important job of a designer is to decide which resources should be scarce in order to increase the player's engagement levels and which resources should be readily available so that the player does not feel the game is too frustrating.

Resources can come in many forms beyond items, experience, and money:

- Limited lives: Three lives is typical in traditional arcade games.

- Units: Games may start you out with a default amount and reward good playing with more.

- Health: Often health packs or pickups are a finite resource (and this can add tension).

- Powerups: Player rewards include more powerful guns, special equipment, or moves. These can be permanent or made into a scarce resource by making them good for only one use or time dependent.

- Time: Players must complete a level or puzzle in X minutes or seconds (to create a sense of urgency).

- The inventory/ encumbrance system: How many items can a player carry? How much weight can a player bear? (Players can also win rewards in the form of more slots in an inventory or more items allowed to be carried.)

Resources can create nuanced depth in a game that can allow the player to go deeper into the experience. Balancing the resources—whether they are food, money, experience points, or weaponry—is critical in creating a solid game. Consider the types of resources and how they can be managed in your game to drive the player experience.

CASE STUDY: ART MEETS INTERACTIVE NARRATIVE IN *KENTUCKY ROUTE ZERO (KRZ)*

Cardboard Computer is a Chicago-based, three-person game development studio consisting of Jake Elliott (Designer), Tamas Kemenczy (Designer), and Ben Babbit (Sound Design). In January of 2013, they released the first act of their five-act video game, followed by the second in May of 2013.

Tone and Aesthetic of the *KRZ* World

"*Kentucky Route Zero* came from our collaboration in an art exhibition with another Chicago-based artist, jonCates. We created an experimental text adventure about Will Crowther, the designer of *Colossal Cave Adventure* (1976), and called it 'Sidequest.' After we had shown this work, we remained interested in the concept and started trying to explore a few different game ideas, and eventually came back around to the setting of Mammoth Cave in Kentucky (also the site of *Colossal Cave Adventure*). We iterated on the idea and experimented for a few years until it took shape as something like a slow-paced and theatrical point-and-click adventure."

"The earliest part of our process was to do a bunch of writing and create a sort of 'tone' trailer." (You can see that trailer on this book's website: www.bloomsbury.com/Salmond-Video-Game.) "The trailer set the tone but the aesthetic is different from the game we eventually created in a lot of ways. The art direction is more angular, and geometric, but as we iterated we arrived at the final aesthetic in response to the way the game design was shaping up. For example, we found the characters were usually small enough on the screen that you couldn't make out the details on their faces. So why even have faces? The current art direction is a lot more flexible and distinct, so we're happy to have moved away from the realism we had originally intended for the game."

2.11
Early animation test and character design. As the game developed, Jake and Tamas pushed the camera and point of view of the player further out so details in realistic characters were lost. Instead, they went for a far more simplified and abstract aesthetic.

2.11

WHEN YOU
BUILD A
GAME, YOU
CONSTRUCT   THE FIELD   THE GAME   THE RULES   THE   THE   PLAYER
A UNIVERSE   OF PLAY   MECHANIC   OF PLAY   OUTCOMES   OBJECTIVES   RESOURCES   CASE STUDY: CHAPTER
                                                                  OF PLAY   OF PLAY   AND   KENTUCKY   SUMMARY AND
                                                                                              CONFLICT   ROUTE ZERO   DISCUSSION
                                                                                                                           POINTS

Production Creates Change

"Originally the game was going to be a platformer, with a heavy emphasis on conversational dialogue. Then when we were building the initial stages, we introduced mouse controls. Suddenly the environments got smaller and more theatrical, and tweak-by-tweak it started to look more like a classic point-and-click adventure in the style of the LucasArts or DoubleFine games. For *Kentucky Route Zero* this happened as part of the evolution of developing the game and learning how to use the tools we had. One issue with this process is that players bring expectations to that style of game and come looking for inventory puzzles or a specific style of humor, which *KRZ* doesn't have. At this point (March of 2014), we have got two acts out, with the third coming quite soon. Act one was the least charted territory for us; we were working out the game mechanics and implementation as we went. So we learned a lot about specifically how to make *KRZ* as we made it."

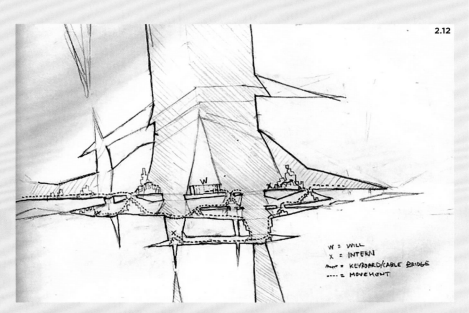

2.12

2.12
An early production sketch gives the artist a sense of the intended proportion and scale. The image below is still early in the production process before the team switched to its final aesthetic.

Workflow

"We're new media artists and don't have any kind of background in professional game development, so all our workflow has been made up as we go along. The flexibility to be able to write a bunch of Blender & Unity scripts to create a workflow as we go has been pretty crucial. Ableton was just what Jake was familiar with for sound design, coming from an experimental music practice. Now we work with sound designer and composer Ben Babbitt, who is mostly using Logic and music hardware. We've had to do a fair amount of custom work—we don't use any of Unity's default shaders, for example. A lot of our process has evolved in response to Unity's quirks, since we've been using it since the beginning. Our workflow was very fluid; we've never worked within larger development companies, but many independent studios like ours make prototypes or use game jams as a way to sketch. Sketching is important!" (Game jams are small, usually local, get-togethers where developers can come together to work with others, discuss games, or show off their works in progress.)

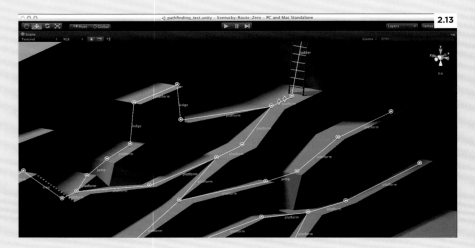

2.13
Learning Unity was part of the workflow and production process. This image shows a late game character pathfinding route (what the game mechanic sees as areas the character can move into and interact with, or a predetermined course an animation would follow).

WHEN YOU BUILD A GAME, YOU CONSTRUCT A UNIVERSE

THE FIELD OF PLAY

THE GAME MECHANIC

THE RULES OF PLAY

THE OUTCOMES OF PLAY

THE OBJECTIVES OF PLAY

PLAYER RESOURCES AND CONFLICT

CASE STUDY: *KENTUCKY ROUTE ZERO*

CHAPTER SUMMARY AND DISCUSSION POINTS

"As the project grew, we needed a sound designer, so we invited Ben Babbitt on board, and over time he's taken a more active role in development. We're still exploring and experimenting with workflow, but a few things that have been constant:

- We use a github.com source code repository to share the project.

- Tamas does the artwork (environments, characters, animations) and designs and programs character and camera movement within the scenes.

- Jake does the writing and dialogue programming.

The roles are fluid and there are a bunch of aspects that we might switch between us as needed. For example, when setting up interactive characters, props, and events in the scene; switching between scenes at the right time; and so on—that's done by one or the other, depending on circumstances. We have a lot of code and structure in place for the game now, but still try to find ways to experiment and introduce new problems to solve."

2.14

2.14
The final game aesthetic grew from iteration and the tone set in the original Kickstarter trailer. The characters were simplified as the environments became more of a central "character" of the game and better suited to the abstract, minimalist aesthetic.

CHAPTER SUMMARY

When creating a game world, you have so many options that it can be overwhelming. One way of short-cutting instead of creating a world from scratch is to work on a licensed property (such as a game based on a film franchise or book). If you are working on a licensed property, your world is going to be restricted to the characters, rules, and world already created by others. This can be useful when starting out because it allows you to get on with creating a working game without doing everything from scratch. This could also be restrictive because the property owners may want to provide a lot of input.

If the game is all your own, starting can be a daunting task. Many bands start out covering songs they already know so that they can learn to play together, and using other people's work is a great focus point before starting on original material. It can be the same when designing a game. There are plenty of myths, fictions, and tales that can be the start of a new game, but each myth exists in its own universe and world. Once you begin to build the world, you have to put in place the physical attributes, rules, and mechanics of this space. They have to be consistent, and they have to make sense within the context of the world you have created for the player.

WHEN YOU
BUILD A
GAME, YOU
CONSTRUCT   THE FIELD   THE GAME   THE RULES   THE   THE   PLAYER   CASE STUDY: **CHAPTER**
A UNIVERSE   OF PLAY   MECHANIC   OF PLAY   OUTCOMES   OBJECTIVES   RESOURCES   *KENTUCKY*   **SUMMARY AND**
                                                                   OF PLAY   OF PLAY   AND   *ROUTE ZERO*   **DISCUSSION**
                                                                                                CONFLICT   **POINTS**

DISCUSSION POINTS

1. **Deconstruct the game world of the video game you have played most recently. How does it break down—from the overall aesthetic to the experience and gameplay? How do you define the world as different from other game worlds?**

2. **Continue to analyze the video game you have most recently played: How does the mechanic of the game world inform the gameplay? What elements are consistent and which elements break that consistency? (This could be as simple as a cut-scene that breaks the player out of their agency.)**

3. **Using an old arcade-style game, define the rule sets of that game. How do they become more complex as the gameplay experience ramps up? (There are many open source and licensed versions of arcade-style games online, such as *Space Invaders*, by Taito, and *Pong*, by Atari.)**

CHAPTER THREE
VIDEO GAME ANALYSIS

Chapter Objectives:

- **Begin thinking like a game designer.**

- **Learn to deconstruct games to make new ones.**

- **Recognize the biases you bring as a designer.**

3.1
Gone Home, wireframe mesh developed
by The Fullbright Company (2013).

THINKING AS A
GAME DESIGNER

Simple Wins

In the first part of this chapter, we will begin to examine the other side of the screen across from the player: the mind-set and skill set of the game designer. New game designers often start with the question "How can I make a game?" whereas a more productive question may be "How do I improve on that as a game?" or even better, "How can I make that into a game?" These questions have the useful attribute of shifting us from the seemingly impossible task of creating something unique and new toward an achievable outcome.

As in all design, defining the problem is the key to moving forward into production. As an example, in the last chapter's case study (*Kentucky Route Zero*), the developers at Cardboard Computer wanted to make an updated version of the old "point and click" and text-based games from the 1980s, which is the period in which they started to fall in love with video games. This concept was the jumping off point, and through the iterative design process (making many versions, improving them with each step), the idea evolved into a game that is far more complex than the simpler games it is based on.

When you design video games, you have to stop playing them and start analyzing them. You have to find out what it is about the game that you enjoy, what you do not like, and what the game designer is trying to communicate to you. Designers no longer play games; they have to look at games clinically to pull back the veil of entertainment and see the systems that work together to create the video game. Analyzing a game is important. How can anyone make a game without knowing what existing games are made of? Most people have a "great idea" for a game, but it's not until they sit down and really think about how the game will play over minutes and hours that the enormity of the task becomes clearer. This chapter will get you over this initial hurdle and help you to better understand and deconstruct a video game.

When starting out as a video game designer, it is useful to focus on the basics. Redesigning (or "modding") existing games to include new ways of playing or to merge genres of games is a simple way to examine rules, play, and mechanics as a designer. In my courses, I set for students a simple task: improve or alter a game from your childhood. This could be tic-tac-toe, hangman, or chutes and ladders. Every time I do this I get different results: One group makes chutes and ladders into a drinking game (you drink when you land on a chute) and another crosses hangman with a movie trivia game. Some groups include new rule sets that enable players to hinder other players' progress, while others want to make the game more collaborative to even the field of play. The really important step is that each student group has to play their reworked version of the game in front of the class. This enables everyone to have input, and the game testing quickly reveals areas that students have not thoroughly thought through as well as those that work.

These basic exercises serve to pull apart a simple game and enable the designer to examine the rules, interaction, and mechanics and then invent new possibilities. This is fairly easy when using simple games such as hangman, but video games are much more complex. Game "fun" and experiences are subjective, yet game designers have to be able to look past that and analyze the components of how the game actually works to be able to begin to make their own.

UNDERSTANDING BIAS

Game designers are players too, with their own favorite game genres and styles, and these are the ones they are most likely to want to create. However, when playing as a designer, it is important to play games that are unfamiliar and from genres that are outside of your usual experience. If you want to make a role playing game (RPG), do not exclude a platformer or sports game from your design research. The sports game may have a really interesting method of handling player statistics that translates well into a character skill-tree. Or a player's dodge mechanic from an NFL football game may translate well into a zombie game as the player's character has to weave between enemies. For example, some of my students have taken the successful elements from two different card games and then mixed in role-playing elements from games such as *Dungeons and Dragons* to create an online RPG that is a combination of all three. The more games and genres you examine and deconstruct, the more likely you are to find inspiration and begin to create innovative and interesting games.

3.2

3.2
There is value in researching all genres and types of game mechanics. You never know what will inform your game; for example, a solid dodge mechanic in a football game could transfer well into a stealth game. *Madden NFL 25*, developed by EA Tiburon (2013).

Addressing Bias

Only playing familiar games can lead to pitfalls that a designer may not even be aware of when analyzing a game. It is natural to take note of where a game is broken—where there is some bad path-finding or "too stupid" A.I.—but the deconstruction of a game should begin before the first loading screen and is known as *addressing bias*. Bias shows up in how young designers tend to design for their own age group and find it hard to create projects for much older people, and the reverse is also true. These are biases that designers have to become aware of and get past when deconstructing a game and then going on to design one.

Bias is hard to design out of any project; in effect, you are learning how to play a game for the first time. When analyzing a game, you need to ask yourself questions that examine each aspect of the game, such as: How do the game's control systems work? How useful are the initial interface screens? Are they simple to use or confusing and complex? Would a new player understand how to enter the game world from a load screen (if there's no "Press A to start" instruction)? How good is the game at guiding the player into the experience and converting them incrementally into embracing the game's mechanic and premise? This is the first step in video game analysis: getting past everything that's a "given" or a convention that "everyone knows" and realizing that any barriers to entry in a game may color the entire experience for a new player.

3.3

3.3
Developers cannot assume everyone knows how to use one of these. Although familiar to many, a player picking up a PlayStation controller who has never used one, or a player who is more used to keyboard and mouse controls, is going to have to be taught the connections between buttons and interactions.

THINKING
AS A GAME
DESIGNER

UNDER-
STANDING
BIAS

STARTING
THE ANALYSIS
PROCESS

BIAS
INFORMS THE
MECHANIC

FIRST ORDER
OPTIMAL
STRATEGIES
(FOOS)

GAME
CONSISTENCY

INTERVIEW:
JAMES
PORTNOW

CHAPTER
SUMMARY AND
DISCUSSION
POINTS

Recognizing Bias

Avoiding bias is not just about getting beyond designing only the games and genres you like. Notice any biases towards certain game control conventions. For example, some people play predominantly on a PC using mouse and keyboard; others prefer a PlayStation or Xbox controller. The bias here is the expectation that when playing a game using a particular console's controller, the buttons will be mapped in a specific way.

On an Xbox console, there are two triggers: left and right. The conventions in a first person shooter game are that left brings up an aim (also known as "iron sights") or an aiming animation and right shoots. A or X are the "action" buttons; they open doors and crates, and they enable talking and varying levels of interaction in the environment. Once a player adopts these conventions, they become habitual and very hard to challenge without the player becoming frustrated. These are *learned biases*. Designers and players have them, and they are not bad; however, designers must recognize them and consider how much the player takes for granted— and how that can work positively for a seasoned player and negatively for a new player.

3.4

A designer has to see the game through the eyes of the inexperienced. Video games have tutorials for the same reasons that we have to undergo driving lessons to get a license: They make us comfortable with the controls and conventions of the technology we are using. (We will cover game tutorials in Chapter 10.)

3.4
Even people who drive every day have to learn how to drive a simulation. As a designer, you must test and then retest how intuitive the controls are and create simple tutorials that ease the player into the game, such as *Forza Motorsport 3*, developed by Turn 10 studios (2009). You cannot assume that only driving game aficionados will want to play your game (or restrict yourself to designing just for those people).

STARTING THE ANALYSIS PROCESS

Part of understanding bias and video game conventions comes from examining a game's menus and button assignments before diving into the game. This does not seem obvious at first, but it provides insight into the game creators' overall design strategy. In a well-designed video game, the most important actions are mapped to the most frequently used buttons. Secondary and tertiary actions are there to be discovered by the more ambitious players and may never be used by the majority of players. Drilling down into the menus and options gives insight into what the player has control over in the game and offers insight into the deeper levels of gameplay imagined by the team. The developers know that most gamers will never look beyond the first level of the "how to play this game" menu or tutorial, but deeper menu systems exist for those players who look for a more involved experience or who want to play in a specific way. Not every game has these deeper layers, which is another reason it is worth playing a variety of games to get a sense of where deeper levels of controls or button customizations are appropriate and useful (and when they become an obstruction to play).

For example, in the game *Sleeping Dogs* (United Front Games, 2012), as players complete missions they receive more complex combat abilities. These abilities are mapped to timed button presses and combinations, and the game can get fairly complex in those combinations. The designers knew that many players would not want to bother learning the more intricate patterns, so they can still make it through the entire game with one or two well-timed rudimentary attacks. The depth is there in *Sleeping Dogs* if you want it, but it's not required in order to have an enjoyable experience.

THINKING AS A GAME DESIGNER

UNDER-STANDING BIAS

STARTING THE ANALYSIS PROCESS

BIAS INFORMS THE MECHANIC

FIRST ORDER OPTIMAL STRATEGIES (FOOS)

GAME CONSISTENCY

INTERVIEW: JAMES PORTNOW

CHAPTER SUMMARY AND DISCUSSION POINTS

BIAS INFORMS THE MECHANIC

There are many different cognitive biases, and these can inform game design. Video game designers (as well as creators of other forms of entertainment) use cognitive biases to increase players' immersion and engagement in the game. Having some general knowledge of how most players think enables designers to make shortcuts in their game world design. These are some of the main biases:

Priming: This is used by magicians and advertising people alike. When a game presents an idea, action, or outcome repeatedly, players are more likely to follow the suggested pattern or directive. For example, when a mentalist is trying to put an idea into a subject's head, she may use the word try and the word cycle over and over again; chances are good that the subject will think of the word *tricycle*. Priming can be used in puzzle design: Giving the player several symbols scattered throughout a level primes the player to align those same symbols on a combination lock without having to present exhaustive instructions. It feels "natural" to the player to do this because of the priming.

Availability: This is why people buy lottery tickets even though the chance of winning is astronomically low. People tend to overestimate probability based on memorable occurrences. The lottery organizers publicize the few winners, not the masses of people who lose; thus, the model of winning becomes the most "available." Designers will draw upon what is most available in the player's memory as a method of interaction. For example, when a player needs to open a crate and has already used a crowbar to whack an enemy, the designer can count on the player being likely to smash open the crate (even though in real life a person would probably use the crowbar to ease open the crate's lid). The availability bias tells us that if you smash enemies with the bar, you smash crates open, too.

Anchoring: People tend to rely on one trait or piece of information to "anchor" their decisions. For example, many people will connect the mileage of a car with its condition. In some cases, a car with high mileage has been maintained well and a car with lesser mileage has been driven into the ground; nevertheless, most people will buy the low-mileage car. People tend to undershoot differences based on internalized baselines. In games with boss fights, designers tend to exaggerate the features of the boss to separate it from other enemies. The boss can look very powerful and menacing, but the player is going to anchor the challenge in what they have encountered with previous enemies. Designers tend to make the bosses look more powerful than they really are to compensate for this bias, and when a player defeats this seemingly incredibly tough boss, this a positive effect on the player.

The halo effect: Our overall impression of someone or something influences how we generalize about the person. For example, we may associate attractiveness with being more intelligent. This bias is linked to the anchoring bias; we are biased on our opinion of people based on our first impression. In a game, better-looking items may be made to work better than those which seem flimsy, or more attractive non-player characters (NPCs) may seem stronger or smarter to players than they actually are. The halo effect is subverted in some games to upset player expectations.

FIRST ORDER OPTIMAL
STRATEGIES (FOOS)

Designers craft a wish fulfillment experience for the player so, after becoming aware of your own biases and those the designers are using to draw you into the game, the next step in game analysis is to look at how the player is introduced to the gameplay itself. One approach to look out for when examining immediate engagement is the use of what are known as *First Order Optimal Strategies* (FOOS). This is a term coined by game designer and educator James Portnow. FOOS are low in skill but have a high level of positive outcome for the player. To put it another way, a FOOS is one seemingly powerful move, weapon, or tactic that a new player can adopt and use easily in the game with immediately positive results. Game developers recognize that coming into a game as a new player and facing super-powered enemies or other more advanced players can be a negative experience. The FOOS attempt to balance this; they provide players with an easy route towards positive in-game feedback while they learn the system and become better at the game.

3.5

As a designer, you need to look out for these because as an experienced player you may not even notice them. It is sometimes worth asking a non-gamer friend to play a game for the first time so you can observe and analyze the person's reactions and behaviors. Most games will have FOOS in them in some form, but FOOS are not consistent across genres. In the video game *Sleeping Dogs*, the first combat scenario you encounter teaches the heavy hit combo (on-screen prompts show which buttons to press). This is effective in beating up the bad guys quickly and players can use it the same way throughout most of the game. The strategy does not work on tougher bad guys; they evade or side step the attacks. This encourages the player to learn new techniques or to strategize differently within the game and to stop relying on the FOOS.

3.5
First Order Optimal Strategies enable players new to a game to feel powerful and accomplished. These FOOS should fall off as the player gets deeper into the game and the challenges become harder. *Sleeping Dogs*, United Front Games (2012).

Another example is in the game *Batman: Arkham Origins* (Warner Bros. Games Montréal/Splash Damage, 2013). Early on in the game, thugs and bad guys can be hit by Batman's batclaw device. This is useful because players can stun or trip up a few bad guys to "soften them up" before going into melee combat. This is an obvious FOOS, but it is balanced in later parts of the game as the bad guys dodge the batclaw. This forces players to lessen their reliance on the device as a singular tactic and to adopt new approaches to the combat so that the game never becomes too easy, routine, or predictable. This far into the game, the players are engaged; they feel powerful and accomplished; and when these tactics no longer work, they are more willing to experiment and more accepting of having to change up their gameplay.

3.6a

3.6b

3.6a
Designing flexible in-game strategies engages the player in what could become a boring rote process to get through a game. Being able to use items in multiple ways as shown here in *Batman: Arkham Origins* enables the player to develop new strategies.

3.6b
In *Call of Duty: Modern Warfare 3* (Infinity Ward, 2011), the "nootube" is a grenade launcher attachment for a weapon that is powerful enough to level the playing field a bit for inexperienced players when up against more able players.

GAME CONSISTENCY

The next step in analyzing video games is to examine the consistency of the gameplay. For example, why does Mario's jump ability feel so solid and capable (*Super Mario 64*, Nintendo, 1996) compared to the badly designed flying mechanic in *Superman* (Titus Software, 1999) for the Nintendo 64? How is the wayfinding (navigating around a level) better in *Half Life 2* (Valve, 2004) compared to the difficult-to-understand map in *Fable III* (Lionhead Studios, 2011)? Examining these elements often brings up what are known as *systemic breaks*. A systemic break is a part of a game where the system fails to work as intended.

As previously stated, games are systems. More so, they're designed systems; they're supposed to work consistently within the parameters designed by the team. This can even include emergent gameplay (unintended play elements, such as rocket-jumping in *Quake* (Id Software, 1993), where players point rockets at the ground and jump at the same time in order to travel further than would otherwise be possible) and exploits (finding a bug or system break that can be used to the player's advantage). Systemic breaks are different because they contribute to an overall negative experience. Systemic breaks are not to be confused with bugs, such as clipping through walls, characters getting stuck in geometry, or the game crashing on a certain level. (No game is ever free of bugs.) Systemic breaks are parts of a game in which the game seems to be playing against the goals or objectives of the player. For example, if a game has a skill-tree for a player that works on experience points, then this implies that points are a resource and hard to come by and must be earned by the player in order to level up. If the game design then gives out lots of experience points too easily, the entire reason for the skill-tree and leveling up makes no real sense; this would be a systemic break.

Consistency in a video game also requires never lying to a player; the game must gain the player's trust. When deconstructing a game, look for mechanics that feel natural, that make sense within the context of the game world. For example, does it make sense that in a game your character is detected by guards when running fast but not right after they have assassinated someone (*Assassin's Creed*, Ubisoft Montréal) or that if a character is human and can climb, that small obstacles, such as suitcases, would hinder their progress (*Alien: Isolation*, The Creative Assembly, 2014)? If an element in a game does not work as it would logically within the rules of the game-world, this will distance the player from the game and pull them out of their immersion, which can negatively affect their enjoyment of the game.

THINKING AS A GAME DESIGNER

UNDER-STANDING BIAS

STARTING THE ANALYSIS PROCESS

BIAS INFORMS THE MECHANIC

FIRST ORDER OPTIMAL STRATEGIES (FOOS)

GAME CONSISTENCY

INTERVIEW: JAMES PORTNOW

CHAPTER SUMMARY AND DISCUSSION POINTS

TIP

EMPIRICAL RESEARCH

Analyzing games means studying games in a methodological, empirical manner, which means acquiring knowledge by observation or experimentation. To do this, you must learn how to observe a game while playing it, which is not easy. Playing as a designer means taking a lot of notes. For example, when playing a horror game such as *Resident Evil* (Capcom, 1996) or *Dead Space* (Visceral Games), a player may become cautious before entering a room or feel nervous when out in the open and exposed. As a designer, you have

to ask yourself: "Why does that scare me?" "How did that audio put me on edge?" and "What game elements have made me apprehensive—how did they achieve this?" Trace back your progress and really look around at the level design, lighting, audio effects, and interactions that have brought you towards a specific emotional state. Becoming aware of how a game creates and paces out an experience is a critical first step in understanding the emotional impact of a game (more on emotion in games in Chapter 5).

3.7a

3.7b

3.7a
For *Dead Space*™ to work, the player has to feel tension and a level of fear almost all of the time. This tension is created through level design (dark corridors, uneven light sources) and audio as well as by mixing up when enemies may or may not appear, so the player is always on edge.

3.7b
Resident Evil helped define the survival horror genre and uses atmosphere and the environment to produce tension. It was also renowned for having enemies jump out unexpectedly at the player. This created an enormous sense of tension in the player.

The Rollercoaster as
Video Game Metaphor

When you play as a designer, the experience is similar to being on a rollercoaster and analyzing the ride at the same time. There are points in a well-designed coaster that enhance the experience, from expectation (the "ascend" is usually a slow journey to the top) to fear (at the first exhilarating drop). Once the first drop is over, we experience an adrenalin rush as the ride produces "airtime," which makes us feel as if we are coming out of our harnesses, and all the while the coaster twists and turns so fast that we can't predict what will happen. Then there is the "block": the area of the ride that pauses just for a few seconds before carrying us on to more exciting parts. The block is important because it gives us just enough time to reflect and consider what has gone before, to dwell for a few seconds within the adrenalin rush of excitement, before we are shot off once more. At the end of the coaster, riders feel exhilarated, relieved, happy, joyous, and perhaps a little sick.

3.8

3.8
A rollercoaster as analogy for a video game: It is a system with multiple moving parts and "scenes" with feeling-states, as are many games. Analyzing a myriad of experiences helps designers build a solid repository for their own design practices. Questions designers ask: "Are all of these people having a positive experience?" and "How does the experience change based on the rider's behavior (screaming, shouting, standing up) and the position of the seat?"

THINKING
AS A GAME
DESIGNER

UNDER-
STANDING
BIAS

STARTING
THE ANALYSIS
PROCESS

BIAS
INFORMS THE
MECHANIC

FIRST ORDER
OPTIMAL
STRATEGIES
(FOOS)

GAME
CONSISTENCY

INTERVIEW:
JAMES
PORTNOW

CHAPTER
SUMMARY AND
DISCUSSION
POINTS

That brief pause on the block allows a moment of reflection and builds anticipation for the next part of the ride. All of this is similar to pacing in a game. As a player/designer, you must look at the pacing of the game you are deconstructing (we will examine pacing more in Chapter 5). How often does the game use "safe points" where no action takes place or where the player is out of harm's way? How are these areas used and communicated to the player? How is the narrative exposition handled? Is it accomplished via NPCs, a voice-over, or cut-scenes? How often are you, as a player, forced to disengage from the action in a game to watch a cut-scene? The notes for even a short game can get quite long, but to study and deconstruct a game, you pause to write down the elements of the game in order to better understand them.

Returning to the metaphor of the rollercoaster ride as game deconstruction, to know the ride properly the designer has to experience it multiple times. Designers have to know every nuance of the experience. For example, how does each experience differ when it is repeated multiple times? How does knowledge of the ride change the experience for the rider? A game designer does not just play a game once; he or she must get to know the game from every conceivable angle. This is how empirical study works: The same "experiment" is performed (the game is played, the rollercoaster is ridden) and the variables are recorded each time, even though the overall mechanic is the same.

3.9

3.9

Mass Effect™ (BioWare, 2007–2012) is a branching narrative game that allows the player to make allegiances, enemies, and decisions that affect some outcomes in the game. Players will have a different experience depending on the choices they make in the game. The focus on inter-character relationships encourages a deeper, more emotionally rewarding experience for the player. These character interactions also serve to better pace the action in the game.

JAMES PORTNOW

CEO, Rainmaker Games; Director, Games for Good

How do you feel bias tends to affect the inexperienced developer?

"I see too many novice developers build what they think they would like, without thinking about how to make that approachable to someone who isn't inside their head. This is the one of the biggest things I see sink projects by inexperienced teams."

"It's incredibly hard to be honest with oneself; after all, there's no one easier to lie to than you, but it's one of the game designer's most important tasks. You must really look at your work as if it were someone else's and be as critical and as demanding as you'd be if someone else were building it."

How would you break down game development into critical elements?

"Too often we build games in isolation, thinking that by playing games, by working on games, we can build games, but our job is actually to craft experiences, and to do that you have to have them. So when people ask me where I draw inspiration, it's just from living, whether it's drinking in the great books that our species has produced over a thousand generations or letting myself really feel the heartbreak of a love I've lost. It all feeds into the game."

"I'd say the most important things for any new developer to be aware of are: scope, communication, and the speed at which you get your product into the hands of people outside of the team. If you can keep a handle on these, scope small, communicate well as a team, and get your game out for people to test as soon as possible, you'll do fine."

Playing as a designer is an important step in understanding the relationship between the player, the developer, and the game.

"I remember analyzing *Gun.Smoke* (Capcom, 1985); it was the first time we had really taken the time to properly break down that old NES (Nintendo Entertainment System) classic. We spent about an hour on the first five minutes and examined how the designers had created the interest curve. We wanted to know what it was that kept us playing; it opened up a world of understand about how interest curve could be crafted by clever enemy placement and wave design alone."

3.10
James Portnow is probably best known for his involvement in the YouTube channel *Extra Credits*. The channel covers all manner of video-game–related subjects and has even become its own independent publisher.

CHAPTER SUMMARY

This chapter examines the process of moving away from being a player of video games to becoming a designer who really studies and analyzes them. Although designers may use themselves as a model for their audience, making the games they would want to play, this can be restricting, leading to repetition and stagnation in genres. When analyzing games, get an overview of the intentions of the game developer; avoid becoming frustrated with elements of the gameplay that affect just you.

Analyzing the mechanics, the aesthetics, and the interfaces of games you know well and also games you rarely play provides insight into how a game really works. Sometimes being a spectator of a game, or giving a game to someone who has never played it, is a solid methodology for better understanding how the game converts non-players to players. As a game developer, you must understand not just the intentions of the designer but also the process of development and how the player engages with the game mentally and physically. There are multiple approaches towards critically analyzing games, and once you have begun to view games from the player-as-developer perspective, you can begin to examine the motivations video game players have for participating in the games they play.

THINKING AS A GAME DESIGNER

UNDER-STANDING BIAS

STARTING THE ANALYSIS PROCESS

BIAS INFORMS THE MECHANIC

FIRST ORDER OPTIMAL STRATEGIES (FOOS)

GAME CONSISTENCY

INTERVIEW: JAMES PORTNOW

CHAPTER SUMMARY AND DISCUSSION POINTS

DISCUSSION POINTS

1. **What particular biases do you bring to familiar games as opposed to unfamiliar games? For example, do you play sports games exclusively or not at all? If not at all, why not? Examine and list your rationales for why you play or do not play specific games or genres.**

2. **Which games break conventions in interesting or frustrating ways? If you've been frustrated by a particular game, how would you attempt to solve that problem, in mapping controls, in player interaction with interfaces, or in other ways?**

3. **Which games have affected you emotionally and how? These could be games that scared you or games that always seem to make you happy. How do they achieve this emotional shift in you? Is it somewhat universal—are other players you have observed also scared or also happy?**

PART 2: GAME DESIGN

CHAPTER FOUR
UNDERSTANDING THE MOTIVATIONS FOR PLAY

Chapter Objectives:

- **Recognize player types.**

- **Understand player motivations.**

- **Explore games as experiences.**

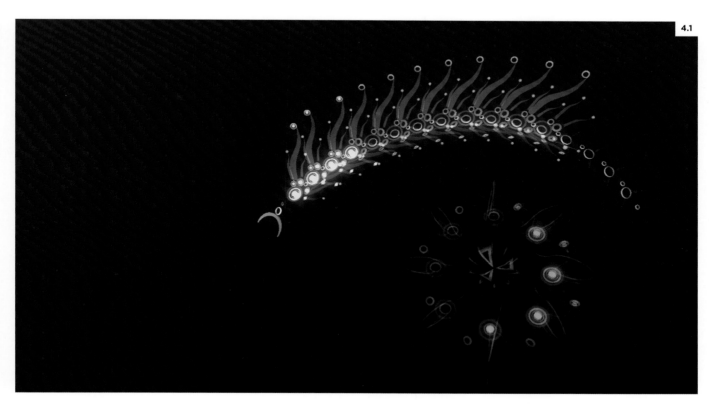

4.1
flOw, developed by Thatgamecompany (2006).

PLAYER-FOCUSED
GAME DESIGN

In this chapter, we will focus on the psychology of the player and delve into the experiences and emotions players seek when entering the field of play (or "magic circle," as discussed in Chapter 2). In Chapters 1 and 2, we examined why we play and how we play; in Chapter 3, we examined the process of video game deconstruction. In this chapter, we'll consider the different types of players, their motivations, and how we can better understand those for whom we make games.

TIP

NEW MODELS FOR NEW FORMS OF PLAY

Understanding players today is very different from the standard practice even a decade ago. With always-online games (for example, multiplayer online battle arenas, more commonly known as MOBAs, such as *Dota 2* (Valve, 2013) and *League of Legends* (Riot Games, 2009), as well as multiplayer-focused games such as the *Call of Duty* franchise), video games have become more akin to services than simple entertainment. From a designer perspective, games that play online are a treasure trove of *metrics* (methods of measuring) and *analytics* (looking for meaningful patterns in data) for the designer and development team. This has shifted the industry's focus away from individual players and turned it instead towards wider community engagement. New careers, such as online community managers, have emerged as part of this shift in focus towards service and prolonged engagement. The development of real-time metrics means that instead of guessing, development teams can make informed decisions about their games based on real data from players. This has changed how players are understood, and it is why the traditional definition of the "taxonomy of play," as introduced in this chapter, has become an increasingly irrelevant and incomplete model. Designers now look for a more psychological and engaged profile of players who change and evolve with the technology (the OCEAN model, see page 70); this provides a more open and fluid understanding of players individually and as groups.

BARTLE'S TAXONOMY OF PLAY

For around a decade, the video game industry has been using a well-established model for thinking about what motivates players. It's known as the "Taxonomy of Play" and was created by game designer Richard Bartle (1996). It was originally designed for an early incarnation of Massively Multiplayer Online Role Playing Games (MMORPGs) or Massively Multiplayer Online (MMO-style) games known as Multi-User Dungeons (MUDs). Bartle's model developed from his observations of players in his games and their reactions to different scenarios. He grouped players into four basic player types (Killers, Socializers, Achievers, and Explorers) as a way to inform his design process.

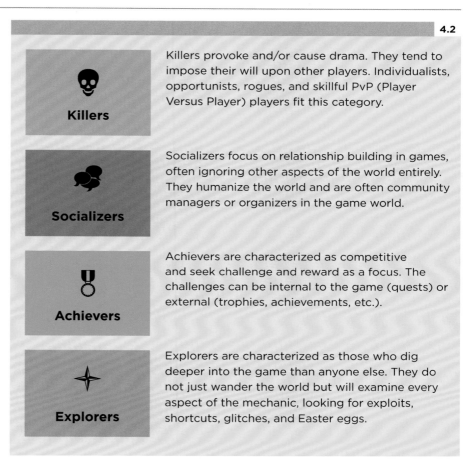

4.2

Killers

Killers provoke and/or cause drama. They tend to impose their will upon other players. Individualists, opportunists, rogues, and skillful PvP (Player Versus Player) players fit this category.

Socializers

Socializers focus on relationship building in games, often ignoring other aspects of the world entirely. They humanize the world and are often community managers or organizers in the game world.

Achievers

Achievers are characterized as competitive and seek challenge and reward as a focus. The challenges can be internal to the game (quests) or external (trophies, achievements, etc.).

Explorers

Explorers are characterized as those who dig deeper into the game than anyone else. They do not just wander the world but will examine every aspect of the mechanic, looking for exploits, shortcuts, glitches, and Easter eggs.

4.2
Bartle's original player types.

Bartle's players would fall somewhere in each category. Some players would, of course, exhibit multiple traits, while others would reveal one major trait. The model labels players so that designers could think about how much a "Killer" would enjoy a certain aspect of a game and which parts an "Explorer" would be interested in. Out of this simple categorization came what is known as the *Bartle test*, which is a series of questions and a scoring system that classifies players based upon their preferences. For example, a player could score 100% Killer, 50% Socializer, 40% Achiever, and 10% Explorer, which would be indicative of a player who prefers fighting other players (such as in Player Versus Player servers in *World of Warcraft*) rather than one who wants to cooperate with others.

Developers, designers, and marketers have used this model and questionnaire outside of its intended use for MMORPGs in an attempt to quantify how much of a game relates to these player types. Designers would conclude that if a game fit some or all player types, it stood a good chance of being successful. The problem is that the Bartle test created a form of "check-box" design process; some viewed it as that elusive "formula" for making a game that is certain to appeal to all types of players. Bartle's player types were a sound model, but these models created issues when applied wholesale to every game, from puzzles to RPGs and FPS games.

In improving the Bartle model to make it more inclusive and to reflect different styles of games, Bartle and others examined players with crossover characteristics or traits. For example, a "Killer" player type may share "Explorer" characteristics, as this player may look for in-game exploits that will aid in dominating other players (e.g., in older multiplayer games where a player could "spawn camp"). The player types became less rigid in the new model and developers became more aware that players may change their types in different game genres; for instance, a player who is an "Achiever" type in a puzzle game may become a "Killer" type in an FPS game.

The Bartle model and its test work well within their intended applications (MUDs and MMORPGs), but these four player types have been applied to games of all genres over time, and it has become obvious that the model lacks nuance. It is based less on psychology and the study of how we think and more on observations of players of a specific game genre. Designers need a model based on who players are today and one that works across all game genres.

BARTLE'S PLAYER TYPES MADE FLUID

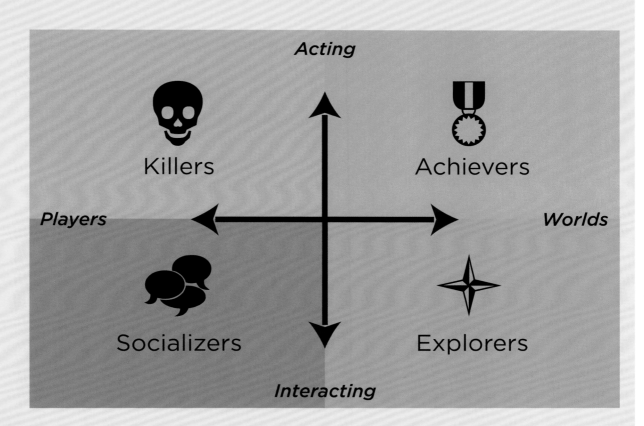

4.3 Bartle's player types, modified.
The horizontal axis characterizes a preference for focusing on other players or on the world (such as in *Call of Duty* multiplayer versus *SimCity*). The vertical axis characterizes a preference for *interacting* or *acting upon*. Achiever types prefer acting upon the world (for example, *The Sims*) and Socializer types prefer interacting with other players (*The Sims* online). As the model shows, these are not exclusive boxes; thus, a Killer type can be social (in teams or clans) as well as one who chases down achievements in the world (high scores, better weapons, etc.). These axes are a map of how fluid player types can be across different genres.

THE BIG FIVE
PERSONALITY TRAITS

Game developers and academics (including Bartle himself) have begun to examine the uses and abuses of the Bartle model in an attempt to evolve it beyond its original intended purpose. One group that tackled creating a new model head-on was an interdisciplinary think-tank called Project Horseshoe. One of its members, Jason VandenBerghe, a creative director at Ubisoft Montreal, gave a talk in 2012 at the Game Developers Conference (GDC) and introduced their new model. Jason suggested disposing of the Bartle types for all games and instead using motivations for play extrapolated from personality studies of psychologists.

Since the 1980s, psychologists have developed a theory of human characteristics (with solid empirical data to back it up) based upon five personality traits. These are known as the Big Five, or OCEAN. The model is particularly interesting because it seems to work across all ages and cultures.

The Big Five, or OCEAN, traits are:

Openness (to experience): These traits include creativity, adventure, curiosity, desire for variety of experience, and preference for novelty.

Conscientiousness: Tendency to be dependable, self-disciplined, not spontaneous, organized.

Extraversion: Energetic, assertive, sociable, seeking stimulation from others, talkative.

Agreeableness: Cooperative, friendly, compassionate, good tempered.

Neuroticism: Experiences negative emotions easily; has a range of emotional stability; experiences anger, anxiety, depression, and vulnerability.

Humans are complex beings, and the richness that the OCEAN model brings when set against the Bartle test is in highlighting the fact that players' actions in a game can change based on the game's context. The OCEAN model provides deeper insight into players' motivations before, after, and during play.

Explaining the New Model

The OCEAN model is not absolute, much like the later version of the Bartle model; it is based on a sliding scale or spectrum of traits. Players can personify several traits at once to varying degrees. One way to better explain the Big Five personality traits is through character analogues. (This is also how many character backgrounds are constructed, as we examine in the discussion of character design in Chapter 7.)

Using the *Lord of the Rings* (book or movie) characters, we can see how the different character traits map to the OCEAN model:

Openness
High: Frodo Baggins
Low: Samwise Gamgee

Conscientiousness
High: Strider/Aragorn
Low: Peregrin Took

Extraversion
High: Meriadoc Brandybuck
Low: Boromir

Agreeableness
High: Gimli
Low: Elrond

Neuroticism
High: Gollum
Low: Gandalf the Grey

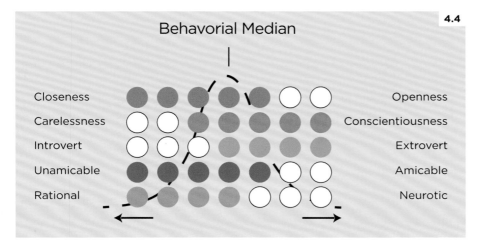

4.4

Behavorial Median

Closeness						Openness
Carelessness						Conscientiousness
Introvert						Extrovert
Unamicable						Amicable
Rational						Neurotic

4.4
The Big Five model is a bell curve; there are extremes at both ends, as you would expect with personality traits, but the majority of people tested lie within the middle. This model also allows for players who share traits across multiple categories and those who score higher and lower across multiple categories.

PLAYER-FOCUSED GAME DESIGN

BARTLE'S TAXONOMY OF PLAY

THE BIG FIVE PERSONALITY TRAITS

THE FIVE DOMAINS AND PLAYER MOTIVATION

PLAYER ARCHETYPES

DESIGNING ETHICAL VIDEO GAMES

INTERVIEW: BRANDON SHEFFIELD

CHAPTER SUMMARY AND DISCUSSION POINTS

Translating the OCEAN Model for Game Design

Because it is a spectrum of traits, some people can be high in one area and then low in another and still be a likeable or interesting person. Having a high neurotic trait does not make a character evil, necessarily (Gollum is an extreme example), but it will make their interactions with others more complicated and their reasons for playing in a specific way more apparent. We all know people in real life who are neurotic about certain things—perhaps superstitious or quick to become moody—but who can be great friends.

People who score low or high on the OCEAN scale (remembering that low does not mean "bad" and high is not "good" or "better") map these character traits from their real life onto their gaming personas. Simply put, we take much of who we are, consciously and subconsciously, into our games. This may sound obvious, but using the OCEAN model allows us to look at empirical data from psychology studies rather than generalized assumptions.

With the advent of the OCEAN model, Bartle's four player types have become five character traits. The problem is that the OCEAN model is a general model for psychologists and was not developed for video games specifically. This is where Project Horseshoe has provided five player motivations—five "domains" of play that bridge the gap between video games and the OCEAN psychology model. The domains are effectively translations of the Big Five that reinterpret the psychological model to make it more useful for game designers. Instead of Openness/Closedness and so on, the five domains are *Novelty*, *Challenge*, *Stimulation*, *Harmony*, and *Threat*. These traits better map onto video games and styles of play.

4.5
Project Horseshoe's five domains or motivations of play: Using the OCEAN spectrum model of high, low, and in between, the domains are mapped onto video game player traits and game mechanics. These domains directly map the psychology model to the "language" of a video game.

Novelty
Experiences
High: *imaginative, unique*
Low: *predictable, conventional*

Challenge
Self-Control
High: *high amount of challenge*
Low: *easy, optional challenges*

Stimulation
Social/Active
High: *social, active, multiplayer*
Low: *calming, restive, no social*

Harmony
Community
High: *cooperation, no violence*
Low: *combative, individualistic*

Threat
Negative Emotions
High: *difficult to master, tricky*
Low: *easy to master, easy*

THE FIVE DOMAINS AND PLAYER MOTIVATION

Designers want to know how their players think and what motivates them to play. Video game design is an expensive, high-risk business. A game may be technically sound but for some reason just not resonate with players (*Beyond Good and Evil*, Ubisoft Montpellier, 2003; *Grim Fandango*, LucasArts, 1998; *Psychonauts*, Double Fine Productions, 2005). Other games may be unfinished or only in pre-release and become hugely popular (*DayZ*, Dean Hall, 2012; *Kerbal Space Program*, Squad, 2011). For obvious reasons, game designers want to find out if their game ideas and prototypes are likely to elicit a high level of interest and emotional involvement from players.

At this point, you may be wondering why we bother with all these models and surveys. Surely people just play the games they want to, and play how they want to, and that's that? The purpose of these models is to create a useful tool set for game designers because they have no idea what you, or your friends, or other players really want. Imagine a game where you play as a teenage girl who wanders around an empty house trying to find out why no one is home. That sounds like a pretty boring game (it's the premise of *Gone Home*), but once we model the game against the five domains, the game takes on a far more interesting shape. There is high novelty (a majority of game characters are male, but this main character is female), medium level of challenge (find out why her family has left the house), low level of stimulation (it is not fast-paced, breakneck action), low harmony (the narrative is designed for one player), and high threat (the big empty house during a thunderstorm is cringingly tension-filled).

Essentially the five domains re-purpose the OCEAN model to make sense as a tool for game designers. A "conscientious" player does not make as much sense in the context of a game world as a player who features high or low on the "challenge" spectrum. So the translation looks like this:

Novelty = Openness of experience

Challenge = Conscientiousness

Stimulation = Extraversion

Harmony = Agreeableness

Threat = Neuroticism

4.6
Examples of the five domains of play.
Novelty: Differentiates imaginative experiences from expected, repeating, or conventional experiences.
Challenge: Self-control; what the game asks of the player.
Stimulation: Physical reaction within player, emotional state.
Harmony: Player to player interactions.
Threat: Trigger of "negative" emotions in the player.

Novelty

High: Civilization V *or* The Sims. *Games are never the same twice.*

Low: FIFA *or* Madden. *Rigid rule set, same mechanic.*

Challenge

High: Dark Souls, *methodological, measured approach.*

Low: Lego Batman, *limited/no mastery, is still fun.*

Stimulation

High: Dance Dance Revolution, *high energy and socialization.*

Low: Proteus, *calming, experiential, solo play and low energy.*

Harmony

High: LittleBigPlanet, *sharing and cooperation—part of the game.*

Low: Mortal Kombat, *individual victory, no collaboration.*

Threat

High: Gears of War, *intense, visceral and fast-paced gameplay.*

Low: Candy Crush, *repetitive, non-violent, positive feedback.*

As a designer, you can match elements of your game to the personality traits of the players you want playing your game. This is a far more nuanced model to use when thinking about game design because it allows for more flexibility and enables you to better direct your game concepts using empirical data rather than guesswork. Remember that High and Low are not positive and negative; designing to hit high and low scoring people could make for a fantastic game experience. A fantasy adventure that takes a single player into a world that is beautiful to look at and explore (stimulation) that also has action and mastery (challenge) but only if the player really wants to pursue them (novelty) would be *Skyrim* (Bethesda Game Studios, 2011).

OCEAN Personality Test (example)

4.7

Openness to Experience(s)

● ● ● ● ● ○ ○

Scoring high suggests people who are original, creative, curious, complex. Lower scoring suggests a personality that is more conventional, down to earth, uncreative, narrow interest patterns.

%: 84

Conscientiousness

● ● ● ● ○ ○ ○

Scoring high suggests people who are reliable, organized, disciplined. Lower scoring suggests a personality that is more disorganized, negligent and not dependable.

%: 69

Extraversion

● ● ● ● ● ○ ○

Scoring high suggests people who are sociable, friendly, talkative. Lower scoring suggests a personality that is reserved, inhibited, quiet.

%: 70

Agreeableness

● ● ● ● ○ ○ ○

Scoring high suggests people who are good natured, sympathetic, empathetic, courteous. Low scoring suggests a personality that is critical, harsh, callous.

%: 57

Neuroticism

● ● ○ ○ ○ ○ ○

Scoring high suggests people who are nervous, highly-strung, insecure. Low scoring suggests a personality that is relaxed, secure, calm.

%: 32

4.7
These are my test results from an OCEAN personality website. This chart goes some way into explaining what elements of games I am most likely to enjoy and which ones I would not. For example, I enjoy RPGs with large open worlds and choose-your-path adventures, such as *Skyrim*. I am not so fond of games that require a great deal of mastery or are stressful to accomplish, such as *Ninja Gaiden* (Team Ninja, 2004) or *Bayonetta* (Platinum Games, 2010).

PLAYER ARCHETYPES

We have been considering models for most of the chapter, but a model based on one person does not offer enough depth to take the guesswork out of the question "Will anyone like this game?" As you build a game concept, you can map the sorts of people most likely to enjoy or engage with the puzzles, action, or narrative of your game, and these imagined people are called *player archetypes*, or *player personas* (*personas* are used most often in marketing and other design industries). You can create player archetypes to guide your game design decisions based on their imagined personalities and game preferences.

Todd Howard, executive producer at Bethesda, who developed *Skyrim*, talked about a process they use called "spotlighting." The design team took each proposed feature of the game and put it into a "spotlight" in front of player archetypes in order to decide how crucial to the overall game experience this one aspect was. For example, what if the horses could carry equipment (and thereby bypass the encumbrance limitation of the player)? This would seem to be a useful addition to the game, but when you begin to look at this decision through the eyes of the player archetypes (challenge, novelty, threat), it meant that the horses became too important in the game; rather than being just a means of transport, they would become roaming inventory systems. Then what happens when they die or can't enter a room or town? This design feature would amplify the negative aspects of what the horse is capable of, so it was removed. The most important part of the *Skyrim* experience has to be the player and their character.

The archetypes are not the perfect players, the ones who would love every aspect of the game. By using the OCEAN and player domain models as a guide, you can begin to build a game that is player focused and, therefore, is much more likely to deliver an overall positive experience. I tell my students that knowing your audience and researching them are important parts of the design process. The challenge is to balance your findings and research against your own creativity and drive to create a compelling game.

There is a danger of building a project too much around the opinions of others and allowing them to steer your process. All of these processes and models are to guide you towards thinking about and designing the experience you want for the player; they can be used as much or as little as the project demands. Another issue to be aware of when using player archetypes and character trait models is making too many assumptions and generalizations. This can lead to employing negative stereotypes, creating a game that lacks any form of inclusion and, in the worst-case scenario, a game that is denigrating or insulting to certain audiences.

4.8
Player personas or archetypes (who the players are) and scenarios (what the player does in situation X or Y) are useful in guiding a project in its early stages. If the game is starting to become unfocused, the design team can use the archetypes to ask, "What would Player X want to experience or see?"

PLAYER-
FOCUSED
GAME DESIGN

BARTLE'S
TAXONOMY
OF PLAY

THE BIG FIVE
PERSONALITY
TRAITS

THE FIVE
DOMAINS
AND PLAYER
MOTIVATION

**PLAYER
ARCHETYPES**

DESIGNING
ETHICAL
VIDEO GAMES

INTERVIEW:
BRANDON
SHEFFIELD

CHAPTER
SUMMARY AND
DISCUSSION
POINTS

4.8

Name	Matthew Magee
Job Title/ Responsibilities	Barista
Demographics	22 years old In a relationship Undergraduate in Art (BA)
Motivations	Matt is interested in games that enhance his fitness levels. He sees himself as a casual gamer, but also one who plays a lot on long commutes to work. He has a smartphone and a tablet device on which he plays games. He also invested in a console but struggles to find games that interest him.
Goals	To be excited by games that fit in with his perception of self. Interesting, deep, artistic, creative, and surprising.
Frustrations	Lack of diversity in games, the general "geekiness" attached to the game, sexism in games—he likes to be able to have his girlfriend watch him play games and these tend to turn her off.
Environment	Matt lives in a small loft apartment in a major multicultural city in the USA. He is comfortable with technology in his world but does not see it as totally fulfilling.
Quote	I want a game that makes me feel.

Name	Rachel Riley
Job Title/ Responsibilities	Part Time Retail, Hot Topic
Demographics	17 years old Single High School Senior
Motivations	Rachel is a bit of a loner; she sees herself as different from her classmates—more intelligent and deeper than her peers. She does not socialize much; instead, she spends a lot of time online in communities for MMO and RPG games.
Goals	Rachel is very comfortable in the multiplayer space but wants to feel more connected with her fellow players. She feels emotionally attached to her clan and online friends but also wants to balance her life with the outside world as she moves towards college.
Frustrations	Getting hit on in the game space constantly; not being treated as a serious gamer because she is female. Wanting to prove her skills to her peers and others. To be understood as a passionate, clever, and interesting player.
Environment	Rachel lives in rural Pennsylvania in a small village of a few thousand. She is most comfortable with PCs over consoles or tablets. Her parents worry that she spends too much time online and try to restrict her playing time.
Quote	I want to be taken seriously as a gamer.

DESIGNING ETHICAL VIDEO GAMES

Sometimes in the rush to get a game prototype up and running or a game out the door, designers can fall into the trap of purposely or accidentally using negative stereotypes in their products. This can happen in games based upon assumptions drawn from limited personal preferences or experiences or based on poorly designed player archetypes. Designers, like many of us, use generalizations and assumptions when creating their products. Games are complex and hard to make, and creative people will often use themselves as a shortcut from which to model an intended audience. Given that most game designers are male (this is slowly changing, thankfully) and (in the west) white, this can lead to some very problematic design choices that are not necessarily deliberate but do nothing to include other genders, sexualities, or ethnicities.

4.9a
How much violence and sexuality you put into your game is a design choice. Games can be used to "just" entertain or to be a catalyst to inform and bring about change. Every decision needs to be balanced by input from as many people as possible. *Grand Theft Auto V* (Rockstar North, 2013).

4.9b
Non-violent games are plentiful and very popular. From the Mario games to *Journey* (Thatgamecompany, 2012), games that offer an alternative to guns and destruction do very well and have broad appeal.

Video Games Are a Transformative Medium

You are doing something amazing; you are creating something where there was nothing before. Games transform those who play them. As we explored in Chapter 1 and Chapter 2, games are part of our culture and video games raise the entertainment bar by being interactive and incredibly engaging. As a video game designer, you have an awesome responsibility to your players, and this is not a responsibility you should take lightly.

We play games for a variety of reasons, but mostly it is for some form of emotional release. We could use a multiplayer death-match to vent our frustrations about our boss, or we could play *Mario Galaxy* (Nintendo, 2007) because it always makes us happy. We could play a game to learn more about ourselves by swapping gender or ethnicity and perhaps gain some new perspective, or we could just play to relax. All of these scenarios are accepted as part of gaming, so it must also be true that if games can serve an emotional need, they must in some way change us as we play. So designers need to be aware of what we are presenting to our players. What are we trying to say and how we are saying it?

Over the course of a game's development, many pressures can be brought to bear on designers to overuse specific cultural norms or to push certain viewpoints because they are thought to appeal to a specific demographic (the young, white, male player). It is all too easy to stray into developing a game that reflects the limited background of the designer. A tool you can use to prevent this, or at least to check it, is inclusive conversations. This is a deliberate thought process and not hard to implement. If, for example, you are part of an all-male design team, it is important to invite female designers or players into the conversation to gain some perspective. The same goes for ethnicity, age, and sexual orientation. Make inclusion part of your design process and your games will be the better for it.

4.9a

4.9b

PLAYER-
FOCUSED
GAME DESIGN

BARTLE'S
TAXONOMY
OF PLAY

THE BIG FIVE
PERSONALITY
TRAITS

THE FIVE
DOMAINS
AND PLAYER
MOTIVATION

PLAYER
ARCHETYPES

**DESIGNING
ETHICAL
VIDEO GAMES**

INTERVIEW:
BRANDON
SHEFFIELD

CHAPTER
SUMMARY AND
DISCUSSION
POINTS

Inclusion

Stereotypes are lazy and are often offensive to those being portrayed; the video game industry is slowly improving because players have diversified and grown bored of adolescent themes and titillation. There has also been a noted and welcome increase in negative reaction against offensive stereotypes. Games can be used to educate us all; as cultural artifacts, they teach us about our own world and ourselves. As a creator, you can get it right or get it wrong.

Your game will influence your players based on your ethical positions. As a designer, be inclusive and respectful of everyone and their input will only serve to make your game better. One place to look for discussions on issues in gaming is the International Game Developers Association website (IGDA.org) and their special interest groups (SIGs), as well as the website for this book, which has links to articles and sites covering these subjects in more detail (www .bloomsbury.com/Salmond-Video-Game).

4.10

4.10
Games such as *Shadow of the Colossus* (Team ICO, 2005) usurp player expectations and meta-narratives. The twist of hero/anti-hero in the game pulls at the tropes and stereotypes used in video games and other media that so rarely question the consequences of violence.

Being the Self-aware Designer

Violence, sex, and gore-laden themes in video games have produced many articles for the news media. Certain video games are singled out, though their content is often no more extreme than that found in movies or on TV. For every *Hitman: Absolution* (IO Interactive, 2012) with its adult themes, there is a *Pikmin* (Nintendo, 2001) or a *Mario Galaxy*. In fact, far more games are released with the "E for everyone" ESRB rating than with the "M for Mature" rating (in 2013, 46% of games were rated E and 12% were rated M). Design choices can affect the bottom line of a game. Although monetary reward is no reason to make a game ethical, there is a very real effect on games that have a distorted moral compass. Having an M rating on your game restricts the audience (although the ratings board in the USA may be more accepting of violent themes over sexual themes, which is somewhat reversed in Europe) for your game and the potential for profits. Being inclusive makes financial and ethical sense; if your game turns off women because of its themes, that is 50% of the general population that will not buy your game. If your game denigrates or insults certain ethnicities, the media backlash or interest group pressure can damage your game or even get it pulled from virtual or store shelves.

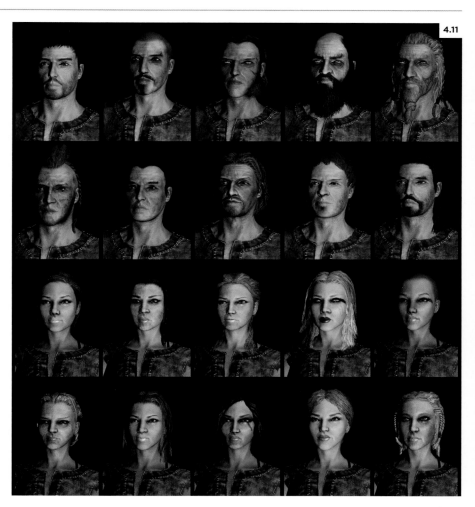

4.11

4.11
Giving the player a choice of gender and/or race, as shown here in *The Elder Scrolls V: Skyrim*®, opens up possibilities for the player to explore his or her own personality and becomes a performance in itself. Forcing a player to be a white male character limits exploration and discourages different modes of play.

PLAYER-
FOCUSED
GAME DESIGN

BARTLE'S
TAXONOMY
OF PLAY

THE BIG FIVE
PERSONALITY
TRAITS

THE FIVE
DOMAINS
AND PLAYER
MOTIVATION

PLAYER
ARCHETYPES

DESIGNING
ETHICAL
VIDEO GAMES

INTERVIEW:
BRANDON
SHEFFIELD

CHAPTER
SUMMARY AND
DISCUSSION
POINTS

That is not to suggest that you should
only consider ethical options if you can
use them to your advantage; you can
make those decisions because they are
the right thing to do. Approaching game
design from an ethical standpoint does
not mean self-censorship or making a
game that is somehow diluted. Other
forms of entertainment (notably
television and film, although there are
exceptions) have broad, mass appeal and
are still entertaining, insightful, and
valid works of art.

4.12

4.12
In video games, designers can set for players
ethical conundrums and then lead the player
towards "doing the right thing" by offering in-
game advantages for the player who chooses
a more righteous path over those who choose
darker paths. In *Fallout 3* (Bethesda Game
Studios, 2008), players choose whether or not
to save the junkyard dog and have him follow
the main character. If the dog is killed, the player
has lost a useful companion.

INTERVIEW

PART 2:
GAME DESIGN

CHAPTER FOUR
UNDERSTANDING THE
MOTIVATIONS FOR PLAY

BRANDON SHEFFIELD

Director, Necrosoft Games

You're Director of Necrosoft Games, which has just released Gunhouse on PlayStation Mobile. The games came from game jams. How important are platforms like that for game development?

"Game jams are important for creativity; they are a good way to work with developers you don't usually work with, to try out new ideas quickly, and to experiment with things you otherwise might ignore. This is why companies like Capy Games and Double Fine host in-house game jams with their own developers—a lot of interesting ideas or mechanics come out of this that could apply to future games or be turned into an entire game on their own."

4.13
The final version of *Gunhouse* was the result of a year of prototype, playtest, rework, repeat.

Could you give us some insight into the development cycle for *Gunhouse*?

"For *Gunhouse*, the first iteration of the game came about during the first MolyJam game jam. Thereafter, I had the opportunity to do some games for Sony's new PlayStation Mobile platform, and since I could use this as a prototype, I went with that as one of them. From there, it was basically iteration after iteration, trying to get the game to feel the way I wanted it to. It would take ages to describe everything I did to get from there to here, but suffice it to say the final game in almost no way resembles the original prototype, even though I used the same artist. The cycle was essentially: prototype, playtest, iterate, then repeat. For an entire year!"

"For *Gunhouse* and our upcoming title *Oh, Deer!*, they're both PlayStation Mobile games, we had to use the PSM suite. There are a few libraries in there that we use, but for the most part we were constrained to that and whatever C# ingenuity we could muster. We use Photoshop and some animation programs for the pixel art, but my artist actually hand-draws all of our non-pixel art, scans it in, and adds color in Photoshop. We animate that in Spriter, by Brash Monkey, which works in a similar way to Flash, and is super cheap, with a responsive team behind it."

As a developer and games journalist, what do you feel is the best way to get noticed by the games press when launching a game title?

"The best thing is to have an original or interesting story. Talk about the trials and tribulations, or the actually unique things your game offers, or anything else. E-mail people whose writing you like and send them builds of the game. Talk to journalists at game conferences and get to know them. When your game comes out, though, you have to have a story and an angle. If you don't have anything about your game that's unique enough, you probably shouldn't expect much press coverage!"

You've talked about large developers and publishers being risk averse. What effect does this have on the future development of video games?

"In the grand scheme, it just means large developers and publishers will continue to make, on average, less interesting, more homogenized products. But games will continue to innovate on the whole, so long as there are people who are passionate about them. I'm not at all concerned about the future of games as a medium, regardless of whether larger developers take part in that future."

"While the new *Madden NFL* (EA) title may not take a lot of risks, there will be a whole lot of smaller titles out there taking more risks than a bigger company would even consider. It balances out—and you'll notice some of the larger companies are trying to dip their toes into that water still, themselves."

CHAPTER SUMMARY

Models used to better understand and anticipate your players can be great research tools. Once you have considered the player and your ethical stance on your game concept, you can begin to craft the experience you want the player to have. It is important to understand that these models only tell a part of the story of the player; they cannot model or map out an actual human being and anticipate reactions and actions (this is what play-testing is for). The game experience comes out of the player and is ultimately shaped by that individual. (There is another model used in the creation of games that helps us to understand this relationship, the Mechanic-Dynamic-Aesthetic (MDA) model, which you can learn more about on this book's website: www.bloomsbury.com/Salmond-Video-Game). The game and player interdependently create an experience, and that is what we will explore in the next chapter: crafting experiences.

DISCUSSION POINTS

1. If you were to create an OCEAN profile for yourself, how closely would it relate to the way you play games? How would the profile differ for a friend or relative, and what genres of games would they prefer based on it?

2. Think of the game you have most recently played. Consider a level or a few levels and think about how the five domains map against your experience in that game. How does this relate to your imagined OCEAN profile?

3. When looking at the last three or four video games you have played, how do they rate ethically when viewed or played by different genders, sexualities, or ethnicities? Would making the game more inclusive improve it, not make any tangible difference, or ruin it?

References

Bartle, R. (1996), "Hearts, Clubs, Diamonds, Spades: Players Who Suit MUDs." Available online: www.mud.co.uk/richard/hcds.htm

Howard, T. (2012), Bethesda Games, "Why We Create, Why We Play." D.I.C.E. 2012 keynote address, Las Vegas, February.

VandenBerghe, J. (2012), "The 5 Domains of Play: Applying Psychology's Big 5 Motivation Domains to Games." Speech, Game Developers Conference, San Francisco, March.

PART 2:
GAME DESIGN

CHAPTER FIVE
VIDEO GAMES ARE EVENT-DRIVEN EXPERIENCES

Chapter Objectives:

- **Recognize the relationship between game events and game experiences.**

- **Understand emotional play.**

- **Explore the concept of flow.**

- **Craft experiences.**

5.1
Final Fantasy XIV: A Realm Reborn, developed by
Square Enix (2013).

EXPERIENCES COME
FROM EMOTIONS

When you think about an experience you have had, although you may be able to remember details, you will best recall the emotions of that experience. When you finish a video game, what are the elements that come to mind first? Is it those frustrating areas you took five attempts to get past? Is it the confusion you felt over those hard puzzles? Or perhaps it was the amazement when you stepped out into the light of a new world? When you describe your game experience to others, you are most likely to use emotions to describe the game.

Experiences come from emotions, and emotions are created by the mechanic of the game. Missing a jump, missing a target, beating an enemy when your character is close to death: These are all the mechanic of the game driving the emotional experience for the player (for more on this, read about the MDA Mechanic-Dynamic-Aesthetic model of game design on the book's website: www.bloomsbury.com/Salmond-Video -Game).

5.2

Designing emotion into a game is no easy task. Part of the issue is the nature of interactivity, or player agency, itself. The player wants to feel in control—to play his or her own way—and players do not want to feel manipulated by the designer into feeling one way of the other. Film has it relatively easy when creating emotion. Films usually have human or human facsimile actors, and people spend a lifetime getting good at responding empathically to our fellow humans. When we see someone cry, it makes us upset; when we see someone laugh, it can make us smile. Have you ever witnessed a yawn travel around a room? Live (and lifelike) experiences intensify emotions. Films even use emotional words to describe their genres: horror, thriller, romance.

5.2
Movie genres use emotions to define and describe themselves.

EXPERIENCES
COME FROM
EMOTIONS

USING
THE GAME
MECHANIC
AS AN
EMOTIONAL
TRIGGER

EMOTIONS
TRANSMITTED
THROUGH
STORY

DESIGNING
AN ENGAGING
EXPERIENCE
OVER TIME

PACING

ARC, SCENE,
AND ACTION

CASE STUDY:
ATMOSPHERIC
EXPLORATION
IN *GONE HOME*

CHAPTER
SUMMARY AND
DISCUSSION
POINTS

Because they are interactive, video games can add to the emotion lists of other media and include visceral reactions and senses that players draw from the personal experience of playing.

The *sense of achievement:* Video games allow us mastery over an in-game skill. They enable the player to feel powerful (wish or fantasy fulfillment).

The *sense of empowerment:* Games are empowering experiences; they allow players to perform acts that they could not perform (or should not perform) in real life, and this is especially true for younger gamers, who have more limitations set on their lives than adults.

The *sense of experimentation:* Video games enable players to not just play out fantasy roles but also experience other aspects of their personalities (male or female, good or evil, etc.) through role play in certain games.

5.3a

5.3b

5.3a
Video games such as *Dishonored* (Arkane Studios, 2012) empower players and are engines of powerful wish fulfillment as the player takes on the role of master soldier righting a wrong in a dystopian world.

5.3b
Because players have agency, they can connect with and project onto a game's character. The character of Lara Croft in the reboot of *Tomb Raider* (Crystal Dynamics, 2013) is at once vulnerable and powerful. Players can identify with the character of Lara and feel excited, tense, or anxious along with the character.

Where Do Emotions Come From?

Our unconscious mind drives our emotions. We are rarely aware of the emotional trigger that creates a specific emotion that we feel. Instead, we have an internal set of parameters that, when met, set off an emotional response. We have little or no control over this; we just find a certain comedy funny, or we find a particular scene in a film sad. We get annoyed in one situation but not in another, even if they're very similar. When approaching crafting emotions into your game, what you can do is map out the basic emotions that we all share and then define the emotion you want to trigger in the player. You can then begin to look at which parameters you would need to add to a game in order to provoke that emotion in many people.

5.4

5.4
Basic emotions in video games.
These emotions can be sprinkled throughout a game; they can be subtle or explicit, depending on the game scenario and how you want the player to feel while playing. Now that we have an outline of the basic emotions and some of their permutations, we need to be able to apply this knowledge to a video game scenario.

Anger/Rage—The frustrations born of a well-balanced element in a game where the player wants to give up but comes to close to winning.

Contempt—An NPC who is inherently evil and your nemesis or people who you, as an evil or maniacal tyrant, feel are beneath you.

Disgust—Graphical fidelity helps to produce a sense of visceral disgust in a player, but so too an audio and the subject matter (phobias, fear of death and disease, etc.)

Interest—This is learning within the game space, that 'aha' moment in a game when the world makes sense (*Portal*).

Distress/Anxiety—Will the player make it to the end of the level? Will they beat the puzzle in time? How do my companions feel about me?

Fear/Suspense—Obvious in games such as *Silent Hill* or *Resident Evil*. Can also be evoked in mystery games (if I accuse the wrong person, the game ends or my reputation is tarnished) or within the mechanic of a shooter (big boss battle, very little health left, running low on ammunition).

Guilt/Grief—Could the player have done more to save that character? Loss of items or companions (*Skyrim*, *Final Fantasy VII*).

Joy/Happiness—Doing silly things within a game world just for the sake of it (*Katamari Damacy*, *Noby Noby Boy*).

Surprise/Wonder—That moment when you step outside of a confined space into a much larger alien/fantasy world (*Halo*, *Skyrim*).

EXPERIENCES
COME FROM
EMOTIONS

USING
THE GAME
MECHANIC
AS AN
EMOTIONAL
TRIGGER

EMOTIONS
TRANSMITTED
THROUGH
STORY

DESIGNING
AN ENGAGING
EXPERIENCE
OVER TIME

PACING

ARC, SCENE,
AND ACTION

CASE STUDY:
ATMOSPHERIC
EXPLORATION
IN *GONE HOME*

CHAPTER
SUMMARY AND
DISCUSSION
POINTS

Crafting an Emotional Experience

Game designers often begin sketching out their game by asking one question: "What wish are we fulfilling for the player?" This is a very similar process to designing an emotional experience. Games are essentially a series of events, and events by themselves are pretty boring without the context of an emotion. For example, a player walks through a marketplace to get from point A to point B—that does not sound exciting. If your character is searching for the people who cheated her out of money and is now seeking retribution, then the walk becomes an exciting quest. This is why emotions are such an integral part of experiences for game designers. It is the introduction of human values into an abstract environment that creates emotions.

Experiences and the emotions they provoke have to be parceled out over the series of in-game events, like scenes in a play or acts in a movie. (Some games even have explicit chapters or acts in them.) Emotions are difficult to orchestrate and control, but using events allows the designer (and the player) to compartmentalize story beats, areas of tension and release, and moments of comedy and action. If you are creating a horror or suspense game, a player cannot feel fear and trepidation the entire time; this state would become overwhelming and exhausting. Emotions need to be paced in the same way that narrative and interest curves are mapped (as we explore later in this chapter).

You can use event triggers to elicit emotional states:

Learning: Humans constantly learn and seek out knowledge. Levels of mastery in games have to be acquired over time, and these are emotionally rewarding when achieved. Becoming better at a game is known as *acumen*, which is the acquirement of skills.

Narrative: As with film, in games we empathize with almost anything that has a form of human personality trait. Narrative and characters are part of the learning emotional state. We want to find out about other players or other characters (novelty, stimulation) as we do with companions in real life. Good character and narrative design evokes deep emotions.

Sociability: Sharing our experiences with others as we play (Twitch TV, Gameplay sharing, etc.) or after we play, as well as playing with others (harmony). This can be play for the sake of play as well as play for social or peer group standing.

Challenge: This is tied into novelty, challenge, conscientiousness, as well as threat or neuroticism. Challenge is a large part of what games focus on, but there are different ways to approach engaging the player emotionally and providing challenge without being adversarial.

Note the crossover between these event triggers and the five domains of play and OCEAN traits from the previous chapter.

USING THE GAME MECHANIC AS AN EMOTIONAL TRIGGER

Flow—Getting into the Zone

As you can see from the four emotional event triggers, emotions occur at a point of change. We do not recognize our emotional state constantly. You could say that we feel "OK" most of the time. Then something in the environment changes—someone taps us on a shoulder, which makes us jump, or we read a sad passage in a book that makes us want to cry. Change events trigger emotions, and, as we know, video games are a series of events.

Change, control, and connection are used to create emotional states in players. Change states resonate that much more when they relate directly to the player. For example, when a player sees the impending demise of his or her character, this is a "life vs. death change" that creates an anxious state. That same state could become a "victory vs. defeat" change (if the player wins, they don't die) that results in nervous anticipation or exhilaration. All the while these states are fluctuating, there is a third meta-state created as the player takes damage or heals: the "healthy vs.

unhealthy" change state which creates relief, anxiety, uncertainty, and respite emotions. Games are very state focused. From safety to peril, from unskilled to skilled—all of these events trigger emotional responses in the player because they reflect the way our real world works. Emotional event states are extensions of the real world and they can be used by designers to subtly manipulate the player's emotions. Beating a level in a game takes you through a variety of emotions, from frustration or stress ("why is this so hard?") to relief (you have finally worked out the enemy's attack pattern or weak spots) to a sense of accomplishment (as you win) and then, finally, to satisfaction (in your accomplishment).

The irony is that as a player you may not be consciously aware of these emotions if the game is balanced correctly. There is a mental state that game designers can invoke in players that is also an emotionally "suggestive state." This is when the player is so involved with the game that they enter a state of deep focus; this is a state known as "flow."

A Hungarian psychologist, Mihaly Csikszentmihalyi, was trying to explain happiness. In doing so, he developed his own theories surrounding the human condition of complete and energized focus on a pleasurable activity; he called this state of mind "flow." Csikszentmihalyi (1990) developed theories focused on getting into a flow state, also known as the "flow zone," or what most people today refer to as "the zone."

Flow works because our nervous systems can only process about 110 bits of information per second. Listening to someone talking and processing what they are saying requires around 60 bits per second (this is why humans can't hear more than two people talking at the same time; everything else gets filtered out). When we're really involved with an engaging project, such as creating music, writing, or playing a game, people do not have enough processing power left over for other input, and they "zone out." When engaged with a really process-intensive task, self-identity vanishes and we become unaware of our body's needs. Hunger, thirst, a sense of surroundings—all go away for this period of focus.

EXPERIENCES COME FROM EMOTIONS

USING THE GAME MECHANIC AS AN EMOTIONAL TRIGGER

EMOTIONS TRANSMITTED THROUGH STORY

DESIGNING AN ENGAGING EXPERIENCE OVER TIME

PACING

ARC, SCENE, AND ACTION

CASE STUDY: ATMOSPHERIC EXPLORATION IN *GONE HOME*

CHAPTER SUMMARY AND DISCUSSION POINTS

TIP

FLOW STATES AND PACING

A player begins a game and is happy just to be able to achieve simple tasks such as moving around and picking up objects and exploring the game. This is the first state of flow (Begin Play). An increase in challenge results in the player breaking out of flow (as the player becomes frustrated or their character dies), but as the player becomes more adept (Skills Improve) the flow state can begin again because the challenge is surmountable and achievable over time (Challenge Met). The flow state is in constant flux; the player needs to match their mastery of the game against tougher challenges, and once they master the challenge this will lead back to the flow state. Breaking in and out of the flow state is natural; it would be exhausting to be in flow constantly, and this is where events and pacing are important. For example, after a hard boss battle in an action game, there is often an animated cut-scene, and this allows the player to mentally "rest" and paces the game before starting up challenges again.

5.5

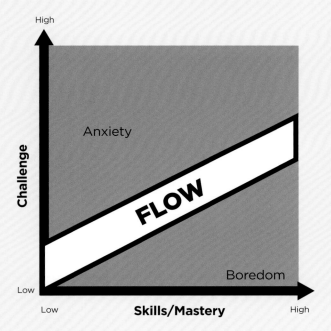
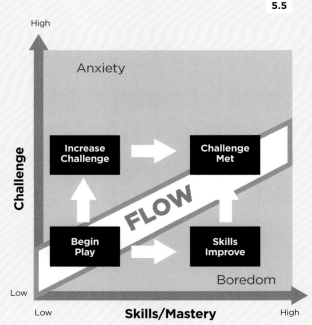

5.5
Sustaining a flow state.

Like emotions, flow is spontaneous. Csikszentmihalyi found that people rarely recognize when it occurs. It is a deep level of player immersion; the player is no longer thinking mechanically about playing the game and is instead playing at a semi-autonomous level. They are playing and reacting unconsciously, and this makes player reaction time faster because the player's brain has "switched off" unimportant distractions to allow for deep focus. Being in a state of flow enhances the enjoyment of the task to the point of it becoming a Zen-like "ecstatic" moment. Csikszentmihalyi found that there were particular elements that had to be in place for flow to occur. The challenge had to be high and the level of skill the person had to bring to the task was also high. Their mental state had to be between arousal (awareness and enjoyment of the task) and control of the task. Apathy, boredom, and worry had to be low, with anxiety ("Will I complete this boss level? Have I got enough power?") and relaxation ("I've done this a few times now; I know what to expect in this battle") fairly high.

Flow is an important part of video game design, and not every game will have obvious flow moments, although flow is part of the challenge-reward-play-fun cycle (read more about this aspect of the MDA model at www.bloomsbury.com/Salmond-Video-Game). Games that have strong physical mechanics can produce flow fairly easily, from *Dance Dance Revolution* (Konami, 1999) to *Guitar Hero* (Harmonix, 2005) because being aware of where your hands and feet are usually leads to a fail state. Other games are designed as pure flow games (*Geometry Wars*, Bizarre Creations, 2003). Flow states are emotional states triggered by events, and they form the focus of some games while they are just a part of some larger games, along with other emotional triggering events, such as narrative and aesthetics. (As examples, *WipEout HD* (Psygnosis, 2008) is an entirely flow-focused game, whereas intense action events in *Gears of War* can create flow for short periods.)

5.6

Shoot-em-ups (schmups) such as *Geometry Wars: Retro Evolved 2* (Bizarre Creations, 2008) have so much going on in the gameplay that the only real way to achieve a high score is to get into a flow state. The controls are simple, so reaction time is more important than strategy.

Everyday Shooter (Queasy Games, 2007) is another flow-based game that has a simple mechanic and aesthetic coupled with fast-paced and "twitch" reaction states.

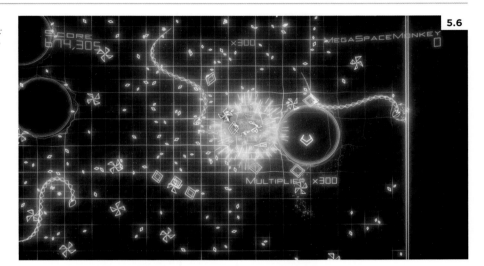

5.6

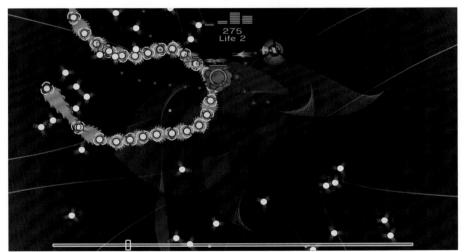

EMOTIONS TRANSMITTED THROUGH STORY

Experiences can be enhanced and nuanced by the use of a story. We are very used to storytelling and being involved in a fiction, and video games can provide players with engaging narratives, character story arcs, sexual tension, and other fictional elements. Players can form very real bonds with characters that are scripted or non-scripted (characters played by real people). A well-crafted companion can create a deeper emotional connection, whether that is when saving them, marrying them, fighting with them, or just hanging out with them and discovering their story.

We are conditioned from a very early age to engage with and tell stories, and it is part of what makes us human. However, story is not enough by itself, as limited interaction in a game, even with deep narrative, would become boring after a while. Match a compelling narrative with a solid mechanic and you have the potential for a great emotional video game within its genre (although not all video games need a story).

TIP | **THE POWER OF STORY**

When creating video games for my courses, students often start with the mechanics and aesthetics—even the emotional experience. This is fair enough, but the question I ask of my students is "Why would anyone play this game?" That's a hard question to answer when, at the outset, a player is looking at a platform or first person game not that dissimilar from many they have encountered before. It is at this point that I introduce my students to back-story and narrative structures by way of Disney World. Walt Disney constructed back-stories for every aspect of his Disney theme parks; everything had to have a narrative reason to exist.

Essentially, Walt Disney was creating a video game world; it may be based in our world, but it is completely fake. It is a virtual world, in a sense. Walt Disney wanted every scratch and bump on Main Street streetcars to have a reason to be there; imagineers wrote long and involved histories for the streetcars and other seemingly insignificant parts of the world. This was because Walt Disney knew the power of story. He knew that even if a guest never came across the back-story behind why a streetcar was that shade of blue, the history made the world more real. It also gave a reason and purpose for every element of the world to exist, and the details weave together into a larger Disney narrative that permeates every park.

5.7

5.7
The environments themselves tell stories (as we examine in Chapters 8 and 9). The aesthetics of a level or an environment are visual shortcuts to establish spaces that are dangerous and populated by foes (such as in the downloadable extension content, the Pitt, of Bethesda's *Fallout 3*), or calm, tranquil, and more suited to moments of reflection or character interaction.

Emotional Experiences

As a game designer, you are working with two important factors, the physical and the cognitive, to create emotions. How we internalize and name these factors is important. For example, as a player, if you enter a boss battle with fairly low health, you know the battle will be tough. The fight begins, your heart pounds, your hands get sweaty, and you become more and more excited. If you were to stop at that exact moment and transport yourself to a party where you see a girl/guy across the room whom you have always wanted to date *looking directly at you*,

the physical experience could be exactly the same: sweaty hands, pounding heart. However, in the first instance, you might call it excitement and challenge; in the second instance, you might call it fear and trepidation.

The difference is in how we internally label those emotions. One is excruciating and one is enjoyable, even though the physical reactions are the same. These ingredients are what we have in our armory when developing games. We try to put the player in a state of flow, cutting off the outside

world; we then heighten that state by giving the player reasons to be drawn into this situation (narrative, action) and then we use mechanics to work within that narrative to elicit emotions from the player. The game can heighten these emotions with taunts from enemies, a timer clock that is counting down to a fail state, or an opportunity to throw the pass that might connect and win the game.

5.8
This is how flow works in most games. Next time you play a game, be conscious of when you enter a state of flow and how long it lasts. What breaks you out of it? What gets you back into that mental state?

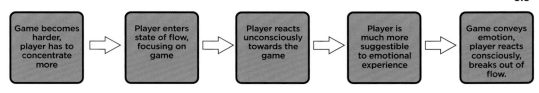

5.8

5.9

5.9
Flow states are points of extreme focus or concentration and can take many forms. A mission where detection by guards leads to a fail state can ramp up the player's focus as they attempt a flawless route through a level. In *Dishonored* your character can easily become overwhelmed by stronger guards, so a more stealth-based approach is wise and adds to emotions of excitement, cautiousness, and relief.

Design assets can also provoke emotional states; in the game *Skyrim*, the designers have used the convention that the more armored or powerful-looking the enemy, the more the player is going to react when encountering them. The convention is subtly layered so that often players will not know if they are powerful enough to take on an enemy. When they fail in combat, the failure drives players back into the game's system: Players want to increase their skill levels and weaponry to come back and try again.

DESIGNING AN ENGAGING EXPERIENCE OVER TIME

Keeping the player engaged with the game experience is a challenge. How do players remain interested in a game? We will discuss other elements of player engagement, such as reward systems, in Chapter 10, but it is important to introduce another model to use when designing an experience for the player. To keep an audience reading, watching, or interacting, media use what are known as *interest curves*. These are how writers and directors plot the pacing of their movies, and it is how game designers keep you playing a game hour after hour.

Exploring Interest Curves

Interest curves for video games plot in much the same way as those for films and television. The difference with video games is that they tend to be much longer than a film (even "short" video games last 6–20 hours) and are actually more comparable to books and episodic television. Another difference is that when we examine interest curves for games we are examining the *experience* the player is having based on the mechanic and the rules. Narrative-based, linear games such as *The Last of Us* (Naughty Dog, 2013) or *Dead Space: Extraction* (Visceral Games, 2009) do have similar interest curves to movies. *The Last of Us* has well-balanced interest curves within each chapter; each main level is referred to as a chapter, and the game is split into 19 chapters and 3 acts.

A well-paced game will oscillate between action and rest points, but every peak will be slightly higher than the previous one until the final all-out ending. The trajectory should not be a 45-degree line; it is a crescendo, and it needs to fluctuate with peaks and troughs so as to not exhaust the player. This does not apply to all games, naturally; it is hard to build an event into a game such as *The Sims* (Maxis, 2000) or *Minecraft* (Mojang, 2009), which use rewards, achievement, pleasure, and knowledge building as engagement and pacing mechanisms. The player in a game such as *The Sims* is constantly building and learning the game mechanic while attending to their Sims, so the pacing effectively comes from the player. MMOs such as *World of Warcraft* have major events and storylines occurring that have similar pacing elements to drive players towards re-engaging with the game.

5.10
An example of the interest curve for the movie, *Star Wars Episode IV: A New Hope* (Lucasfilm, 1977). This is simplified, but you can see that there are multiple peaks and valleys in the action/adventure movie that ramp up towards the penultimate scene. Narrative or action video games plot a very similar interest curve.

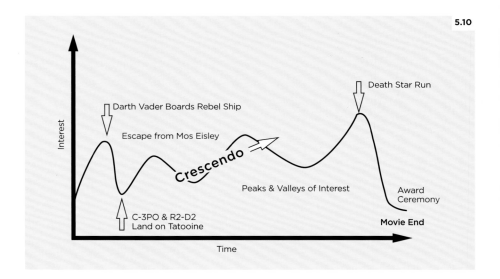

5.10

EXPERIENCES COME FROM EMOTIONS

USING THE GAME MECHANIC AS AN EMOTIONAL TRIGGER

EMOTIONS TRANSMITTED THROUGH STORY

DESIGNING AN ENGAGING EXPERIENCE OVER TIME

PACING

ARC, SCENE, AND ACTION

CASE STUDY: ATMOSPHERIC EXPLORATION IN *GONE HOME*

CHAPTER SUMMARY AND DISCUSSION POINTS

Video game interest curves are not only applied across the game in its entirety; they are also plotted into the levels. The interest curve within a level works in much the same way as scenes in a play or episodes in a television series. Interest curves are almost like fractals in that designers plot them for the entire game (the meta curve) as well as for the level and for the scene. Each curve will contain an element of the overall story of the game. For example, in *Assassin's Creed* the aim is ultimately to defeat the Templars. Each level has a main quest line, such as killing a major Templar. Each scene leads to clues that uncover where that Templar is hiding.

One of the principles of level design is that it is a form of storytelling and pacing. What the character can see or access, how other objects in the level relate to the character, and how that level relates to the larger game are important parts of the level design process (level design is covered in Chapters 8 and 9). Interest curves are, in part, a way of controlling player engagement throughout the game and interest curves are manipulated by the designers through the use of pacing elements. In *The Last of Us*, it is important that the designers know how to place the high action scenes (of fighting off the infected) against narrative exposition and then balance that with peaceful moments (which might include a giraffe).

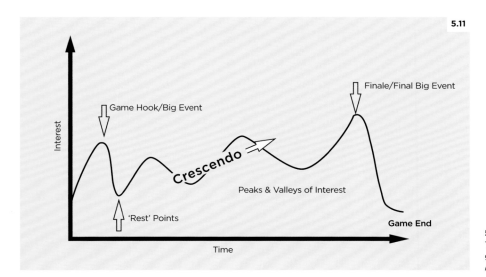

5.11

5.11
This is the interest curve for most narrative video games; it would work for *The Last of Us* or the *Resident Evil* (Capcom) franchise.

PACING

An interest curve is the outcome of pacing and can be modeled in single player as well as multiplayer games. For example, it is fairly obvious how narrative drives the action and engagement within *The Last of Us*, but multiplayer games such as *Call of Duty Modern Warfare 3* (Infinity Ward, 2011) have "chapters" too—they just call them modes. Each multiplayer match is finite and has objectives and pacing (reloads, hiding, running, strategizing, and so on). The lobby areas serve as a pacing point, too; they are a time to reflect in order to "de-brief" or to ready the player for the next match.

Pacing Is Used to Establish Tone

Pacing and the interest curve are a form of persuasion mechanism. In creating that first peak, you are setting the tone for the rest of the game. It is a convention that we have learned from movies and television, and it is prevalent in action/adventure video games. The first peak will introduce a main character, his or her world, and often the main mission or reason for the player/hero to exist (the dragons are back, the world has been invaded, etc.). For example, in the opening scene for *Uncharted 2: Drake's Fortune* (Naughty Dog, 2009), the player is introduced to Nathan Drake waking up inside a crashed train, which we

then find out is on a very precarious ledge. This is exactly the sort of perilous situation that the character is going to be getting into repeatedly throughout the game. Nathan then has to escape the train before it plummets to the bottom of the ravine. It's a series of timed jumps and dodges that introduces a lot of mechanics to the player. Once Nathan escapes the train wreck, the action stops and the player is given a cut-scene of Nathan in a tropical bar, far away from the action we have just witnessed. The game switches to story exposition as a way of pacing the game.

5.12
Uncharted 2: Among Thieves sets the tone of the action/adventure game immediately by dropping the player into a train wreck action scene. The consequent escape and "luck" of the main character, as well as the mountain environment setting, immerses the player very quickly into the pacing of the game, which will be action, then pause, then action once again.

5.12

EXPERIENCES COME FROM EMOTIONS

USING THE GAME MECHANIC AS AN EMOTIONAL TRIGGER

EMOTIONS TRANSMITTED THROUGH STORY

DESIGNING AN ENGAGING EXPERIENCE OVER TIME

PACING

ARC, SCENE, AND ACTION

CASE STUDY: ATMOSPHERIC EXPLORATION IN *GONE HOME*

CHAPTER SUMMARY AND DISCUSSION POINTS

5.13

5.13
God of War II (SCE Santa Monica Studio, 2007) is an opening sequence that establishes the epic scale of many of the boss battles Kratos encounters. This battle is a primer for the player because the game's premise is a betrayal by Zeus. The Colossus of Rhodes battle introduces many of the mechanics of the game and works as a primer for its scale.

ARC, SCENE, AND ACTION

As a designer, you should play and deconstruct games to examine their curves and pacing. Pacing is split into three parts: arc, scene, and action.

Arc: The piece as a whole—the total interest or engagement curve (in literature or film, it would be the story arc).

Scene: These are the subsections of the game; this could be a level or even a part of a level. For example, a building in a city level where a major combat scenario takes place (or the falling building escape sequence in *Gears of War 2* (Epic Games, 2008), which is part of a larger level). Each scene has its own engagement curve, which should be the same in every scene. This does not mean the content remains the same; instead, there is some predictability to each scene. For example, in the *Gears of War* series, the player fights through many smaller areas to reach what is essentially a larger arena at the end of the level. There are often several scenes (sometimes with cut-scene animations) to get to these parts, but they follow a predictable pattern.

5.14

5.14
Writing arcs and narratives for video games such as *Kentucky Route Zero* (Cardboard Computer) are far more challenging than traditional media because of the nature of interaction. It is common for players to expect to move between scenes and plot arcs as well as revisit conversations and plot points.

EXPERIENCES
COME FROM
EMOTIONS

USING
THE GAME
MECHANIC
AS AN
EMOTIONAL
TRIGGER

EMOTIONS
TRANSMITTED
THROUGH
STORY

DESIGNING
AN ENGAGING
EXPERIENCE
OVER TIME

PACING

**ARC, SCENE,
AND ACTION**

CASE STUDY:
ATMOSPHERIC
EXPLORATION
IN *GONE HOME*

CHAPTER
SUMMARY AND
DISCUSSION
POINTS

Action: This is a specific moment of the gameplay, usually linked to the mechanics. The engagement curve in the action part can be the wind-up of a special power or the feeling of wielding a certain weapon in the game. This is very specific to each game and is a part of pacing that many people miss. Pacing elements can be built into how long it takes to bring up a certain type of gun and aim it or how long it takes to swap out inventory items (too quickly provides no tension in an important fight, too slow frustrates the player over time) or how long a player takes to heal in the middle of a zombie attack. Actions may last a second or a few seconds; even so, every action—from a jump to an axe wield—should be examined in relation to the overall engagement curve.

All of these parts of the interest curve are important, but it is arguable that action is the most important because this is what the player is doing the most. A bad jump curve or a too-slow aiming curve can ruin a game or at best make it feel "off." Engagement curves can be applied to many aspects of your game and are at once very broad (the arc) as well as very specific (action). When designing these elements, it is well worth researching curves from other games to get timing, pacing, and engagement that feel right for your game. When analyzing other video games, a spreadsheet can be a useful tool in tracking pacing and interest curves. This may not seem like the most creative of tools, but when you think about plotting time and events-in-game against when players become bored, confused, or excited, a spreadsheet is a great way of keeping all that data together. You can set up time frames for each chapter's acts (or just time spent in the game) and begin to track moments of excitement, flow, interest, and other emotional states.

CASE STUDY:
ATMOSPHERIC EXPLORATION IN *GONE HOME*

Gone Home: The Concept

The Fullbright Company is an independent video game studio founded in Portland, Oregon, in March of 2012. Its co-founders are Steve Gaynor, Johnnemann Nordhagen, and Karla Zimonja. The team has worked in various capacities on *BioShock 2: Minerva's Den* (2K Marin, 2010), *X-COM Enemy Unknown* (Firaxis, 2012), and *BioShock Infinite* (Irrational Games, 2013). Their closest collaboration was as the small team responsible for the *BioShock 2: Minerva's Den DLC*, with Steve Gaynor as the writer and design lead.

In this Case Study, Steve Gaynor provides insight into the process of atmospheric design in *Gone Home*.

"We were especially focused on the first-person atmospheric exploration and story discovery aspects of the games we had worked on in the past, and we wanted to make that the whole game. Once we had that concept we had to give it a form. As we are a small team, we knew that one location would be more achievable than a vast sandbox world. Once we had fixed on a house as an environment, it then threw up other questions: who owns the house, who are the family, and what is their story? It's really important to start from the perspective of 'what is the player doing and how is that engaging, regardless of the specific content or environment they're in?' Exploring a place to find out what happened there is inherently interesting as a trope. Once we had this core concept, we could begin to build out specifics."

5.15

5.15
The title screen for the Fullbright Company's first game evokes a horror or suspense narrative.

EXPERIENCES COME FROM EMOTIONS

USING THE GAME MECHANIC AS AN EMOTIONAL TRIGGER

EMOTIONS TRANSMITTED THROUGH STORY

DESIGNING AN ENGAGING EXPERIENCE OVER TIME

PACING

ARC, SCENE, AND ACTION

CASE STUDY: ATMOSPHERIC EXPLORATION IN *GONE HOME*

CHAPTER SUMMARY AND DISCUSSION POINTS

Production of *Gone Home*

"*Gone Home* was about 17 months of production. The three co-founders of the studio worked on the whole game from March, with the 3D artist (Kate Craig) coming onto the team in July. It was very much a collaborative project with a small core team; for example, we had Chris Reno compose the music, and other artists produce posters and other assets."

"We knew from the experience of working on other games that plans tend to change as you make the game, so we wanted to just get on with it. We were all excited about the game we wanted to make; pre-production was listing the specific features we wanted to make that idea a reality and playable. We had all begun talking about this game while we were working on the *BioShock* franchise, so some of the conceptual groundwork had been done. Before we all moved to Portland, OR, Steve wrote up a design document that covered all of the main features of an exploration-based narrative game. Once we had gone back and forth on the background, characters, and aesthetic, we knew how the game would work, so we started building the physical space the player would explore very quickly.

The game was created using the Unity game engine, mostly because it is a robust production solution and we knew it would be capable of making the sort of game we wanted to make."

5.16

5.16
One of the very first art assets the player sees sets the tone for the tension and mystery of the narrative. The note reads, "Katie, I'm sorry I can't be there to see you, but it is impossible. Please, please don't go digging around trying to find out where I am. I don't want ~~Mom and Dad~~ anyone to know. We'll see each other again some day. Don't be worried. I love you. – Sam"

"For assets, we used Maya for 3D and Adobe Photoshop or Illustrator for the 2D art. Karla did almost all of our 2D art with Kate using Photoshop for textures for the 3D assets. Johnnemann used Visual Studio for the programming. Audio was edited using Audacity, and Notepad ++ was used for editing scripts. The plan was to use industry standard or free software wherever possible."

"Rapid prototyping was a key part of the pre-production process; we wanted to know that you could use art assets in the way we had envisioned—clicking on a note and being able to read it and flip it over or go back to it in the environment. It was a fairly fluid process. As the environment and mechanic took shape, Steve started writing the audio diaries and note content and we would place it in the game; if it worked, it stayed; if it felt wrong, we would put it aside. Because the environment was relatively simple, there wasn't the sense that everything had to be completely right up front. Our pre-production process was to establish an agreed-upon baseline for the game, something we could all use, and then we could evolve the story, environment, and atmosphere as we were in production. The success of the development cycle was that we had a clear, well-featured plan from the beginning that we didn't go too detailed on and that was fairly complete, and we stuck to the plan and focused on making that design as good as it could be. It was very much implementing towards a vision we all shared."

Designing the Emotional Experience

"When we were thinking about creating tension within the environment, we were fortunate to take advantage of a familiar setting. We used a big dark house in the middle of a storm at night. That's a very concrete environment to work from because everyone's been there. Most players would have been in an unfamiliar house that's empty, and we knew we could tap into that visceral emotion. Drawing from personal experience to color the game's reality is a shortcut. Given that this is an environment people have experienced either as a child or adult, it taps into that fear and unease very easily because you're reminding the player of that emotional state through the game. It allows the player's imagination and assumptions to do the work for us to a large extent. We could then back that up with creaking floorboards and 'haunted house noises' as well as the music at the beginning and the pacing with the note on the front door. Everything points towards 'ominous' without us having to give the player any additional information. The goal was to use that unease and sense of tension to draw the player into the experience and make them feel compelled to find out what happened."

EXPERIENCES COME FROM EMOTIONS

USING THE GAME MECHANIC AS AN EMOTIONAL TRIGGER

EMOTIONS TRANSMITTED THROUGH STORY

DESIGNING AN ENGAGING EXPERIENCE OVER TIME

PACING

ARC, SCENE, AND ACTION

CASE STUDY: ATMOSPHERIC EXPLORATION IN *GONE HOME*

CHAPTER SUMMARY AND DISCUSSION POINTS

"We then transitioned that initial 'buy-in' (on-boarding) to the player paying attention because they've become invested in the characters and story and want to find out the relationships, over the feeling that a monster or serial killer is going to jump out at them at any point. It's a subtle transfer; the tension is always there to an extent, but we wanted the player to become invested in the investigation and exploration aspects over time. We wanted to disabuse them of the notion that this is a pure horror game and instead that it's important to discover the characters."

5.17

5.17
The atmosphere is delivered purely through the setting, the environment art, and the player's own mental projections into the game.

CHAPTER SUMMARY

Designing a game mechanic that can be played is fairly easy; there are many games that do just that because it is the path of least resistance and a designer can control all of the game elements (jump, shoot, flap, etc.). Designing a game that elicits emotions from players is much more difficult. Thinking about the feelings you want to invoke in the player is harder but potentially much more compelling and memorable for the player. For great examples of games that focus on creating an experience, examine games such as *Flower*, *flOw*, and *Journey* (Thatgamecompany). The issue many game designers have is that most players say they just want to have "fun" in a game. Fun is subjective and what is fun for one person may not be for another. What the player really wants is a rewarding experience. Video game design focuses on providing compelling, event-driven experiences in which the player forgets about playing the game and becomes absorbed in a personal experience with the game.

EXPERIENCES COME FROM EMOTIONS

USING THE GAME MECHANIC AS AN EMOTIONAL TRIGGER

EMOTIONS TRANSMITTED THROUGH STORY

DESIGNING AN ENGAGING EXPERIENCE OVER TIME

PACING

ARC, SCENE, AND ACTION

CASE STUDY: ATMOSPHERIC EXPLORATION IN *GONE HOME*

CHAPTER SUMMARY AND DISCUSSION POINTS

DISCUSSION POINTS

1. Which games have elicited the most emotional states from you? What were the emotions and how did the game achieve them? This could be feeling happy because *Mario Sunshine* (Nintendo, 2002) reminds you of your childhood or scared because *Dead Space* is so claustrophobic and has many jump-scares.

2. As an exercise in understanding interest curves and pacing, plot the interest curves of a short game as well as those of a much longer game. Even comparing a game such as *Angry Birds* (Rovio Entertainment, 2009) against *The Last of Us* can provide insights into how those games create continued interest for the player.

3. Going back to the games that have managed to create the most emotional responses in you while playing: How did the games' designers create that emotional mindset and connect with you? Does that mindset still exist if you replay the game now or has it changed?

References

Csikszentmihalyi, M. (1990), *Flow: The Psychology of Optimal Experience*, New York: Harper & Row.

PART 3:
SYSTEMS AND
DESIGNING WORLDS

CHAPTER SIX
PLANNING, PREPARATION, AND PLAY-TESTING

Chapter Objectives:

- Use planning and preparation models.

- Appreciate iteration as part of the design process.

- Create design documents.

- Understand play-testing and quality assurance.

6.1
GoldenEye 007: Reloaded, developed by
Activision (2011).

THE PREPARATION PHASE

Lack of Experience

Over the last five chapters, we have been discussing and exploring the conceptual aspects of video game design. We'll now move into the practical side of video game design, and that starts with preparation (sometimes referred to as pre-production). Preparation is everything and while this is especially true with big games, it's also true for smaller games. Crashing on with a game's development without thinking it through is going to lead to unforeseen consequences later in the development process. The lament of many delayed games is that they've been held up by "unplanned development issues." Proper planning enables realistic deadlines to be created based on conversations with all the "stakeholders" (everyone involved in the design process).

The problem when starting out in video game design is that the knowledge you need to plan and build timeframes successfully is based on experience. This chapter is a guide to some of the common pitfalls and best practices that will enable you to be, at best, forewarned and, at worst, prepared to make mistakes and build that into your production timeline. You cannot plan for every eventuality, but you can learn to avoid making mistakes by adopting a model of efficient planning. Even a small amount of planning before getting on with prototyping and asset creation means that potential wrinkles can be ironed out as much in advance as possible.

This is why taking video game design courses is useful—not just for the expertise of the lecturer but to get you into the mindset of what is achievable within a given timeframe and what's likely to get cut due to deadline constraints. In every course I have taught on game design, the students come up with great ideas for games that

would take teams of people years to create. The students then have to work on simplifying and narrowing the focus of their concept towards an achievable, deliverable game. This process is, in itself, an incredibly useful lesson to learn. Making a prototype or "proof-of-concept" game can be achieved in a short amount of time. Events such as the Global Game Jam (participants have 48 hours to create a playable prototype) are a good example of extreme focus. In the game courses I have taught, my students have created a playable prototype in six to eight weeks using game engines such as Unity, Clickteam Fusion 2, Game Maker, or GameSalad. If the task is to mod a game or build on an existing genre, a game demo can be completed in a few hours.

Creating a prototype is a good start, but it is not the entire game. A prototype of an FPS concept or an RPG style game is good to get the creative juices flowing, but if you want to create a fully realized playable game of any scope, it is going to take some time, iteration, and planning.

THE
PREPARATION
PHASE

PLAYER
NUMBERS AS
MECHANIC

INITIAL
PROTOTYPE
PHASE

THE
ITERATION
LOOP

DESIGN PHASE
1: FIXING ON
THE VISUALS

DESIGN PHASE
2: CHARACTER,
CAMERA,
AND CONTROL
DESIGN

PRODUCTION
TESTING

PRACTICAL
APPROACHES
TO TESTING

INTERVIEW:
KATE CRAIG

CHAPTER
SUMMARY AND
DISCUSSION
POINTS

Plans Are Good, but Plans Change

When working with my students we often start out by recreating existing games as a way to learn about different mechanics. In the classroom setting, we create a copycat game, a version of an existing (usually very simple) game to get students started on the deconstruction of a game. The students have to use their own art assets and audio and also alter at least one facet of the mechanic. This gives a sense of how long even creating simple and straightforward variations on an existing game can take.

Once a copycat game has been made, we set about planning a new game. Building an understanding of the production process is important in choosing your route towards creating your game. Every game is different and every team is different. Some games have very short production periods (as we saw in Chapter 5, *Gone Home* was a few months, but the team had already been working together for a while and had solid skill sets) and other games have extended production timeframes. For example, the games *Portal* (Valve, 2007), *BioShock*, and *Fallout 3*

(Bethesda Softworks) had infamously long production periods. The original *BioShock* pitch document is up on the Irrational Games website and is available at: http://irrationalgames .com/insider/from-the-vault-may/. It is markedly different from the game that was eventually launched (it was originally a science-fiction shooter game based on *System Shock 2* (Looking Glass Studios, 1999). The key is to develop an approach to planning that works for the team and that is flexible enough to evolve when outside pressures bear down on the process.

6.2

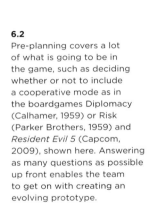

6.2
Pre-planning covers a lot of what is going to be in the game, such as deciding whether or not to include a cooperative mode as in the boardgames Diplomacy (Calhamer, 1959) or Risk (Parker Brothers, 1959) and *Resident Evil 5* (Capcom, 2009), shown here. Answering as many questions as possible up front enables the team to get on with creating an evolving prototype.

PLAYER NUMBERS
AS MECHANIC

From a game developer point of view, the first question when thinking about the mechanic of the game and planning a prototype is "How many players are there?" First person shooters can have solo single-player modes as well as cooperative play and multiplayer, whereas *Mario Galaxy* is a game designed for a single player. Thinking about the number of players in advance is an important part of conceptualizing the game's development as it defines the primary mechanic and is difficult (or expensive) to change later on. When designing for player numbers, it is important to understand what the number of players really means for the game. Fixing the number of players defines much of the game—every aspect of the design flows from that set of player interaction patterns.

In their book *Game Design Workshop*, Tracy Fullerton and Christopher Swain (2004) explore the relationship between game mechanic and players as "player interaction patterns." These are derived from the perspective of board games but hold up well when translated to video games. Fullerton and Swain's interaction patterns are:

- Single player versus game (*The Last of Us*, *BioShock*, *Dishonored*)

- Player versus player (*Gears of War*, *World of Warcraft*)

- Multiple individual players versus game (Horde modes, MMORPGs)

- Unilateral competition (two players versus one player)

- Multilateral competition (MMORPGs, *Call of Duty* multiplayer)

- Cooperative Play (*Resident Evil 5*, *Gears of War*, *Left for Dead*)

- Team Competition (*World of Warcraft*, *Gears of War*, *Madden NFL, FIFA*)

When designing a video game, the key player mechanic decisions should be:

1. *How many players are required for the game?*
   This is either solo or multiple. Cooperative games can be played by one player but are designed specifically with two or more players in mind; single player games are designed for one player. Player numbers define the game mechanic, rules, and field of play. Tacking on multiplayer capability once development is underway is an expensive and often badly implemented idea.

6.3

6.3
Resident Evil 5 was designed from the outset as a two-player game (co-op). If played solo, the game would use A.I. for the Sheva character to accommodate the individual player.

2. *How many players are allowed?*
A game such as tic-tac-toe can be played by two people or by a single player against a computer opponent. Other games are flexible up to a point; for example, the board game Monopoly requires two to eight players. It cannot be played solo and it cannot have nine players. Each game's mechanic is designed to serve the needs of the number of players and is balanced to accommodate those numbers. Monopoly isn't necessarily more fun with eight players than it is with four; it scales well for both (although it does not scale down well below four).

3. *Do the players have uniform roles?*
Chess and Monopoly (Magie, Darrow, 1903) have set player roles that never change. Chess is player battling player; there is no cooperative mode or multiplayer team mode. Games such as Diplomacy or Risk set player against other players as they collude to support or defeat each other. Here the roles are constantly changing between friend and foe; this shifting is designed into the mechanic of the game and defines it. In video games, especially in role playing games (RPGs), characters can have multiple roles. One player could be a healer who is also a fighter, or a thief who is also a mage, and so on.

6.4

6.4
Titanfall™ (Respawn Entertainment, 2014) is a multiplayer-only game, one that requires multiple players to be online at any time for matches to take place. Console game developers have not traditionally adopted this route because once the game slopes off in popularity it becomes pointless to play.

INITIAL PROTOTYPE PHASE

The first step is the game idea: Think about the world, the narrative, what experiences you want the player to have, and how that will become a game. At this stage, you can borrow heavily from existing tropes (save the world, wish fulfillment) and even mechanics because you are experimenting and trying to figure out the best shape for the game. Once you have an embryonic game idea, you can move towards a simple prototype to test the idea's viability.

The best prototypes start out with sketches—sometimes on paper but more often digitally. The advantage of digital is that, when working in a team, the prototype updates and documentation can be shared 24/7 from anywhere in the world. Using free tools such as Google Docs enables better interaction and no one member of the team can lose or forget to bring that important piece of paper to a meeting. There are so many free and free-to-use game engines that are simple to learn and get started with quickly. Design ideas should move quickly into a playable prototype, so that development questions can be answered and lessons learned. Video game design today is very much focused on creating a first playable prototype and then using that to inform the subsequent planning. The basic rule is to get a game engine and get something on the screen as soon as possible, and then evolve it.

A quick prototype will also enable you to focus on what the game actually is. A good test in the initial stage of design is to think of a 30-second "elevator pitch" for your game. If you can't explain what your game is in that time, you don't really know what you want or what you are making.

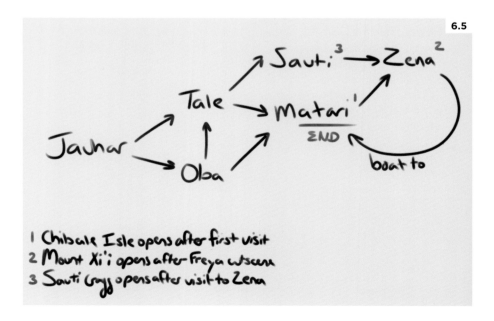

6.5

6.5
Victoria Pimentel, a student who created an RPG game, sketched a multi-path narrative roughly on paper before committing to choices that she would then implement digitally.

6.6

- THE CHIEF STOPS
- THE CAMERA MOVES UP TO HIS FACE AND PUSHES IN

6.6
This is a storyboard planning a cinematic from the game *Halo 3* (Bungie Inc., 2007). Although this is a storyboard for an animation, the same process can be applied towards simple interaction and for fixing camera angles and perspectives.

THE ITERATION LOOP

From graphic design to fashion design and video game design, all design has iteration built into its process. Iteration is: "Make something, test it, learn from it, repeat."

There is an ideal loop when planning a game. See Figure 6.7 below.

The cycle is not set against time, because early on in prototype development the iteration cycle will be very fast, with multiple changes. As the prototype improves, the iteration slows down, and there are smaller, more refined changes taking place.

The formal process usually includes the following steps.

Concept Development:

- The high concept or brief description of the game.

Design Phase/Pre-production (pre-production is a contentious term):

- Concept or proposal document (small document of game's selling points, profitability).

- Game proposal/plan (larger, more in-depth document, including gameplay, genre, hardware platforms, features, setting, story, target audience, estimated schedule, team requirements, risk analysis).

- Prototype.

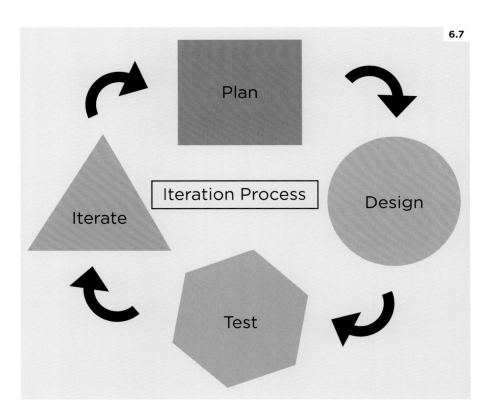

6.7

6.7
The iteration cycle: Plan – Design – Test – Revise.

Production:

- Design of the game, implementation of the vision of the designer or team.

- Programming, more complex and expansive prototypes. Working in final game engine.

- Level creation.

- Art production.

- Audio production.

- Testing and quality assurance (QA).

Milestones (often set by the publisher but can also be set internally):

- First playable. A game version that contains gameplay and art assets that reflect what will appear in the final game.

- Alpha. Key gameplay mechanics are implemented and most assets are implemented. Alphas are "feature complete" but could change based on testing and feedback.

- Code freeze. No new code is added to the game. Instead, focus is on bug correction and fixes.

- Beta. The game is complete with all features and assets, only fixes are based on testing feedback. It is essentially a shippable game.

- Code release. All discernible bugs are fixed and game is ready for shipping and/or console manufacturer review. QA further tests the game to ensure quality and stability.

- Gold master. Final build of game for release.

Post-production:

- Maintenance. Once the game is released and played by the public, bugs and issues with hardware occur and need to be addressed with patches.

- Localization. If the game is released to multiple markets, teams will work on translations, updating content, new voice overs, etc.

All of these phases of planning, design, and production are important. The next sections emphasize a few that warrant further detail because they are areas where designers can trip up.

117

DESIGN PHASE 1:
FIXING ON THE VISUALS

If the prototype seems viable, it is time to bring in an art team and to start working on the art style. It is important that the artists have seen the prototype so they can make judgments on whether the art style works effectively with the mechanic. For example, it might not make sense to have a rich, medieval third person hack 'n' slash game aesthetic in a side-scrolling platform game where the camera never really picks out any of that detail. From the prototype, the artists will also get an idea of the level of detail they will or will not need to create based on the player's perspective. As the prototype is the base mechanic of the game, the artists can begin technical conversations about the constraints and limitations of the game engine.

This could be the polygon budget (how detailed the models should be for the intended platform to run smoothly); the maximum texture resolution (for 3D) games; and then other elements, such as the size and scale of in-game objects, number of animations, number of states per object (for example, if the game character or environment has undamaged and damaged states), and levels of detail (much of this is covered in Chapters 8 and 9). This is where artists and designers have to research fully the technical aspects of their game and the platform on which it will run. The PC may seem to be the easiest, but it is by far the most customizable, so there needs to be at least minimum, intermediate, and high technical specification sets.

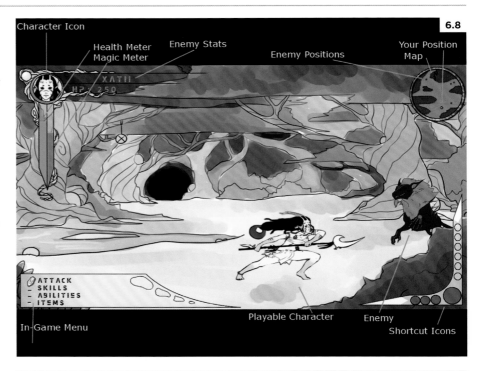

6.8
Draft screen from a student game by Victoria Pimentel. In this document, Pimentel is planning an RPG-style game using rough graphics to get a sense of layout and how much information she can fit onto the screen before it becomes overwhelming to the player. Draft art assets such as these are presented to other members of the team and/or other stakeholders to get objective feedback.

THE
PREPARATION
PHASE

PLAYER
NUMBERS AS
MECHANIC

INITIAL
PROTOTYPE
PHASE

THE
ITERATION
LOOP

**DESIGN PHASE
1: FIXING ON
THE VISUALS**

DESIGN PHASE
2: CHARACTER,
CAMERA,
AND CONTROL
DESIGN

PRODUCTION
TESTING

PRACTICAL
APPROACHES
TO TESTING

INTERVIEW:
KATE CRAIG

CHAPTER
SUMMARY AND
DISCUSSION
POINTS

From the creative perspective, there are other considerations in developing the look and feel of the game world environment, its population, and the game's interfaces. Art, like programming, takes a long time to accomplish. A late decision to go from a medieval environment to a science fiction dystopian future would be a disaster—which is why you go back and forth with sketches and asset development before fixing on the final aesthetic that will work within the technical constraints of the engine and hardware. Art is important because the level design, character design, and environmental mechanics have to align with the aesthetic to make for a consistent game.

6.9

6.9
When creating my game *The Diaries of Professor Angell; Deceased,* the aesthetic went through multiple iterations before fixing on 1920s America. This setting informed the narrative and historical aesthetic for an exploration game (in the genre of *Gone Home, Everybody's Gone to the Rapture*, The Chinese Room, 2015, and *Cradle*, Flying Cafe for Semianimals, 2015) that uses text and interactions to uncover the machinations of a cult based on H.P. Lovecraft's mythology.

DESIGN PHASE 2:
CHARACTER, CAMERA,
AND CONTROL DESIGN

When thinking about the mechanic, it is important early on to involve the perspective of the player. How does the player interact with the game? What can they see and what can they interact with, and how? This part of the prototyping process is mechanics based and breaks down into three parts:

Character design isn't just about the look of the main character, it's also about how the player interfaces with the world and how the character moves, jumps, shoots, and so on. In this context, "character" can refer to any game element: It could be a car or a tank as much as a human or Mario. Just as we ask about the mechanic that defines what the game is, we must also ask, "What is the game's 'character'"?

Camera design works in the same way: Choosing a focal plane and exploring how the camera tracks the player's movement are vital components and inform the connection between player and world. The camera could even be considered a character because how well it supports the gameplay defines the game. A change as seemingly simple as bringing the camera in a few feet can make or break the entire game. There are, of course, technical conditions: Where does the camera get "stuck"? How does it cope with following the character through a door? How fast should it move? And so on.

Fixing an aesthetic and a camera design early on establishes much of the game. Choosing between first-person and third-person perspective may seem arbitrary to an outsider, but the decision creates a fixed narrative point, an aesthetic perspective, and a specific connection with a character. Also, a third person requires more work as you need to show a character that animates, moves, fights, and so on.

Control design can rely on conventions (or bias) that adhere to the platform, such as left mouse click to fire on a PC, right trigger on an Xbox 360 controller, and so on. Or the controls could be completely different; for example, the game *Brothers: A Tale of Two Sons* (Starbreeze Studios, 2013) uses both thumbsticks on console controllers to move two characters around the environment. Thus, some games may require a control system that the player has to spend some time getting used to, and designers have to create more assets, such as tutorials or in-game instructions, to compensate.

6.10
Telltale Game's *The Walking Dead* (2012) has many surprises, plot twists, and tension, so it would make sense for them to have used "Kleenex" testers. These are testers who are used once because they have never played the game before and are not used again.

PRODUCTION TESTING

No Egos Allowed

Even when creating early prototypes, designers must test the game because eventually it needs a fresh set of eyes—testing just among the design team can lead to over-familiarity, thus missing obvious problems. In this next section of the chapter, we will consider some best practices for play-testing your game. This is not an exhaustive list, and different studios have different approaches towards testing. What is common to them all is that testing is in service of producing a better game and experience for the player.

The most honest play-testing approach is simply to give the game to testers and observe them. Testing is focused on making your game better—not forcing the tester to love your game. As a designer, you have to give the testers room to play their way, and you have to observe and take a lot of notes. Your game should never be tested by just one person; however, at an early prototype stage it would be counter-productive to have lots of people testing the game because it is most likely broken and unstable. Those outside the design team will create lots of negative feedback. A small group of four or five is able to provide enough variance in gameplay styles and tastes to give you useful

feedback for a prototype. If every person gets stuck at exactly the same place or cannot fathom your puzzle, it is time to revise and then re-test. If four out of five get past that point and one fails, you are more likely on the right track.

If you are testing the game fairly early on, you are going to want to use each tester just once. As soon as a tester is familiar with this build of the game, she or he can never have that initial reaction again. Amass a number of potential testers, some of whom will play the game once and then never play it again until it is complete (or at least until it is much further along in development).

6.10

Try Not to Fixate on the Negatives

At first testing, you are most likely to ask testers questions like, "Does the game feel right to you?" rather than getting into specific detail. When you are observing the players and asking them questions related to the game, it is important that you do not fixate on one tester's negative (or positive) findings; if you do, it becomes difficult to apply the findings to improve the game. For example, even though I have been teaching for over ten years, it surprises me still when students take comments in critiques to heart. The purpose of an instructor's critique (and tester feedback) is not to break the student down, but instead to build the student up and make the student a better designer. The critique is not always heard that way because the work often feels personal.

It is hard to take a step back and look at what a tester is saying and then analyze it in context. When you are taking on the testing process, you have to look at all the results in as detached a manner as possible. Usually testers, like the team, want the game to be great, but individual opinions can be counter-productive if they are taken completely at face value and in isolation, so you need to look at overall comments and feedback. On the other hand, you cannot afford to be arrogant about your game and assume that the testers are just stupid for not understanding your obvious genius. The testers are your audience—always remember that.

Getting What You Need

Once you bring in people from the outside to play-test, you need to know what insights you want to get out of them and what feedback is going to be most useful to you or your team.

The first question to ask is how much of the game you are going to show. Different play-testing scenarios may require different parts of the game to be tested. For example, if you have puzzles in the game that may be too easy or too hard, it is not worth having the tester play through several minutes or hours of the game to get to the puzzles. You need to create skip points that take the tester to where their feedback will be most useful. Perhaps you want to test combat scenarios, or some jump-scares in a horror game. You may also need a full play-through of the prototype so you can get an overall sense of the flow of play from the tester. You have to go into each testing scenario knowing what you want to get out of it. Play-testing is, for the most part, asking people if the experience they are getting out of the game is the same as the experience you are trying to design.

There are different approaches and varieties of game testing dependent on the size of the game and studio developing it. There are also specific testing routines that occur at certain times during the production process, such as soak testing, localization testing, beta testing, and load testing. I will focus on the predominant and most useful approaches in this chapter and encourage you to visit this book's website (www.bloomsbury.com/Salmond-Video-Game) to find out more about testing.

Focus Groups

These are used more by marketing people to determine people's perceptions, opinions, beliefs, and attitudes towards a game (usually the prototype). Focus groups can be useful because there is group interaction; one tester may immediately dismiss the game mechanic or setting but be persuaded by a fellow group member. Of course, the opposite can happen, and this free and open conversation is important to gathering data.

THE PREPARATION PHASE

PLAYER NUMBERS AS MECHANIC

INITIAL PROTOTYPE PHASE

THE ITERATION LOOP

DESIGN PHASE 1: FIXING ON THE VISUALS

DESIGN PHASE 2: CHARACTER, CAMERA, AND CONTROL DESIGN

PRODUCTION TESTING

PRACTICAL APPROACHES TO TESTING

INTERVIEW: KATE CRAIG

CHAPTER SUMMARY AND DISCUSSION POINTS

Quality Assurance (QA Testing)

Depending on the size of the game, the QA team may be in-house or outsourced to a private company. QA testing begins with the first playable prototype and ends with post-production. QA testers are looking for game bugs, which are reported using a bug-reporting system (sometimes a spreadsheet, sometimes software such as Atlassian's *Jira*) and sent back to the design team and programmers. Bugs break down into A, B, and C. A-level bugs are critical and would prevent the shipping of the game. B-level bugs need to be fixed but do not prevent the game from being played, unless there are multiple B-level bugs. C-level bugs are small or obscure problems that can be handled easily or in a post-release patch.

The QA team is also looking at compliance issues if the game is going to any console. Each console manufacturer has strict technical requirements for their platforms. A QA department does not get too heavily involved with the technical side, but will be looking for standard formatting of error messages, how trademarks and copyright material is handled—as well as potentially reporting content that falls outside of the desired ESRB rating intended for the game. There is also compatibility testing on the PC platform, which has the testing team run the game on several different configurations of PC hardware.

Usability Testing

Usability focuses on maximizing effectiveness and player satisfaction. Usability issues are myriad, but could be as simple as one color on a map being used to communicate multiple messages (confusing for the player) or a lack of feedback when something bad occurs or when an item cannot be used (players need feedback). Usability issues occur in all aspects of the game and relate directly to what may frustrate the player or prevent a positive experience. This sort of feedback usually comes from usability experts; once this initial test is completed, the usability testers invite players from the intended demographic to play the game.

The expert will then give a player specific tasks in the game and encourage the player to think out loud while playing. The usability expert will often interrupt the player to ask specific questions and will then analyze the results post-play. Experts test the game by first analyzing their own reactions based on their knowledge of other games and then inviting others in and observing their reactions to the game. The usability team will provide the designers with a detailed and prioritized list of problems as well as solutions (this is a useful shortcut).

6.11
A usability tester focuses on elements of a game such as inventory systems and interfaces and provides feedback on how easy or intuitive they are to players. *Diablo III* (Blizzard, 2013).

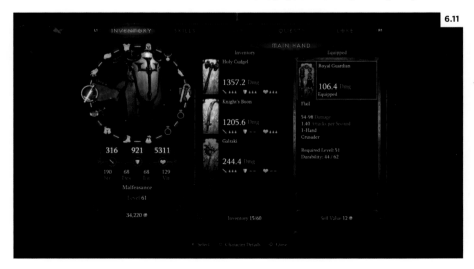

6.11

PRACTICAL APPROACHES TO TESTING

There is no one right or wrong way to play-test your game. You have to find the approach that works best for you and delivers the results you find most useful. Game designers tend to use a variety of approaches because each one can catch different feedback. Screen recording may allow the player to get more lost in your game and be a better reflection of a "normal" player, but that also means they are not so consciously seeking problems. Questions allow the player to reflect on the game during and after they have played it, but there is the issue of interrupting gameplay.

Screen Recording

Invite people in to play your game and then record the gameplay. This is a way to catch bugs and monitor player behavior and offers the advantage of being able to rewind and pause the play-testing. Screen recording can provide a more honest level of feedback because the tester can easily get lost in the game and forget they are there to test it, which can offer a valuable insight to how others will approach your game.

Questions for Testers

There are several considerations when putting together a play-testing methodology. It is not enough to ask, "Is this game fun?" because that is only going to give you a small amount of data (yes, no, and maybe). When observing testers there are questions you ask them and, more importantly, questions you ask yourself. This is a short list that acts as a starting point; each game has its own set of specifics that need to be play-tested. Developing your own questions is a good idea; just be careful not to make the questions "leading" ones. For example, "Do you have any issues with the game?" implies that there are issues from the beginning; a non-leading example is "How was your experience with the game?".

When play-testing, you may also want to think about where you set up the test. It can be intimidating for testers to come into a studio (especially if that studio is your bedroom or a room in your house) and feel comfortable being critical. Testing can occur in neutral locations or even online (although an issue with online is that you need to make sure no one is going to leak your game). Early release versions of games that are played and improved have become a recent model for success, with games such as *DayZ*.

THE
PREPARATION
PHASE

PLAYER
NUMBERS AS
MECHANIC

INITIAL
PROTOTYPE
PHASE

THE
ITERATION
LOOP

DESIGN PHASE
1: FIXING ON
THE VISUALS

DESIGN PHASE
2: CHARACTER,
CAMERA,
AND CONTROL
DESIGN

PRODUCTION
TESTING

PRACTICAL
APPROACHES
TO TESTING

INTERVIEW:
KATE CRAIG

CHAPTER
SUMMARY AND
DISCUSSION
POINTS

QUESTIONS YOU ASK TESTERS:

Were you bored during the gameplay?
(This can lead to follow-up questions:
"Where did you get bored?" etc.)

How long do you think you were playing for?
(This indicates boredom/engagement levels.)

Which parts of the game were most fun?

Which parts of the game were the least fun?

When playing level X, what are your thoughts on
its length and relationship to the rest of the game?

Have you come across any puzzles that were
too hard to solve or too easy to complete?
In either case, why do you think they were
too hard or easy?

QUESTIONS YOU ASK YOURSELF:

Do players play the game differently
(assuming you have male, female, and
mixed age groups in your testing group)?

Which group seems to be enjoying the game
more? Do they fit your target audience?

Does the player get lost?

Does the player get frustrated?

How are the First Order Optimal Strategies
(if used) leveling the playing field?

Do players want to play the game again?
If so, why? If not, why not?

6.12

6.12
Survival horror game *DayZ* is one of the most
popular games that was released as "early
access," which gave players an opportunity to
play the game while it was still being developed.
(It is a mod of another game and so was already
reasonably stable.)

INTERVIEW

PART 3:
SYSTEMS AND DESIGNING WORLDS

**CHAPTER SIX
PLANNING, PREPARATION,
AND PLAY-TESTING**

KATE CRAIG

Environment Artist

Kate is a Canadian game artist who has worked in social and independent game development, most recently on the indie game *Gone Home*. Currently an environment modeler at The Fullbright Company, she illustrates comics for the Web and print in her downtime.

How did you become a 3D game artist?

"I've always had a latent interest in game art, but assumed it was a career other people were involved in, that it was too technical, and that I'd need to know programming to work in game development. While knowledge of programming languages absolutely does help, when I learned it wasn't as crucial to game art as I'd thought, I enrolled in a 3D animation course to learn how to model, rig, and animate."

What were the challenges you faced working on *Gone Home*?

"*Gone Home* is set in a single house; the player is gated from leaving, though we did try to imply a greater sense of world through lighting and sound (e.g., the lightning storm outside). Because it's a single location, the ability to drill down and explore each room on a deep level was extremely important. Each of those rooms required many unique game assets, so the sheer number of models to create was probably my biggest challenge. We were lucky enough that we had friends and artists interested enough in the development that they donated their time to help with some of the modeling work."

6.13

6.13
The lounge and a mixtape from *Gone Home*.

You work in 2D and 3D from comic books to game design. How do you feel the processes differ or inform each other?

"They're similar in that they share many of the same tools and skill sets—Photoshop coloring is similar for both texturing assets and flatting pages, for example, but the mindset behind each workflow is very different. In comics, the focus (for me) is whether the art supports the narrative, and whether the conversation or action flows from panel to panel and page to page. Pacing is the main concern, not draftsmanship, and everything that impedes that gets jettisoned."

"In creating game art, each asset is created and viewed as a tile in a mosaic—does this model add to the overall tone of the setting? Does it look out of place and is it built in such a way that it's efficient and not bogging down the scene? There are technical constraints in game art that just aren't there in 2D. If I need to draw a whole mountain range in a single comic panel, that's no problem. In 3D, polygon and texture budgets limit what can be on screen at any one time, so I find myself switching over to a much more technical way of thinking."

CHAPTER SUMMARY

There are those who plan, there are those who over-plan, and those who under-plan. This is why project managers exist and are incredibly valuable. It is their job to keep spreadsheets of timelines and costs, and they will know how much changing an art asset or introducing a new concept will cost in time and money. Planning is a skill set that needs to be developed, but simple prototypes get the game off the starting blocks sooner so the design and production process can begin.

If communication among all members of the team is good, and there is an agreed-upon understanding of what the game is and how it will evolve, the chances of success are very high. Testing is a huge part of the design process success and must be woven into the development throughout the course of the game's life. Being too precious about your game and not wanting to receive negative feedback is completely counter-productive and often damaging to the game.

The key is in knowing what the game is, who it is for, and what you need from testers to make the game better. It is part of the plan-design-test-learn-repeat cycle that must be embraced by all members of the team.

THE PREPARATION PHASE

PLAYER NUMBERS AS MECHANIC

INITIAL PROTOTYPE PHASE

THE ITERATION LOOP

DESIGN PHASE 1: FIXING ON THE VISUALS

DESIGN PHASE 2: CHARACTER, CAMERA, AND CONTROL DESIGN

PRODUCTION TESTING

PRACTICAL APPROACHES TO TESTING

INTERVIEW: KATE CRAIG

CHAPTER SUMMARY AND DISCUSSION POINTS

DISCUSSION POINTS

1. If you were to create a "copy" of a well-known but simple game (such as the arcade game you deconstructed in the discussion points of Chapter 2), what would it be, and what would you alter to update it? For example, explore how making *Pac-Man* (Namco, 1980) a multiplayer experience could enhance or change the overall feeling and playability of the game.

2. Continue the arcade game alteration: Change another feature, iterate on that, and then bring in a feature from a different arcade-style game and see how that works. For example, how would a multiplayer *Pac-Man* play if it also incorporated high-pace elements from games such as *Defender* (Williams Electronic Games, 1981) or *Robotron: 2084* (Vid Kidz, 1982)?

3. How would you test the effects of your additions to the arcade game in order to assess whether they are positive or negative for the players? What metrics would you want to get out of a testing session, and why? Draw up a testing plan based on the outcomes you want and then bring in designers from another team to see what they would test for, based on your game mechanic.

References

Fullerton, T. and C. Swain (2004), *Game Design Workshop: Designing, Prototyping, and Playtesting Games*, San Francisco, CA: CMP.

PART 3: SYSTEMS AND DESIGNING WORLDS

CHAPTER SEVEN
CHARACTER DESIGN

Chapter Objectives:

- Understand principles of character design.

- Build a character profile and back-story.

- Make the character real, with personality traits and relationships.

7.1
Lara Croft concept art, developed by Square Enix
(2013).

THE PRINCIPLES OF VIDEO GAME CHARACTER DESIGN

What Is a Character?

There is overlap between the development of level design, concept art, and character design. The way in which a world is built and the levels within it develop is much the same way that the characters come to populate it. All of these have to be in response to what the game mechanic requires (Does the mechanic require jumps? Are the levels destructible? etc.). Your game has many moving parts, all of which must talk to each other but which are ultimately in service to the world you have created. Jill Murray (2013), the scriptwriter behind Ubisoft Sofia's *Assassins' Creed III: Liberation* (2012), has said that research and knowing the world the character inhabits is vital in creating depth and that it is a good idea to get the world right first, because it's the context in which your characters' lives play out.

"Character" is a dual-purpose word; it describes not only the physical attributes of a person (height, weight, gender, race), but nature and personality as well (kind, angry, violent, happy). These are the "characteristics" of a person or thing. For example in the *Halo* franchise, the character of Master Chief is defined by his stature (he stands at over seven feet tall) and other physical attributes, as well as his armor and impenetrable visor. The character's personality is communicated mostly through his actions as he is a man of very few words. Master Chief seeks justice, honor, and valor in battle and is driven to do the right thing in defeating an alien threat. Those are the character *traits* of Master Chief. In development at Bungie Inc., Rob McLees and Marcus Lehto combined their inspirations—from Clint Eastwood's characters in westerns to a combination of movie tropes (the lone samurai, the one-man army, the last of his kind)—to create the character. Master Chief is recognizable because he blends universal themes and is all the more memorable because of the world he inhabits and his aesthetic qualities.

7.2

7.2
Concept art and early environment art for the game *Halo: Combat Evolved* (Bungie Inc., 2001). This illustration establishes the mood of the game and defines the main features of the Master Chief character.

7.3

7.3
Licensed characters such as Batman (here in *Batman: Arkham Origins* from Warner Bros. Games Montréal, 2013) have predetermined aesthetics and backgrounds. The creative problem to solve in developing new games for a preexisting franchise is making sure that fans and players alike can relate to the character they know from the raft of different media Batman has appeared in.

THE BUILDING BLOCKS OF CHARACTER DESIGN

When designing a character for the player (in this case, the main character), the basic principle is to communicate personality traits that will resonate with the player. Getting those right or wrong is the difference between characters that people want to play with or against— and characters that players just do not care about at all.

The developer Tim Schafer has been creating memorable video game characters for over 20 years. Schafer (2004) defines the tenets of good character design as:

Wish Fulfillment: When creating great characters, understand that games are wish fulfillments, and the main character has to be a conduit for that.

Ego Invest: The player will best identify with a character that seems real and doesn't block the player's actions; a character helps to make the game "mean" something.

Uniqueness: Players will remember a character that is unusual and not bland.

Coolness: The main character should be the "coolest" and get the best dialogue and best equipment, just as the main character in a movie would.

Active Roles: The last blow or significant act should be made by the main character and the biggest reward be given to them.

Motivations: Main character motivations should be simple and universal. The audience wants to relate to the character, so you have to find the simplest, most universal motivations for them, like love or greed. If the character has those broad strokes, an audience can identify with him or her.

Deeply Felt Motivations: The character cannot just go through the motions. You have to remind the player that this character wants their objective more than anything else in the world. If the character doesn't care, then the players will not care.

Be Responsive: Make supportive characters respond to the main character (e.g., the character of Farah in Ubisoft Montreal's *Prince of Persia: The Sands of Time* [2003] gasps when the player nearly falls off a ledge). This will communicate a deeper sense of realism.

Back-story: Know more than you show. You need to know your main character. Where was your character born? What were her parents like? You should know because you will pull from these details in subtle ways.

Supporting Characters: Would you go on a road trip with these characters? Would you want to hang out with them? If yes, then so might your player.

PERSONALITY AND PERSONIFICATION

Personification and anthropomorphism (the ability we have to attribute human characteristics to an animal or object) are useful human traits from a game designer's perspective because they enable us to imbue almost any abstract object with a personality. Even though players know they are looking at animated pixels, characters that are designed well seem real, and players will care about and react to that personification.

Abstract shapes or characters that are more akin to "blank slates" allow us to project into the character because we get so little information back. Humans are very good at filling in the blanks and building on a select few personality traits. Even though we know the character is not real, we can suspend our disbelief and care for inanimate or animated objects and characters. This opens up options for the design of the game and its characters. It is also very useful if you are not an accomplished artist.

THE PRINCIPLES OF VIDEO GAME CHARACTER DESIGN

THE BUILDING BLOCKS OF CHARACTER DESIGN

PERSONALITY AND PERSONIFICATION

CHARACTERS THAT SERVE A PURPOSE

BUILDING THE CHARACTER

MAKING THE CHARACTER REAL

NON-PLAYER CHARACTERS AND RELATIONSHIP MAPS

MOOD BOARDS AND CHARACTER SHEETS

INTERVIEW: JAMES FOX

CHAPTER SUMMARY AND DISCUSSION POINTS

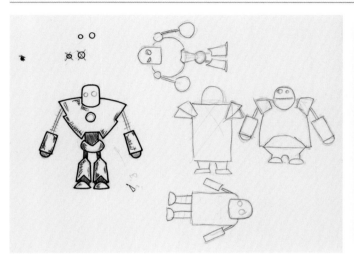

7.4

7.4
Robots are an example of anthropomorphism; they are objects that can be imbued with human or non-human traits dependent on the game narrative. In this example, the artists at Fishcow are working on a robot for *Gomo* (Fishcow Studio, 2013) that will eventually morph into a fairly menacing character in the game.

It begins as a somewhat friendly looking, soft, more rounded character, but as the game takes on a darker tone, so the artwork shifts to include tropes from movies (such as the psychopathic computer HAL in the movie *2001* with its menacing red "eye" and a more "muscular," overpowering presence) and the robot guard takes on a different aesthetic.

7.5a

7.5b

7.5a
Not all strong characters in games are humans. A minor character, "Muggy" in *Fallout: New Vegas DLC, Old World Blues* (Obsidian Entertainment, 2011), is a miniature version of other security robots the player encounters, but this one has an obsession with collecting mugs. This singular trait and his interactions with the player have endeared him to many.

7.5b
Childlike characters with no dialogue and simple movement can become endearing to players. The "sackboy" character from *LittleBigPlanet* (Media Molecule, 2008) drew on a history of doll-like characters players of all ages could relate to. The designers then added variants and different subtle personality traits into the game to further connect the player and character (cheekiness, bossiness, happiness, etc.).

CHARACTERS THAT
SERVE A PURPOSE

When designing a game, you may already have an idea of the personality traits of the character or characters you want to create. They may be adventurous, heroic, righteous—or the exact opposite. As with level design, other media tropes and characters may well inform and inspire your decision. If you are thinking "action war hero with big guns," there is a good chance that part of your creative process is modeled on characters from the Stallone, Schwarzenegger, or Vin Diesel style of films. If you are developing an RPG genre game, there is a strong chance other game characters you have played are going to inspire and inform your process, along with the *Lord of the Rings* books or film adaptations. The design problem is to come up with something new and yet also retain a recognizable core for people to be able to understand your character. For example, a main character may be from an unfamiliar culture, but she is driven by a quest for revenge or justice, which is universally understood.

7.6

The question to begin with is: What purpose does the character serve for the player? The main character is usually the conduit of wish fulfillment for the player. However, to be able to relate to that character, the player has to be able to connect on some level, even if the player has a different gender or ethnicity from the character. The character needs to be memorable in some way and relatable on multiple levels. This works as well with a hero character such as Lara Croft as it does with a ridiculous character such as Homer Simpson. Both are memorable and can be related to for different reasons, and they have persisted and been constantly reinvented because of this.

7.6
The Lara Croft character from *Tomb Raider*, Crystal Dynamics (2013), has been successful because she has traits that people can identify with and that are associated with the action/exploring genre of her game. She defies the negative stereotypes of "weak female" or "princess in distress" and has survived as a game character because of the strength of her personification.

When creating a character, you should begin with what is referred to as the "high concept," as explained by Steve Meretzky (2001), who has designed *Stationfall* (Infocom, 1983) and *Hitchhiker's Guide to the Galaxy* (Infocom, 1984):

Remember the two things you're trying to do with this character: make an enjoyable and interesting character that a player will want to adopt into his or her life for the next few weeks or months, and create a character that will be different and memorable enough to help you cut through the clutter of the several thousand other games that you'll be competing with for shelf, magazine, and player-awareness space. So at this point try to think, what's interesting? What's cool? What hasn't been done before?

The character must serve a purpose for the player, but also have restrictions based on the mechanic or gameplay. The main character (as stand-in for the player) has no history in the game world and as such needs to be given additional information (quests, history, training) by other characters. There are other considerations for creating memorable characters for the player to use or work with. For example, when developing the supporting character of Elizabeth for *BioShock Infinite*, Irrational Games (2013), the question for the animation director, Shawn Robertson (2014), at Irrational Games was: "Can she talk?" The original character design had Elizabeth as a non-talking character. As the development of the character began, the focus was on maximizing the player experience, and the silent version of Elizabeth was not building the relationship with the player that the

designers wanted. So the team made a talking version and immediately the bond was created between the player and the character. This also gave purpose to the Elizabeth character because she now guides and helps the player and can give them information and back-story. This is not the purpose of every character—some may be quest-givers or enemies—but each interaction with the player must be purposeful.

7.7

In the game *Gomo*, published by Fishcow Studio, the main characters are made of very simple shapes (the game is intended for small mobile screens) but must still convey character and elicit an emotional connection from the player. Much of this is done with movement as well as audio; however, as in children's animation, a simple character is more of a "blank slate" onto which the player can project their own personality and emotions.

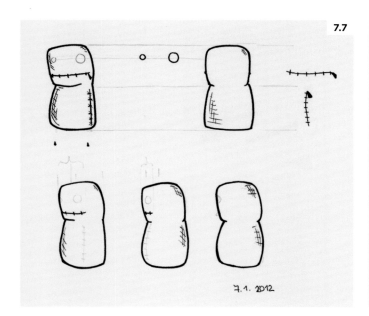

7.7

7.1. 2012

TIP | **WHAT'S IN A NAME?**

7.8

7.8
What if this character, from *The Elder Scrolls IV: Oblivion* (Bethesda Game Studio, 2006), were called Barry? How would that alter the player's perception of the character? Would he be less intimidating? Would the character be perceived as more friendly or approachable?

Naming your character is important; it not only gives the designer better insight into the nature of the character, but it will also help to inform the player. Is your character a Cordelia or a Belinda? A Jason or a Sean? These names bring their own associations: *Cordelia* has an old-fashioned, slightly mystical sound, and it begins with a hard *C*. *Belinda* is a softer name, one that could be associated with a certain decade in high school or the girl next door. Great examples come from literature: J. K. Rowling constructs her character names as a means of defining their personality traits. *Harry Potter* is a soft name and sounds friendly, unassuming, and "normal." *Severus Snape* and *Draco Malfoy* do not have the same connotations at all, and their names have been constructed to reflect their roles and personalities. When designing a character, be aware that the name serves the purpose of setting expectations for the character and the player's relationship to the character.

THE PRINCIPLES OF VIDEO GAME CHARACTER DESIGN

THE BUILDING BLOCKS OF CHARACTER DESIGN

PERSONALITY AND PERSONI-FICATION

CHARACTERS THAT SERVE A PURPOSE

BUILDING THE CHARACTER

MAKING THE CHARACTER REAL

NON-PLAYER CHARACTERS AND RELATIONSHIP MAPS

MOOD BOARDS AND CHARACTER SHEETS

INTERVIEW: JAMES FOX

CHAPTER SUMMARY AND DISCUSSION POINTS

Stereotypes: Uses and Misuses

Stereotypes can be useful shortcuts when designing non-essential characters, but are dangerous when relied on too heavily. Stereotypes are, by definition, generic traits and visuals applied to a person. Farmers with strong rural accents who seem mild-mannered and slightly scared of violence or muscled warriors who find it hard to string a sentence together are both stereotypes that aid a player in identifying the trope the character is fulfilling. This also makes them exactly like every other character that fits that mold and ones that a player has seen many times before. Stereotypes can also be insulting, denigrating, and offensive.

We explored ethical choices in video game creation in Chapter 4; the short version is to be aware whether or not your character design would offend anyone, be they male or female or from different ethnicities or sexual orientations. Stereotypes tend to be insulting because they are overused in media, from "dumb blondes" (Princess Daphne in Advanced Microcomputer Systems' *Dragon's Lair*, 1983) to "clumsy and cute" (Yuffie and Rikku from the *Final Fantasy* franchise by Square Enix) to "African American characters as gangsters or sports stars" (Cole Train from *Gears of War*, Epic Games, Sam B from *Dead Island*, Techland).

Being thoughtful about your characters, and avoiding negative stereotypes, is not a form of self-censorship; it takes far more creativity to design a non-stereotypical character that resonates. It also does not mean that the character you create has to be bland or cannot be used to raise awareness about stereotypes or issues with dominant tropes themselves (the *Mass Effect* games allow same-sex relationships along with inter-species relationships; the James Heller main character from Radical Entertainment's *Prototype 2* [2012] is an African-American ex-marine).

7.9
Players discover very little about the Dixie Clements character from *Rumble Roses XX* (Konami, 2006) during the course of the game. This is in contrast with more developed characters such as Alyx Vance in *Half Life 2* (Valve, 2004), who is a fully fleshed out character with whom the player can form an emotional bond.

BUILDING THE CHARACTER

Once you have a name and know the world the character will inhabit, but before you know what your character looks like (although you will have some notions based on the setting, genre, and early concept art), it is well worth building a profile of the traits and personality that will inform the character's aesthetic.

Step 1: Background

The character of Logan from *Dead Island* (Techland, 2011) has a bio that gives some background and rationale for his personality traits in-game:

A former football star, spoiled by life and successful in every possible way, Logan's ego finally put an end to his bright future. Taking part in a reckless street race with tragic consequences, Logan not only killed a young woman—his unfortunate passenger; he also fractured his knee, putting an end to his sports career. His fall from stardom inevitably followed and he plunged swiftly into a life of bitterness and despair. In an attempt to get away from the demons hunting him, he gladly takes the chance to experience the beauties and wonders of Banoi.

Soon enough though the getaway he was dreaming about turns into a real-life nightmare . . .

This is not an exhaustive bio or profile, but it gives the designers enough back-story and personality to build from when creating dialogue, reactions to other characters, and possible actions. Some character bios run into pages of information, while others (especially if the game is not heavily narrative based, which is the case with *Dead Island*) can be more of a jumping-off point during development.

7.10

7.10
Although not a deep bio, the story behind the character of Logan in *Dead Island* is enough to establish a tragic past based on rash and impulsive actions. It also establishes a potential weakness and sense of regret that can be reflected in his dialogue.

THE PRINCIPLES OF VIDEO GAME CHARACTER DESIGN

THE BUILDING BLOCKS OF CHARACTER DESIGN

PERSONALITY AND PERSONI-FICATION

CHARACTERS THAT SERVE A PURPOSE

BUILDING THE CHARACTER

MAKING THE CHARACTER REAL

NON-PLAYER CHARACTERS AND RELATIONSHIP MAPS

MOOD BOARDS AND CHARACTER SHEETS

INTERVIEW: JAMES FOX

CHAPTER SUMMARY AND DISCUSSION POINTS

Step 2: Build a Profile

The process of character creation starts with a profile. These can be fairly deep and designers can create lengthy scripts for their main characters. You need to write as much or as little as required to know and understand the character. One quick approach to character profile development is to create a social media account for your character. In the profile, you can create a list of the music the character listens to, which films they watch, what games they play, and who their friends are. This works even for a fantasy character; it would be slightly abstracted but will still be useful.

For example, a warrior character who is stereotypically aggressive might listen to heavy metal (clichéd though this is) and watch a lot of wrestling. Or, bucking the stereotype, the warrior may be at heart peaceful and listen to classical music yet be driven to violence by a thirst for justice. A healer character might listen to new age music and have lots of images of calm, natural environments in the profile, or, conversely, they could be emotionally unbalanced by all the sickness and death they have seen and use the profile as an artistic outlet for that. Immediately, these profiles can begin to evolve the character; it is typical to start with clichés and stereotypes and then, as you bring in other elements and juxtapositions, a more complex, believable character begins to form.

This is by no means an exhaustive list, but it is a good start. Knowing the character means developing who they are, their relationships, dreams, and desires; it also includes how they dress, how they move, and how they look.

Some typical questions when writing a profile are:

Where does the character live?

What, if any, was the character's education?

What are the character's personality traits and how are they revealed?

Did the character suffer trauma as an adult or child?

What were the character's biggest triumphs and defeats?

Are there any romantic involvements? Past, present, or future?

Does the character have religious or spiritual beliefs?

What unusual talents does the character possess?

Does the character have any phobias or quirks?

What is the character's financial status?

What does the character want more than anything else in the world?

What does the character fear more than anything else in the world?

How does the character relate to friends, authority, or social classes?

7.11a

7.11a
Each character in Telltale
Game's *The Walking Dead* is
scripted so that a deeper back
story is suggested and alluded
to in the game. By offering
glimpses of a precursor life
outside the current narrative
the characters become more
nuanced and their motivations
for in-game actions seem more
easy to relate to for the player.
It is also a subtle way for the
developers to suggest how the
character should be played
based on insights into their
back story.

7.11b

7.11b
Relationships between in-
game characters can be used
to add emotional depth and
resonance to a story. Believable
relationships reflect the
reality we know and add more
tension when characters are
put into peril. *The Last of Us*
connected with many players
and critics because it explored
the emotional growth of a man
(Joel) tasked with protecting
a surrogate daughter – Ellie)
despite his reluctance to
become involved because of
the loss of his own daughter.
Although these are character
tropes echoed in literature
and film, it is still rare for video
games to add this level of depth
to characters.

THE
PRINCIPLES OF
VIDEO GAME
CHARACTER
DESIGN

THE BUILDING
BLOCKS OF
CHARACTER
DESIGN

PERSONALITY
AND PERSONI-
FICATION

CHARACTERS
THAT SERVE
A PURPOSE

BUILDING THE
CHARACTER

MAKING THE
CHARACTER
REAL

NON-PLAYER
CHARACTERS
AND
RELATIONSHIP
MAPS

MOOD
BOARDS AND
CHARACTER
SHEETS

INTERVIEW:
JAMES FOX

CHAPTER
SUMMARY AND
DISCUSSION
POINTS

Step 3: Research the Aesthetic

Personality, background, and building a profile are important, and these will inform how the character looks, dresses, and interacts with others. When researching visual styles for your characters, you can draw inspiration from comic books, illustrations, film, and, of course, other games. This does not imply that you should make a character that you think other players want. Often people have no idea what they want until they see it, but existing characters can help inform your approach.

For example, no one would have necessarily expressed a strong desire to play a Syrian assassin from the twelfth century, and yet we have *Assassin's Creed* (Ubisoft Montreal, 2007) introducing Altaïr Ibn-La'Ahad. Altaïr is as much informed by his surroundings and history as by his personality traits. Although he follows many tropes from film and literature, such as the lone hero or the man caught up in a cruel world, players connect with him because of the universal themes and personality traits he exhibits.

When developing the look of a character, the concept artist needs to know who the character is because this defines how they will appear to the world. Game developers do a lot of research, (especially if there is a historical setting, but even if the setting is, say, science fiction). What have others created in this genre? What has made those characters stand out (either positively or negatively)? How do those characters fit into their worlds?

Once you establish the aesthetic and character traits, the next step is to start building the character in more detail and making decisions because every aspect of the character is impacted by the game's intended platform, mechanic, visual resolution, and the amount of animation required.

TIP

GENERIC CHARACTERS VERSUS STAND-OUT CHARACTERS

When designing multiple characters in your game, one way to make one or a few characters stand out is to make the others generic. For example, on a ship's crew (such as in the *Mass Effect*, BioWare [2007–2012], games), the characters you can interact with all have some standout features (color of hair, stature, a specific hat, or even slightly different lighting). The rest of the crew are generic; they wear the same uniforms and do not stand out in any way. By utilizing similar poses, standard expressions, standard stances, and so on, the player can identify them as generic "crew members." These kinds of characters add emphasis to the main character; everything that is special and unique about him or her is not brought out in the generic characters, thus making the main character stand out all the more.

MAKING THE CHARACTER REAL

When beginning basic character design, one approach is to use graphic design concepts—these translate well to character design.

Color: You need to contextualize the characters within the environment: What color scheme should they have? Do they need to camouflage because they are prey or predator? Would they stand out against the environment?

Shape: What emotions should their shape communicate? Cute, cuddly, and light-colored like a Tribble in *Star Trek* or menacing, dark, and insectoid like the aliens in the *Alien* movies?

Size: Much as with shape, if the planet is fantastical or more Earth-like, how does that inform the size of the character? Does size relate to power?

Emotion: Use adjectives such as strange, menacing, friendly, dangerous, and so on, and apply them to the characters to inform the poses and mannerisms they would adopt.

Opposition/enemy: When developing character concepts, human or alien, opposition is an important consideration. Are the aliens red to differentiate them from their sworn enemies or predators who are blue? Are the red aliens gentle and peaceful and living in fear of the aggressive and dark blue aliens?

Texture: As with shape, color, and size, texture can subtly define the personality of a character: fluffy, smooth, coarse, armored, pock-marked, soft, and so on.

As the process goes on, a character may become more nuanced, but these initial steps will aid the artist in coming up with concept art that can go through iterations towards the final design.

7.12

7.12
Character shape, color, and form are important and informed by the overall aesthetic of the game (and perhaps by technological shortcomings, such as web or mobile platforms). Early sketches begin to convey the personality of the characters and inform their functions: hero or enemy, friend or quest-giver. The process of designing characters must be open at first, but each character has to be one that can be animated (mouths, arms, eyes, legs, etc.) and designers must consider how much technical constraints are going to affect that. A simple character, such as those in *Gomo* by Fishcow Studio, are going to work easily across multiple platforms because of their low fidelity. Just adding hair or a cloak can cause headaches for the programmers and these decisions must be made in line with the artist's development of the characters.

THE PRINCIPLES OF VIDEO GAME CHARACTER DESIGN | THE BUILDING BLOCKS OF CHARACTER DESIGN | PERSONALITY AND PERSONIFICATION | CHARACTERS THAT SERVE A PURPOSE | BUILDING THE CHARACTER | **MAKING THE CHARACTER REAL** | NON-PLAYER CHARACTERS AND RELATIONSHIP MAPS | MOOD BOARDS AND CHARACTER SHEETS | INTERVIEW: JAMES FOX | CHAPTER SUMMARY AND DISCUSSION POINTS

NON-PLAYER CHARACTERS AND RELATIONSHIP MAPS

Supporting or non-player characters serve another purpose: to support or antagonize the player. They may be the evil that has to be defeated (Lord Voldemort), the friend who helps the player succeed (Hermione and Ron), or the mentor who trains and advises them (Dumbledore).

One approach to developing the interplay between multiple characters is to use the "Interpersonal Circumplex," which is based on a model developed by psychologist Timothy Leary. This map involves the conceptualizing, organizing, and assessing of interpersonal behaviors, traits, and motives between people. The clinical psychologist J. S. Wiggins (1996) evolved this original model and has developed it into a personality map used by a variety of psychological specializations. Its use in character design is in being able to map out the interconnectedness of your main character's personality in much the same way a psychologist would.

By mapping the personality traits against each other, you begin to see how balanced your game characters are and which traits best suit your concepts of the main hero and anti-hero. This circumplex does not need to become too complex, but it can prevent too many characters with similar traits.

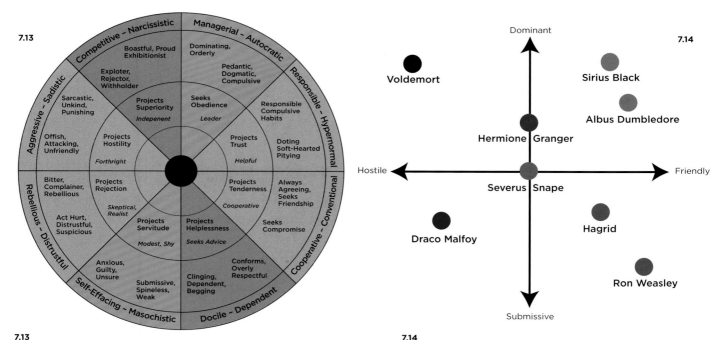

7.13
The Interpersonal Circumplex is a tool that social psychologists developed and game designers use to visualize the relationships between characters. The model has two main axes based on traits: friendliness and dominance. Designers map various characters on the circumplex to map interconnected relationships.

7.14
In this model, you can see an interpretation of the various personality traits of the *Harry Potter* characters, how they relate to each other, and where they might overlap or diverge.

MOOD BOARDS AND CHARACTER SHEETS

When developing the visuals for a character, mood boards are a useful starting place. As with level design, building a repository of images that exemplify your characters allows for more focus and visual direction. In games, as in movies, the clothing and props that characters use say as much about them as their poses and expressions. If the character has clothing and weaponry, it is important that those are developed along with the character; for example, what sort of bow should Lara Croft from *Tomb Raider* have? Or what sort of sword should a user-created character in *Skyrim* be able to wield? Character is further informed by texture and tone of clothing: dark or light, sexy or chaste, flowing or tightly worn? On a technical note, these decisions can also have implications for animators. There is a reason you do not see many capes or scarves on video game characters: They require expensive polygon counts and mapping to look good.

Mood boards are used in all areas of design; they are visual collages that communicate many elements of the character. These could include size, presence, color palette, and clothing. They are a useful visual guide for an artist when developing concept art but can also provide context for the development team.

Once the character begins to take shape, the artist or modeler should create a character sheet; this is the visualization of the character from a variety of angles and poses. This is also an opportunity to build on uniqueness and back-story because the character sheets can suggest a history or present allegiances. This could be a tattoo that identifies the character with a faction later in the game, or a scar that was inflicted by a nemesis or that indicates the character is battle hardened. Tattoos, tribal markings, or jewelry can also denote a rebellious streak or affiliation to a cause, as can weapons, special moves, or specific poses.

7.15

7.16

7.15
Non-Player Character (NPC) designs from *Skyrim*. Clothing and props go a long way in denoting the profession and social position of the character.

7.16
This is an action mood board based on the game *Mirror's Edge* (EA Digital Illusions CE, 2008). The mechanic of the game was based around the free-running sport of Parkour. The way that the athletes dress and move informed the character in the game, and the environments and CCTV cameras imbue a sense of an oppressive totalitarian regime.

THE
PRINCIPLES OF
VIDEO GAME
CHARACTER
DESIGN

THE BUILDING
BLOCKS OF
CHARACTER
DESIGN

PERSONALITY
AND PERSONI-
FICATION

CHARACTERS
THAT SERVE
A PURPOSE

BUILDING THE
CHARACTER

MAKING THE
CHARACTER
REAL

NON-PLAYER
CHARACTERS
AND
RELATIONSHIP
MAPS

MOOD
BOARDS AND
CHARACTER
SHEETS

INTERVIEW:
JAMES FOX

CHAPTER
SUMMARY AND
DISCUSSION
POINTS

Character sheets also denote design choices, which are useful for the animators to work from. This could be where it makes most sense to store a weapon (hip, back, or unseen); what form a magical spell may take and where it is cast from; as well as where costumes fasten, hinge, and move. Props are also important here. If the character has a heavy weapon, such as a battle axe, as well as smaller knives, the player would expect to see a slight or pronounced change in the stance and execution of certain moves. Character sheets can map these elements, and the team can make informed choices on the development of the characters' look before going into the lengthy animation process.

7.17a

7.17b

7.17a
Developing the personality traits and rationales behind a supporting character informs the player of that character's agendas, counter-points, and allegiances in relation to the main character. This is especially useful if the characters are visually similar; it is the traits, personalities, and actions that differentiate them (Elliot Salem and Tyson Rios from EA Montreal's *Army of Two*™, 2008).

7.17b
In the *Tomb Raider* reboot, it is the smaller stature of Lara Croft that in part differentiates her from the other game characters. It also communicates a sense of vulnerability and youth.

JAMES FOX

Director and Producer

With a background in TV, digital, and creative agency work, James Fox has created and developed a wide range of award-winning TV series, websites, and games for a variety of big name brands. Using a wide network of directors, editors, animators, designers, writers, and musicians, James has created content for clients and production partners from around the world, such as the BBC and Cartoon Network.

When designing characters for animation, do you begin with sketches or the personality profile of the character?

"This depends on your starting point. If you are creating a character based on an existing story, then you want to reflect the personality that's already been created. If you are creating a character from scratch, then sketching is a great starting point. Playing with facial expression, pose, and posture you can really get to know the basics of a character before he or she or it becomes a fully fleshed-out person."

Could you break down your process of designing a character: Do you start with face, then body, then eventually clothing, or do you design whole characters and then iterate them towards the final design?

"Character design is all about experimenting. I generally go for the overall shape of the creature/person first. I like geeks and nerds, so most of my initial designs are often lanky or goofy, but that's just me. I always sketch very loosely for ages before I start worrying about specific details, making sure I stay playful and free. Then when I feel like I've got a rough idea of who this person is, I'll focus on the face, and I will repeat the process over and over before I get to something I like. Then when it feels like the character is making his way through, I'll start doing more detailed experiments on the whole character. The secret is to not think too hard, just let things flow; don't be afraid of making mistakes."

7.18

7.18
James Fox's *The Lighthouse and the Lock*, with characters Sloth, Bingly, Owen, Amelia, and Devon.

Is character back-story important when designing the visuals of a character?
"Yes, always. Whether you are designing from a character in a script or from scratch, you need to know the basic personality you are dealing with."

One of the tenets of character design is that they should be distinctive and often exaggerated. Is that part of your thought process when designing a new character?
"Yes. If you can look at a character and immediately know what they are about, then you are onto a winner. Big wide eyes verses small suspicious eyes—who are you going to trust more? Animation is a playground, so pushing things as far as you can is always a good idea."

How much does the environment for the character influence the character design?
"That depends on their relationship to the environment. If a character is unhappy with where they are, they have two choices; get down about it or do something about it. It all depends on the story and the character's part in the story. This is a great way to test out who your character really is, so do a version where they are repressed by the environment and one where they have decided to change it. You'll be amazed how different they come out."

Once you have a character finalized, how does the process of animating that character begin? In the earlier stages, do you plan out how you think the character will walk, talk, and move, or does that come later in the process?
"In the latter stages of design, this depends slightly on how you are going to fulfill the animation (2D, 3D, stop-motion, etc.), but in the early stages the first thing to do is a character sheet. This is a set of poses that shows how the character looks in certain poses and positions. Storyboarders will always start working from character sheets; they are the character 'bible' from which all animation will spring."

Moving from sketch to final animated character, what do you feel are the most important steps in creating a "living" character, one that audiences can connect with and believe in?
"The face will obviously be a focal point; sincerity of character is hugely important so always make sure expressions are really thought out and done well. Just as important is body language. Unlike live action, the acting in animation is often way more exaggerated and expressive, so always focus on this."

CHAPTER SUMMARY

Character design takes many forms. If you are working with a licensed property, then much of the work is already in place. If you are working on your own unique game, you are going to have to create every character. Characters do not always have to be incredibly detailed and back-story rich for the player to have a positive experience (the game *Journey* from TGC is a master class in minimalist character design). The personality of a tiny 8-bit sprite can be communicated as well as that of a fully fledged 3D model if it is given the correct amount of development time and attention.

Character design involves creativity, psychology, research, iteration, and experimentation; balancing those factors will increase the chances that you create a memorable and engaging character for your game. Every aspect of the game world and every character in it must be consistent and relate to one another in a way that makes sense to the player. Even if the main character is a mute "vessel" who never speaks (for example, Gordon Freeman in *Half Life 1* and *2*), then supporting characters and the level design need to be able to draw the player into that world and keep them there.

THE
PRINCIPLES OF
VIDEO GAME
CHARACTER
DESIGN

THE BUILDING
BLOCKS OF
CHARACTER
DESIGN

PERSONALITY
AND PERSONI-
FICATION

CHARACTERS
THAT SERVE
A PURPOSE

BUILDING THE
CHARACTER

MAKING THE
CHARACTER
REAL

NON-PLAYER
CHARACTERS
AND
RELATIONSHIP
MAPS

MOOD
BOARDS AND
CHARACTER
SHEETS

INTERVIEW:
JAMES FOX

CHAPTER
SUMMARY AND
DISCUSSION
POINTS

DISCUSSION POINTS

1. **Examine two characters from a game you recently played. What do you feel are their defining characteristics? How did the designers ensure you connected with the characters? Did they use stereotypes and shortcuts or did they spend some time developing your relationship with the character?**

2. **How successfully are the two characters integrated into their worlds? When approaching your own character designs, how do you plan to make sure that character, mechanic, world, and interaction work together coherently?**

3. **Come up with a few examples of "bad" character design. Why do these characters not resonate with you? If they annoy you, is that by design or unintended? Does the lack of connection with this character affect your relationship with the game?**

References

Character bio for *Dead Island*'s Logan. (2011), June. Available online: http://gamevolution.co.uk/ 2011/06/dead-island-character-bio-logan/

Meretzky, S. (2001), "Building Character: An Analysis of Character Creation." *Gamasutra*, November 20. Available online: http://www .gamasutra.com/resource_guide/20011119/ meretzky_01.htm

Murray, J. (2013), "Diverse Characters: Write Them Now!" Lecture, Game Developers Conference, San Francisco, March.

Robertson, S. (2014), "Creating *BioShock Infinite*'s Elizabeth." Speech, Game Developers Conference, San Francisco, March 20.

Schafer, T. (2004), "Adventures in Character Design." Speech, Game Developers Conference, San Jose, March.

Wiggins, J. S. (1996), *The Five-factor Model of Personality: Theoretical Perspectives*. New York: Guilford Press.

PART 3:
SYSTEMS AND
DESIGNING WORLDS

CHAPTER EIGHT
BRINGING IT ALL TOGETHER

Chapter Objectives:

- Understand level design principles, concepts, sketches, and planning.

- Apply concepts of planning player movement in level design.

- Use level design for storytelling and as emotional resonator.

8.1
Gears of War 3, Aftermath Map,
developed by Epic Games (2011).

LEVEL DESIGN FROM THE GROUND UP

Creating an Emotional Aesthetic

The scope of this book is to introduce concepts and best practices for video game design. In the previous chapters, a lot of ground has been covered, and Chapters 8 and 9 focus that knowledge through the practice of level design. By now you know what your game is, how many players there are, what the mechanic is, and so on. You may even be starting to design your game's characters. Level design is where you begin the process of moving towards a more complete game.

Level design, as with animation, programming, character design, audio design, and so on, is a specialty in its own right. These chapters provide an overview of the level design process that will afford insight into the basic principles of level design and the effect it has on the overall design of the game. Every decision in level design ripples through the entire design team (which is why planning is so important).

From the outset, as with all creative processes, you begin with research. If your game is to be set in a post-apocalyptic Washington, DC, as in *Fallout 3*, you will refer to multiple sources, including images and maps of how it looks now, and then cross-reference those with images from disaster movies or other video games in order to consider how others have visualized similar scenarios.

It is worth building up an image repository of architecture from all over the world, from the past and from the present (do this when you travel and use Google Maps to travel to many more places virtually). Your world may be sci-fi, fantasy, or historical—but the game is being played and understood by human players, so it is useful to ground it in some real-world analogies that help people make sense of even the most fantastic of places. For example, in the fantasy genre level designers and artists may work from sources such as Tolkien (*Lord of the Rings*, EA Los Angeles, 2004), ancient Nordic designs (*Skyrim*), and European medieval architecture (*Fable*, Lionhead Studios, 2004; *The Witcher*, CD Projekt Red, 2007; *Dark Souls*, From Software, 2011) and then mix in elements that work with the game's unique aesthetic. All good designers borrow from the world around them, taking what works within the context of the world or emotion they want to create and mixing it with unexpected or juxtaposed sources to create something new and visually engaging.

LEVEL DESIGN FROM THE GROUND UP

LEVEL DESIGN IS STORYTELLING

PLANNING THE LEVEL

BIRD'S EYE VIEW AND ENVIRONMENT FLOW

PLOTTING THE PLAYER PATH

CASE STUDY: EVOLVING GAMEPLAY

CHAPTER SUMMARY AND DISCUSSION POINTS

8.2
This concept art for the non-existent city of Windhelm in the game *Skyrim* is a mixture of several architectural styles, most notably Norse, but with additions from other medieval European buildings.

8.2

Be Detail Oriented

When photographing and collecting images from environments, focus on more than just the large vistas; consider every element that may appear in a game. For example, if a mechanic's garage is going to feature in a level, you need to get several samples of garages, both exteriors and interiors, as well as their surroundings. The design team should "scout" as many locations as possible. There's only so much detail you can discern from a photograph, especially if it's online. This is why film directors always visit the locations they want to shoot in to get the atmospheric "feeling" and emotions of the physical space. Obviously, if your levels are inside spaceships or contain a mythical land, it is not so easy; so find analogous sites. Spaceships are not that dissimilar to submarines and aircraft carriers. Mythical realms tend to combine the familiar, such as a forest, with the unfamiliar, such as a deep-sea environment.

8.3

8.3
Visiting every part of the world looking for inspiration is not cost-effective, but there are elements of copied architecture in unexpected places. This Roman or Greek style "ruin" is in Edinburgh, Scotland.

LEVEL DESIGN FROM THE GROUND UP

LEVEL DESIGN IS STORYTELLING

PLANNING THE LEVEL

BIRD'S EYE VIEW AND ENVIRONMENT FLOW

PLOTTING THE PLAYER PATH

CASE STUDY: EVOLVING GAMEPLAY

CHAPTER SUMMARY AND DISCUSSION POINTS

8.4

Rather than waiting for people to get out of the way when photographing for architectural features, try to include people in the shot. They provide a measurable sense of scale.

8.4

LEVEL DESIGN
IS STORYTELLING

Games are experience-based interactive products, so the world design and the levels within them have to be thought through from a story-teller's perspective. Even if it is a gruff military-style action game, the player has to feel that every design decision is consistent with the theme of the game. The architecture of France in a WWII game needs to look like 1940s France. Even though players have never seen 1940s France, they will have an idea of it based upon other media sources. Not all games have to be 100% accurate of course, but doing the ground work will sell your level to the player that much more.

A designer must know what the story behind the level is and the purpose behind the environment. If the story is set in 1940s France with the Allies pushing back a German advance, and the player is part of an Allied platoon, this serves as the "why" and the rationale. The purpose of the environment is then multiple. First, it serves an aesthetic function, with streets and architecture looking like a French war zone from a period many people will have seen at some point in film. Its second purpose is to get the player to their goal—without them getting lost, confused, or frustrated because they have no real idea where they are—while delivering game elements (enemies, cover points, puzzles, etc.).

Concept Art and Sketches

Character and level design often run parallel, as the world and those who inhabit it are so closely linked. The concept for a game may be that it is an FPS (*Call of Duty Modern Warfare 3*; *Killzone,* Guerrilla Games, 2004) with Stealth (*Splinter Cell; Blacklist*, Ubisoft Toronto, 2013; *Thief*, Looking Glass Studios, 1998) set in a Victorian-esque world (*BioShock Infinite*): You'd have the setting, gameplay, and tone of the game *Dishonored* from Arkane Studios. In all of these games, the design of the world is as much a character in the game as the playable characters are. Artists and designers will begin level design with sketches and art that communicate the tone and feel of the overall game aesthetic. Concept art will expand upon reference photographs and character designs, begin to flesh out the look of the world, and make decisions on its "character" and back-story before the work of designing the levels begins in earnest. Once again, this is in concord with other members of the design team to make sure that the art direction matches the overall vision and technical limitations of the game.

TIP | FLAVOR

Level design is a form of storytelling and often achieved through set dressing and what is known as "flavor." Lighting, textures, and set dressing can convey meaning to a player. A darker, more downtrodden area can present as menacing, or as a good place to hide, depending upon the context of the game. Other flavor elements are objects that a player may be able to interact with, but that are of no importance to the game, such as cups, computers, switches, and so on. Flavor can also be used to convey subtle meaning, such as the use of posters in the *BioShock* games that offer insight into the mindset of the rulers of Rapture and Columbia.

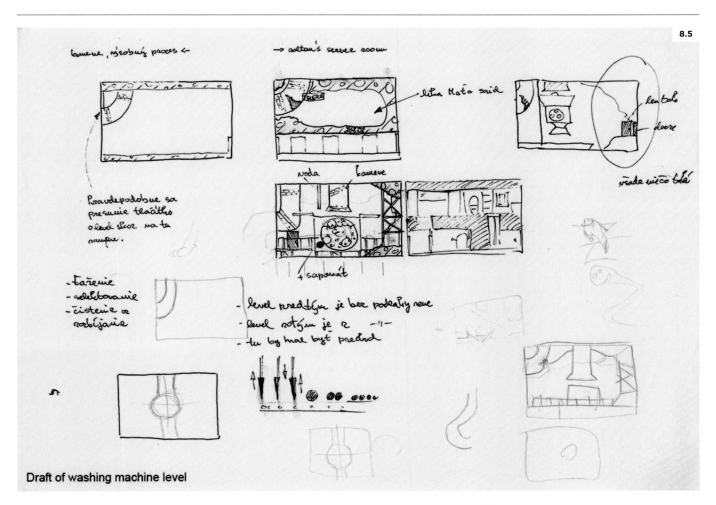

8.5

Draft of washing machine level

8.5
Sketch in early concept design for a level in the game *Gomo* from Fishcow.

PLANNING THE LEVEL

The focus in this chapter is on an RPG or action-style game level design, but the principles apply broadly to other game genres. There are genre-specific considerations, and a puzzle platform game or driving game will have its own specific level design attributes. However, there are some crossover points. For instance, in a driving game there are focal points and references that are similar to line of sight and wayfinding, along with the "game flow" of each track. A driving game will have cambers, turn-in points, short cuts, and so on that, although seen at great speed, map well onto the choke points, looping, and priming you would see in an action game. Most simulation-based driving games are going to be far more restrictive than an exploration, open-world game, but level design is focused on delivering the best experience to the player in a consistent and emotionally engaging way.

When planning a level, part of the design process is in creating a space that invokes an emotion in the player. This could be a claustrophobic dungeon corridor or an open environment for the player to wander around in. Both areas are controlled spaces that guide the player towards an ultimate goal. The design questions spread out from that premise:

- How long should the player spend in the level?

- Is the level ideally walked through by the player (high level of detail) or created to be run through at speed (lower level of detail)?

- Are there areas that will "trap" the player (like a boss battle) until an event has been completed?

- Are there objects to be found or collectibles?

- How much do you want the player to be able to explore the level?

- Where does the player start from (known as a spawn point)?

- Where do non-player-characters (NPCs) walk/stand/animate?

- Which areas are navigable, and which are not?

- Where do the enemies appear from?

- Where are the traps/puzzles/pacing elements?

This list covers the basics. Start simple and begin with a blueprint or "map" of the level layout using simple blocks and lines to represent components in the level. As you revise, the level may become more complex.

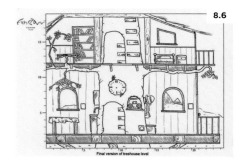

8.6

8.6
These three development process images from *Gomo* exemplify the level development process. The developers at Fishcow Studio sketch out to scale their environments and develop them further as the game becomes more complex. They plan areas of interaction and puzzles, and the gameplay and aesthetic are developed in line with one another. Rapid prototyping is key to developing a solid mechanic within the planned interaction of the game, and sketches are a way for the art team to iterate quickly and feed level design ideas back to the programmers. This does depend somewhat on the structure of the development environment; some teams may be working within a known game engine, so all iterations ("move this here, try that there") can begin to happen in-engine much faster.

Listing the Level Components

Start by compiling a list of the elements you need in a level; these elements are the building blocks for the level, such as buildings, roads, carts, people, doors, etc. What you are looking for especially are assets that can be repeated or reused, simplifying the modeling time and process. For example, if it's a market area (like the *Assassin's Creed* souk) there will be interior rooms, stalls, seats, and tables, and each store may be very similar in shape and size and have the same furniture. Some buildings will be bigger, longer, or more complex in form than others, but these could be two room "blocks" pushed together or offset for variance. It is important to reuse elements as much as possible, because every time the graphics processor has to draw something new, it takes time and processor resources, which can have a negative effect on performance. A modular approach to design is important (more about modular design later).

> **TIP**
>
> **TILE GRAPHICS**
>
> An early example of modular design was the use of "tile graphics" to get the most out of the hardware. Tiles of a certain size were used and reused, and different assets were swapped in and out to create the illusion of a much larger world than the one that actually existed. In early games (*SimCity*, *Pac-Man*), tiles were used to create entire levels, including buildings, landscape/terrain, and even characters. Tiling as an asset reduction strategy is still used to optimize textures in some games today.
>
> Art is "expensive" in video games, and designers are always looking for a trade-off between what looks good and how much load it puts on the hardware. Memory allocation (or memory budgeting) is still one of the biggest technical restrictions on the design process, and artists are given a limited amount of freedom in what they can do. It is important to understand that there are many constraints placed on designers due to hardware and stability; these restrictions have to be built into the creative process.

The asset list for the map needs to include architectural elements beyond just walls and floors. For example, if your level is a marketplace, some stalls may have canopy roofing or tent-like structures attached to them. This adds variety and a more organic feeling to the design. Other rooms may have flat or vaulted ceilings—and so on. Examine the variance and the flow of the buildings of a real city (Google Maps is really handy for this): A city that has evolved over time is going to be very irregular and almost chaotic as opposed to more modern, planned cities such as in the USA. A spaceship or militaristic map will be more efficient and streamlined because of the mindset of those who built it for a specific purpose. All of these variables must be included in the map list because at this point you are creating the physical architecture of the level.

A simple map will include:

- The overview/bird's eye view or layout of the level.

- A level map key. It is good practice to create a key to your map that defines the different wall, roof, and object types (e.g., a red circle = columns, brown squares = doorways, orange circles = archways, etc.).

- Wall types, room types.

- Furniture types.

- Ceiling types: canvas, vaulted, flat.

- Player goals and event triggers marked out (blue dot is a door key, green dot for a treasure chest, yellow is a collectible item, purple is an enemy spawn location, etc.).

8.7

8.7
Many cities have a modular look to them, such as this one in Tunisia; it's the smaller embellishments that add variance. Ancient cultures overlay the new and the old, and the evolution of the architecture over time gives it an organic, somewhat chaotic, aesthetic.

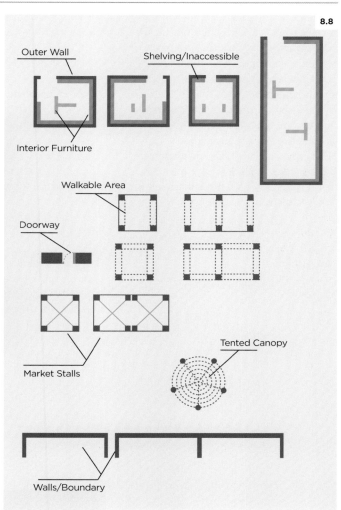

8.8

8.8
A basic list and visuals of some of the components of the market level. These can all be duplicated and recycled to make the level larger.

BIRD'S EYE VIEW AND ENVIRONMENT FLOW

When beginning the design of a level, it is important to think of the flow of the environment and how this relates to the gameplay (for example, "What speed is the player travelling at?" and "How long do they stay in the level?"). This is most easily worked out by the use of the top-down map because you are not concerned with the aesthetics at this point, but instead with how players get to their objective, what they may pick up on the way, where the enemies come from, and so on.

The basics when creating a top-down map would be:

- Environment flow—can the player easily see the objective or keep it in view most of the time?

- Gameplay—how does the environment support or inhibit the player? Will the game camera get caught in the wall/geometry if the space is too tight?

- Are the player objectives clearly defined?

- Is the player able to use landmarks or locations to navigate through the level? What elements of the level are in place to differentiate each location?

- Are there any potential choke/pinch points for the player to pace the level?

- What are the enemy spawn locations?

- Where are objects placed in the level?

- Where would combat take place? Are combat areas well defined and easy to differentiate from non-combat spaces?

- Which areas are player accessible and non-accessible?

- How are the non-accessible areas closed off visually?

8.9

8.9
Dead Space 2™ (Visceral Games, 2011) uses debris, fire, and other level assets to funnel the player down specific pathways. The debris fields seem accessible, but the fire would cause damage, as in the real world, so this does not break immersion in the level.

As this is still the planning and sketching stage, the level can be drawn out and effectively played like a board game. The player has an entry point; what do they see and where are they most likely to go? Working as much out in advance as possible is going to streamline the process of making the actual level. In the following examples, I am using part of the Roman market town of Herculaneum as a map. I used Google Maps to get a bird's eye perspective of the ancient walled town and then started building my marketplace level (with some artistic license) based on that.

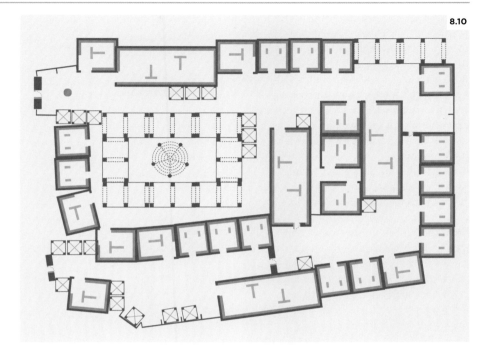

8.10

8.10
This is the overview map (based on Herculaneum) that has been put together using just those few assets from the initial list shown in Figure 8.8. Varying placement and repetition has made the map feel organic. There is a sense of flow, and the route for the player to take is forming; the map also allows for exploration by having more than one way of accessing different areas.

TIP | ART FATIGUE

You need to ensure the player does not suffer from what is known as "art fatigue," which occurs when every element of the level looks the same. It was prevalent in early games such as *Doom* (Id Software, 1993). Every room was square, and though they varied in size, they were essentially the same, and this got boring quickly. It also makes it harder for a player to navigate a level when very little changes between areas.

PLOTTING THE PLAYER PATH

In any game you design, more than one player type exists; there are going to be players who have little interest in exploring beyond finding where they need to go to achieve their goals ("challenge" players from the five domains of play in Chapter 4) and there are other players who are going to look everywhere just to see what they can find and interact with (seeking "novelty" and "stimulation"). The level needs to work for both of these players, so the "novelty" player can find collectible objects that are hidden throughout the level and the "challenge" player can look at shop signage or visual cues to determine where to go to get the job done as quickly as possible. Even given their preferred play style, level designers can subtly coerce "challenge" players to drop out of their mode to grab collectibles or other quest items if they are placed in plain sight. This serves to encourage players to look around more because once they have that one item, the concept of collecting is established in their mind and they are more likely to begin amassing items. That said, a level design that deliberately obstructs players' paths and forces them to explore and pick up every item would be frustrating for many players.

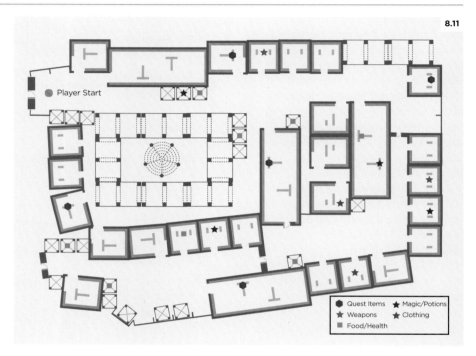

8.11

8.11
A map of a marketplace, complete with a key that lists placement of objects, including quest items, food/health, clothing, and weapons. These are spread out in the level to encourage exploration.

TIP | **COVER**

When looking at varying the placement of elements, it's important to consider what cover options you're offering the player (and this does not only apply to shooting games). A cover corner or vestibule could be used for stealth (hiding) or it could be an area where the designer places an object (such as a collectible) for the player. That object would be easier to find if it's "hidden" in an irregularly shaped area, distinct from the more regular surroundings. This also becomes a learned feature of the level—anything unusual or irregular could be worth exploring—and this adds depth to your gameplay.

Lines of Sight and Paths

Player paths can be well directed because, as the designer, you know exactly where the player will enter a level. It is reasonable to assume that when most players enter a new level on a mission they will follow their line of sight, particularly if they can see a perceived goal in the distance. Even if they are unsure where the ultimate goal is (if it isn't on their map or it cannot be seen in the distance), players in 3D and side scrolling games are used to moving forwards, away from what is behind or to the left of them. This mechanic is embedded into so many games that players have become used to the convention.

Another ploy, if placing an obvious goal in immediate sight is out of the question, is to use a dissimilarity. This could be an object or area that will pique the player's curiosity and draw them towards a goal. For example, a well-lit area within a dark level is enough to say to the player *come here* because psychologically we avoid dark "unsafe" places and see light as "safe," so we are hard-wired to head towards it.

Other conventions may not make sense in the real world, but do work in games. For example, placing a door in the player's line-of-sight when they enter a new level can signal that it is a goal to be investigated. Even if they venture off the direct path, they are likely to come back to it, as it's the first thing they saw and has thereby been afforded extra significance. Some games make this even more obvious by having a very short animation that flies the player through the level to show them their goal when they enter a level, as in *Tomb Raider* or *Uncharted*.

8.12a

8.12b

8.12a
From *Gears of War 3*, this level, known as "Mercy Courtyard," was built to have long lines of sight for the players as well as multiple cover areas and paths through the level and various different areas from which enemies can appear.

8.12b
This is part of the "Chateau" level from *Uncharted 3: Drake's Deception* (Naughty Dog, 2011). It might not seem it, but this is essentially a choke point and ambush point for the enemies in the level. It also has clearly defined goals: The player has to get from one side of the courtyard to the other.

Limiting Lines of Sight

A door at the end of a level works well to focus the player, but what happens when the design calls for multiple doors and the door that is the ultimate goal is out of sight when the player moves further into the level? This is where object interaction and subtle environment design comes into play. For example, a marketplace level might have three open stores in the distance, while the stores closest to the player are closed. This encourages the player to move down the street by limiting their options. Similarly, if all the stores are closed but further down the street there are carts with goods on them, the player is more likely to move towards these because they will be curious about why they are there. Other "flavor" elements or set dressing can also guide the player; for example, road signs may have places on them the player has never heard of but the directional arrows could all point in the direction of the player goal. Interior spaces can use the ubiquitous "exit" signs seen in every hotel and office space to guide the player, and so on.

Knowing what to place in the character's line of sight can be prototyped in the overview map, but has to become more resolved in the game engine. In the blueprint, it is a good exercise to map the probable line of sight as a continuous set of lines for "ideal" traversal of the level. This will inform you where the player is more or less likely to move when they enter a space. For example, as a player enters the marketplace, her line of sight is focused on a sign in the distance for a pharmacy. The player knows she is on a mission to seek ingredients for medicine, so she will probably move towards this store. As she exits that store, she is going to look away from where she has come, and that new line of sight is where you would place the next area of focus (e.g., the carts) that will lead the player towards her next goal, and so on through the level.

Assuming you want the player to spend some time in the level, you will need to break up the line of sight to add to the sense of exploration. This is achieved by moving buildings and other objects back and forth once you have drawn a straight line from where the player enters the level (showing their immediate line of sight). You can then judge where a player needs to move to in order to see around the obscured line of sight. This can be used to build tension in a horror game (with something like a long, badly lit corridor), a sense of exploration in another genre, or unease if there is a chance enemies are hiding out of sight. All of these elements force the player to continually re-establish the line of sight in order to see the goal and add to a deeper level of immersion in the environment.

8.13

8.13
The marketplace level with predicted lines of sight from the player's perspective. We can see likely paths the player will take based on line of sight, so now we consider what we need to place in that path that will be useful or interesting to the player.

LEVEL DESIGN
FROM THE
GROUND UP

LEVEL
DESIGN IS
STORYTELLING

PLANNING
THE LEVEL

BIRD'S EYE
VIEW AND
ENVIRONMENT
FLOW

PLOTTING THE
PLAYER PATH

CASE STUDY:
EVOLVING
GAMEPLAY

CHAPTER
SUMMARY AND
DISCUSSION
POINTS

Priming

Level design can also include an element of foreshadowing: A glimpse of a tall tower through a window or a blocked-off area gives the player an idea of where they need to go. The player is then engaged with figuring out how to get there. This is known as "priming"; it's showing another part of the level while the player is still in the present area. Priming is useful in providing an objective or even revealing narrative without having to rely on voiceover or interaction with other devices.

Loops and Exploration

Towns, cities, and even spaceships are not entirely linear spaces. There are streets, alleys, and cabins with multiple entrances and exits and these are sometimes interconnected. As a level designer, you can use this to your advantage by linking areas together. This means a player can be encouraged to loop back to a previous area of the level without the negative experience of backtracking. For example, you might include a store with a back door that opens onto a small courtyard, and the courtyard might have a gate that links to the rear of another store. This gives the player options when exploring the map, shows that the game can be non-linear, and encourages investigation. Adding loops makes the spaces feel natural to the player because we tend to understand our own world as interconnected. That is a big shortcut for level designers; if the player understands intuitively how the spaces within levels work, the game is going to be more immersive.

Loops may seem to counter the concept of directly steering the player towards a goal, but the player does not have to be entirely goal-directed. Loops offer a form of intrinsic reward (we will discuss rewards in Chapter 10). You as a designer are rewarding the player for exploring—for bothering to take the time to really look around the level. The downside of loops is that they can become a trap for the player. Unless there is a decent amount of variance within the set dressing of the level, the player can easily get lost. If they wander from store to similar store and get turned around, they can easily become frustrated when they want to return to their original goal. This is where visual reference and well-placed "flavor" can help. If each store has at least one item that defines it, the player can use that item as a form of landmark. If they see it twice, they know they've looped around and can retrace their steps or try another route.

8.14

8.14
An example of priming in level design is showing structures that stand out, such as the city of Megaton in *Fallout 3*. Because the structure is visually different from the immediate environment, the player is primed to approach this as an area to be explored in a way that's dissimilar from the wasteland they are currently in. The player is primed to expect NPCs, quest-givers, and dialogue. From a distance, Megaton is the only visible landmark that drives the player towards it (or away from it).

CASE STUDY:
EVOLVING GAMEPLAY WITH *GUNPOINT*

Tom Francis
Designer, writer, programmer

John Roberts
Lead artist

Ryan Ike
Lead composer

Fabian van Dommelen
Background artist

Francisco Cerda
Composer, menu music

John Robert Matz
Composer, main theme

8.15
The fixed camera point-of-view gives the player an overview of the entire level. As gameplay begins, the viewpoint zooms in so that the player can connect with the main character.

The Evolution of *Gunpoint*

Gunpoint is a stealth-based puzzle-platform game created by indie developer Tom Francis. It is set in the near future and players assume the role of freelance spy Richard Conway, who infiltrates buildings to fulfill assignments from various clients. Players must avoid guards and bypass security features with the aid the Crosslink tool, which rewires electrical circuits.

The idea of clicking to aim the character's jump was unconsciously inspired by a game called *Wik and the Fable of Souls* (Reflexive Entertainment, 2004), about a frog jumping and swinging from his prehensile tongue. The general idea of finding creative ways to infiltrate buildings was directly inspired by *Deus Ex* (Ion Storm, 2000), and the rewiring tool in particular was an attempt to expand on that and focus on allowing players to subvert the environment. According to Francis, one constraint was not knowing how to build a game in GameMaker or knowing what the software was capable of producing. Most of the look and feel of the game comes from learning the software during development and having to produce artwork within the constraints of that game engine.

8.16

The aesthetic of the levels is in keeping with the noir detective film genre. The game itself is a mix of traditional and environment-based puzzles in which the player manipulates elements of the level to achieve success.

8.16

On-boarding and Player Feedback

The very first level where you get to use the rewiring ability went through a lot of iterations, but the concept was always the same: Present the player a problem that is a) obviously impossible without rewiring, and b) incredibly simple with rewiring. It's just a locked door, a light switch, and a light. The only way to open the door is to switch to rewiring mode, click on the light switch, and drag its connection to the door—so Francis offered the player those controls and left them to it.

When testers played the game at home and emailed feedback, not many mentioned having trouble with that first challenge. But when Francis watched people play it on the expo floor at the Game Developers Conference, many people misunderstood and tried to connect the door to the light switch, instead of the other way around. Francis therefore reworked the level and the visual representation of connections to stress that these connections are directional, and the changes worked for most people, going from about 50% of players understanding it to about 90%.

The interesting thing was the disparity between the remote feedback and observing players in person. Francis concluded that a lot of remote testers actually were confused by the first rewiring challenge but, because it's logical once you grasp it, they saw it as their own fault that they didn't understand at first (and therefore didn't report the confusion as an issue). As Francis puts it: "That's nice of them, but as a designer it's good to know when something is counter-intuitive. Even if you don't ultimately blame me for it, I don't want you to have that confusing experience on what should be the simplest puzzle."

Balancing the Puzzles

As Francis explains, the game evolved over time: "I hadn't really set out to make a puzzle game, I didn't really want to make puzzles: In the most conventional sense, a puzzle is an obstacle with one particular solution, and my original aim was to mimic the way *Deus Ex* gives you tools flexible enough to invent solutions even the designers hadn't thought of."

"For the Crosslink to be an exciting ability, you had to be doing elaborate, interesting things with it. But if you give the player too many elaborate, interesting options, they'll find and choose the one that's easiest and simplest to them and won't find it interesting or elaborate."

"After a few rounds of testing and reworking the levels, I settled on a formula that seemed to give the best of both worlds. I designed the levels so that just breaking into the building is easy, and there were lots of different ways to do it. Once inside, getting to your objective is trickier, involving danger and guards, but there's a lot of potential for finding your own approaches. Then, to open the final door or get past the final obstacle, I intentionally designed a tough puzzle with only one or two solutions, which would require some mental leap of realizing how you can chain things together."

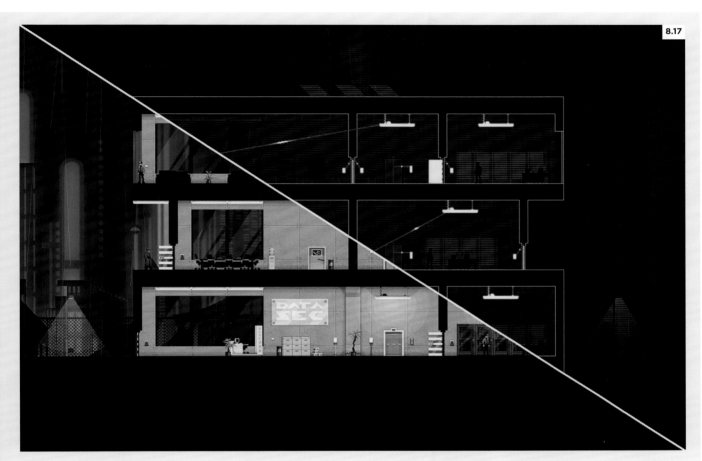

8.17

8.17
This is a split shot showing how the same level looks normally and in Crosslink mode. Crosslink mode is what you switch to in order to rewire the electronic bits of a building: You can see what everything's hooked up to and drag these connections around to make the level work the way you want it to.

CHAPTER SUMMARY

Consider the marketplace examples shown in Figures 8.10 and 8.11. Thus far, we have only looked at how the geography and the layout design impact the player's path through a level. This is an important step, and we can now build upon this to make the level more nuanced as we add non-player characters, enemies, and quest items. As level designers, we can be subtle and teach the player how to navigate simply by providing elements that the player has not yet seen—for instance, by changing the architecture (or just the textures). Rather than use a door as a marker that says "go there," for a player rounding a corner, we can design a wall that looks different from those the player has seen so far. If the marketplace has walls of mostly adobe texture and color, the introduction of a brick or white wall becomes a signifier for a path. This helps prevents art fatigue (because there is really nothing interesting about a series of doors). Solid walls, transparent objects or geometry, and flavor and set design all contribute to a level that guides the player as slowly or quickly as desired towards the goal, which is the point of the game experience.

In the next chapter, we will build on the concepts of level design by examining textures, setting boundaries for the player, and more about the modular design of a level.

LEVEL DESIGN
FROM THE
GROUND UP

LEVEL
DESIGN IS
STORYTELLING

PLANNING
THE LEVEL

BIRD'S EYE
VIEW AND
ENVIRONMENT
FLOW

PLOTTING THE
PLAYER PATH

CASE STUDY:
EVOLVING
GAMEPLAY

CHAPTER
SUMMARY AND
DISCUSSION
POINTS

DISCUSSION POINTS

1. Look at a game you have played recently that has a first- or third-person perspective. How does the level inform and engage via that camera and character point of view?

2. Games such as *The Last of Us*, or *BioShock: Infinite*, or *Brothers: A Tale of Two Sons* (Starbreeze Studios, 2013) frequently use priming for narrative as well as gameplay structure. What do you see as the advantages of priming? Does it break the player out of immersion? Does it help or hinder the player's quest or mission? Have you, as a player, even noticed priming before?

3. Examine some of the different methods that wayfinding systems and loops are used across different game genres. How do they inform the gameplay?

PART 3:
SYSTEMS AND
DESIGNING WORLDS

CHAPTER NINE
THE ENGAGEMENT
ENGINE

Chapter Objectives:

- Incorporate further principles of level design into your game.

- Scale levels, establish wayfinding systems, and use modular modeling.

- Create an engaging level for the player.

9.1

9.1
Concept Art from *The Elder Scrolls V: Skyrim*,
developed by Bethesda Softworks LLC, (2011).

CONNECTING AESTHETICS AND PLAYER NAVIGATION

This chapter is an extension of the principles covered in the previous chapter, and expands into more of the nuts and bolts of level design. We will examine in more depth how to build your design vocabulary and cover the important elements that go into creating an engaging level for your game.

Video games are more open and larger than they used to be; the problem is that it's very expensive to create truly open worlds where the player can go anywhere she or he pleases. When starting out as a game developer, ambition is good, but being too ambitious and unrealistic about the game you are developing can be counterproductive. Keeping your levels smaller and manageable is the key to creating and actually finishing a game. A good way to solve the issue of size versus depth is to use level boundaries.

When implemented well, boundaries can give the player an illusion of openness with no feeling of being blocked into a small area. For example, in much of *Halo 2* (Bungie Inc., 2004) the planet levels seem very open through clever use of large skies and the combination of mountains and dense vegetation, but, in fact, the play space is very small and constrained (this technique has been used in games from *Resident Evil 5* to *The Last of Us*). Boundaries help the player learn the map or enable the designer to control player progress so that players can only enter areas when they are ready or need to (for example, in the *Assassin's Creed* games, there are areas that are restricted until the player has reached a certain level or completed a specific mission in the game). Boundaries also close off areas because there is no content behind the façade, perhaps because of hardware or time restrictions or simply because there is no need to have every building open and accessible (*Shenmue* from Sega attempted to subvert this back in 1999).

9.2a

9.2b

9.2a

The level design in Naughty Dog's *The Last of Us* was visually very open, but gave clearly defined boundaries for the player. The use of high walls, foliage, and piled-up cars contained the player and restricted navigational choices while staying within the aesthetic of the game. This image also shows an example of priming, as the Joel character points to the destination.

9.2b

This traversal part of a level in *God of War* (SCE Santa Monica Studio, 2005) uses the architecture and features such as water to frame an optimal path for the player without using arrows or signage. The lighting also drives the player's eye towards the climbable space and ledges.

Consistency is Critical

When approaching level design, designers often use a Human Computer Interaction (HCI) term, "visibility and affordance." *Visibility* relates to how much information is being given to the player via the interface (visual feedback on health, a map, or the dashboard in a driving game) and *affordance* is the property of an object (a door with a handle that opens or is locked) and how it is perceived by the player. An example of inconsistency in affordance rules would be the use of climbable and unclimbable walls in games from the reboot of *Tomb Raider* to *Resident Evil* and *Uncharted*. In these levels, there are some walls the player can climb over, which are usually differentiated in some way (in *Tomb Raider*, the designers use white marks to show the climbable walls), but in other spaces short fences or even half-walls are unclimbable. When approaching these obstacles, the character just bounces off or does a "climb" animation but goes nowhere. This breaks the affordance rule, because

it makes sense that walls can be climbed, especially low ones. Breaking the affordance rule might also mean that the player is using a lot of trial and error to find out which walls they can scale, and which they can't. *Tomb Raider* does sidestep this by clearly delineating climbable versus non-climbable areas (by including white "scuff" marks on the scalable walls). *Assassin's Creed*, however, has many accessible areas but then other areas that you simply cannot climb for no apparent reason.

Inconsistent boundaries, visibility, and affordance are important issues because in a video game, players are always learning and looking for patterns. If players come across rock X, which they can climb, and then rock Y, which seems the same but cannot be climbed, they will have no way to learn what they can and cannot do. This is the same for visible-invisible barriers; for example, when players see a sizeable opening between two rocks or in a forest, but they will

not fit through it, it will make no sense unless the designer includes a way for players to learn what is a barrier and what is not. Inconsistent boundaries and barriers are not always caused by incomplete design. Many terrains and worlds are built *procedurally*; that is, they are built on the fly using code based on set parameters (for example, *Minecraft* by Mojang).

A solid design approach is to avoid inconsistency through subtle indicators. For example, you might have crumbling walls that are easy to climb over, while higher, intact walls cannot be climbed—this constitutes a subtle, consistent, and logical rule showing players how the level works. Dense forestation, cliff walls, water, or a walled city are all sound approaches to incorporating boundaries within the gameplay. They allow players to focus on the accessible parts of the level without wondering why they can go through a gap in one spot but not in another.

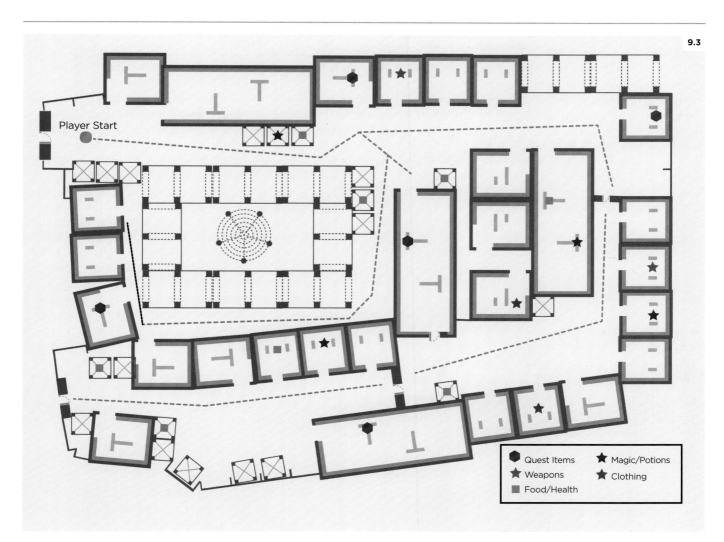

9.3

9.3

The map now shows the marketplace fully bounded by exterior walls (inside a larger city). The player is now restricted within the level boundary in a way that makes sense within the game.

SIZING AND FIELD OF VIEW

Boundaries encompass and define player movement. Another factor to consider in level design is scale. Whether you are establishing the size of an archway, or the extent of a character's field of view, review your reference photographs. Although a camera does not record all of the field of view a person actually has, it is close enough for the purposes of a first-person or third-person game. (This is an estimation process; level designers go into much more exacting detail and use architectural studies of height, width, and so on, from original blueprints.)

When artists and designers go out scouting, they will often put themselves or other people into the photograph to record a sense of scale. It is much easier to use a person with known proportions and extrapolate from that than to guess how wide a corridor needs to be after the fact. For the player to get the best sense of immersion, you need to be able to match the field of view of a still shot or video shot with that of the game. For example, when walking down the middle of a real street, if a live-action camera can see two or three floors of a building, then so should the camera in the game.

It is also a good idea to take photographs of a structure or area from different angles to cover crouching or prone characters. Take close-up shots of objects and textures, as well. If a photo of an object has a certain amount of detail in that close-up shot, the object is going to need roughly that same amount of detail when the player's character gets that close to it in the game. If a texture looks realistic from a distance, but awful when the player gets closer to it, that's going to affect the immersion levels in the game. Being detail focused on sizing will enable the texture mapping to be that much more accurate. It can involve a lot of arithmetic to enable smooth switching between levels of detail in your game.

9.4
Knowing roughly how tall a person is in a shot allows you to extrapolate sizing for buildings or other elements in the level. The same is true for modern buildings; although you may be able to find exact sizing, matching people and building dimensions is a good place to start when building models.

9.4

CONNECTING
AESTHETICS
AND PLAYER
NAVIGATION

SIZING AND
FIELD OF
VIEW

WAYFINDING
SYSTEMS

MODULAR
MODELS AND
TEXTURES

SILHOUETTE
ENVIRONMENT
DESIGN

CHOKE POINTS
AND STRONG
POINTS

INTERVIEW:
MEDIA
MOLECULE

CHAPTER
SUMMARY AND
DISCUSSION
POINTS

Level of detail, dynamic terrain meshing, and continuous Level of Detail (LoD), among others, are all mathematical algorithm approaches to solving platform texturing and detail issues. The basic principle is that the more the player can see, the more work the graphics processor has to do. So to minimize processor work, algorithms will "swap" out textures based on occlusion culling (see box on p. 184)—what the player can see and the player's distance from the object. Distant mountains may be very low polygon models because they do not need to be detailed; closer objects, such as buildings and other characters, are higher detailed. These techniques get very technical, as you might imagine, and even top game designers still ship games that have "texture pop-in": players are able to see the higher quality textures replace the lower level detail ones.

The use of simple 3D objects placed on your blueprint in the game engine with known sizing (7-foot wall, 3-foot high table, etc.) allows you to quickly and

9.5

easily get a sense of what field of view you need from the game engine (28mm camera, 60mm camera, etc.). There are far more technical approaches to doing this, of course, but this a good approach in early level design prototyping. Now that you have a player in a game and some models to move around or through, and you have established the field of view of the player, it is time to consider how the player will navigate through your level.

9.5
Uncharted 3: Drake's Deception (Naughty Dog, 2011) adds "verticality" to its levels, which adds a sense of scale and complexity to the environment.

9.6
Reference images of textures from different distances are also very useful for prototype texturing and modeling. The texture our eyes can see from a distance is refined when we get close, and this is the same within a video game level. Often textures are swapped out by the game engine as a character approaches because it would be very GPU-intensive (graphical processor unit) to load a large level full of high definition textures for every object. Coding is used to "cheat" so that detailed textures only load when the player approaches an object.

9.6

TIP

OCCLUSION CULLING, OVERDRAW, AND FRUSTUM CULLING

Game design is a series of compromises based on the hardware. You are always offsetting graphics, interaction, and rendering against the processing power of the platform. Traditionally 3D engines render objects that are farthest away from the camera (or point of view of the player) and then closer objects are drawn over them. This is known as "overdraw" or Level of Detail (LoD), and it is dictated by the hardware. It is set either in the asset creation software (e.g., Maya, 3d Studio Max) or within the game engine itself.

Frustum culling is a more elegant solution as it disables the rendering of objects that are outside of the camera's viewing area. However, it does still use overdraw for what can be seen (even if there is a wall in front of the player, all of the area behind it is still rendered). This method works well in smaller settings, but in wider open spaces, it still puts a lot of strain on the graphics processor.

Unity and other game engines use a more versatile method called "occlusion culling." This method only renders the elements of the map that the player can see. The occlusion culling process takes a virtual camera through a level when the level is being run and identifies what is visible to the player and what is not. This reduces the amount of "draw calls" (information sent to the graphics card and processor) and frees up precious performance resources.

Occlusion culling does require some manual setup and pre-planning on how the level geometry is created, but it is worth it for the smoother running of the game. For example, if a room is created as one large continuous model (or mesh), it can only be occluded or not (on/off), and this is more expensive graphically. If a room consists of four wall meshes, a table mesh, a chair mesh, a floor mesh, and so on, then they can each be on or off, so the occlusion is going to work better by not rendering those objects that are outside of the view of the player. For further reading on back-face culling and removal of hidden geometry during optimization, as well as other techniques, visit this book's website at **www.bloomsbury.com/Salmond-Video-Game**.

CONNECTING
AESTHETICS
AND PLAYER
NAVIGATION

SIZING AND
FIELD OF
VIEW

WAYFINDING
SYSTEMS

MODULAR
MODELS AND
TEXTURES

SILHOUETTE
ENVIRONMENT
DESIGN

CHOKE POINTS
AND STRONG
POINTS

INTERVIEW:
MEDIA
MOLECULE

CHAPTER
SUMMARY AND
DISCUSSION
POINTS

TIP

FIELD OF VIEW AND THE FRUSTRUM

The viewing frustum is the viewable space in the game from the perspective of the game camera's field of view. A frustrum is best described as parallel planes emanating from the camera into a cone of vision. Sometimes the term "pyramid of vision" is used instead of frustrum. The shape of this field of view varies depending on the size of the camera lens that is simulated.

In addition to the parallel lines of the field of view, the frustrum has two planes, the near plane and the far plane. Usually the game engine does not draw objects closer than the near plane setting or objects further than the far plane. In some cases, such as open world games, the far plane is placed infinitely far away from the camera/player and so all objects within the frustrum are drawn (e.g., in *Skyrim* you can always see the mountains in the distance when outside).

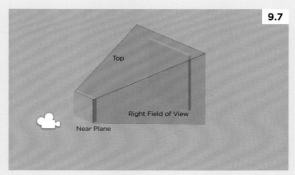

9.7
This graphic visualizes the pyramid of vision; it is the camera/player's field of view in the game.

This more detailed image illustrates what the camera/player can see when focusing on an object in a game based on his or her field of view and distance from the object. The object will appear nearer because of the near plane; this compensates as the player moves towards the object.

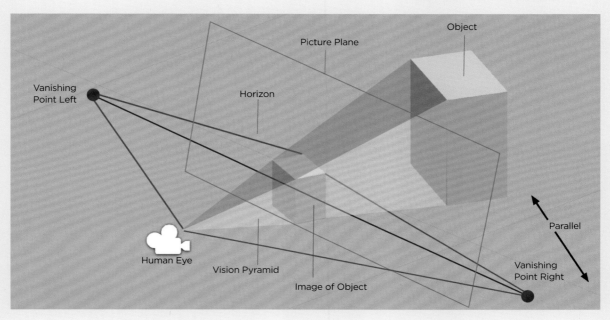

WAYFINDING SYSTEMS

As we've already seen, when creating a new world, level designers need to help players navigate through an unfamiliar space without getting lost (this is particularly true when creating large open or multi-path worlds). We need to help players find their way, using wayfinding tools. One such tool is to create an interactive overlay that the player can see, showing a path from A to B (for example, on-screen directional arrows in *Fable III* or *Dead Space*). This is an advanced technique and one that involves a considerable amount of programming and implementation. Simpler wayfinding is in the use of subtle or obvious artwork and landmarks. It is rare for people visiting a city, even a foreign one, to get out maps continuously because there are elements common to all cities. There is an in-built "meta-city" model most of us share. Cities usually have a business district, a historic district, and a shopping district. In the

marketplace map shown in Figure 9.3, for example, we might group merchant types or housing styles together so that the player is aware they're in a meat-packing area or a low-rent slum; this is a set of visual cues from which players can navigate.

Another wayfinding technique is to vary textures, or use different wall coloring or tiles to underline a change in an area and be used as a landmark. Although this does not occur so obviously in most real-world environments, it is useful in games where the player cannot ask for directions and has a limited sense of direction due to a restricted field of view. Another obvious aid in player navigation is the use of in-game signs or signposts. These are to be used sparingly, though; an over-reliance on signs that people may not bother to read (or have graphics cards not powerful enough to render) can lead to players getting lost. It also removes the sense

of exploration for the player. Obvious signage, such as merchant signs outside of storefronts, work well, as do colored awnings, which also serve the function of adding flavor to the level design. For example, awnings that are red could denote a meat/butcher's store and blue awnings could indicate tailors. These are also much easier to see from a distance or with a quick glance.

A sometimes forgotten part of wayfinding is answering the question of where the player spawns or enters the level should they die, quit, or restart the level. It may always be the exact same place, but it may also be random. These decisions, like many of the decisions we're about to see in this chapter, are critical and need to be agreed upon before time is spent on artwork and animation. If the player restarts the level in a variety of different places, it is even more important to use assets in the level to communicate to the player

9.8a

The city of Bowerstone in *Fable II* (Lionhead Studios, 2010) uses merchant shingles/signs to identify different kinds of stores as well as subtle changes in colors of the buildings to help players navigate.

9.8b

In the game *The Elder Scrolls IV: Oblivion* (Bethesda Game Studios, 2006), although there are markers and interactive maps, the designers still use road signs, knowing that this is a more immersive visual for the player and adds to the reality of the environment because of the analogue with our world.

9.8a

9.8b

CONNECTING   SIZING AND   MODULAR   SILHOUETTE   CHOKE POINTS   INTERVIEW: CHAPTER
AESTHETICS   FIELD OF   MODELS AND   ENVIRONMENT   AND STRONG   MEDIA   SUMMARY AND
AND PLAYER   VIEW   TEXTURES   DESIGN   POINTS   MOLECULE   DISCUSSION
NAVIGATION   POINTS

                                    WAYFINDING
                                    SYSTEMS

where they are, so that they can navigate to where they want to be easily. Another approach is to use wayfinder markers in the interface or on a mini-map that gives rough directional cues. In larger open-world games, the wayfinder or "quest markers" can be set by the player to enable exploration without getting lost. Once again, as a designer you need to analyze different games' wayfinding systems, what works, and what does not, and make decisions about which you want to implement in your game. The simpler and more streamlined the wayfinding system, the better.

9.9

9.9
These level design screens from the *Elder Scrolls IV: Oblivion* show the process of moving from wireframe of solid objects to the inclusion of possible player paths and interactive objects. Some objects require automatic animation (candles, flags, etc.) and others are triggered by the player's exploration.

9.10
In my own game I used prominent features and lighting in the level to signify a goal for the player and to act as navigational cues.

9.10

MODULAR MODELS AND TEXTURES

Level designers are always looking for efficient design processes. The best approach is to use elements that can be made once, and then used time and again. Street lights, archways, walls, awnings, windows, and so on can all be made once and used in a level to add flavor, while also reducing graphic processor draw calls. It is the same with textures, floor tiles, plaster, bricks, etc. All of these work well in modular design because they can be applied to more than one instance of a model. For example, a long corridor with textures of peeling paint and cracked plaster

could also serve as the interior walls of a disused store room elsewhere in the same level. Designers can use modular textures on any item that appears repeatedly, from wood textures on boxes and roof beams to fruit and meat in store windows. Furniture and items can be repeated with the same textures without becoming visually inconsistent.

However, textures can be overused and create art fatigue as much as repeated models in a level. Shorter spaces allow for more texture variance, and long runs can become visually boring. If there has

to be a long unbroken texture (a long path or big courtyard, for example), look to break it up using intersecting textures. The addition of pathways, windows, drainage ditches, or rough ground is great for breaking up any visual monotony without being overly taxing on the hardware.

9.11

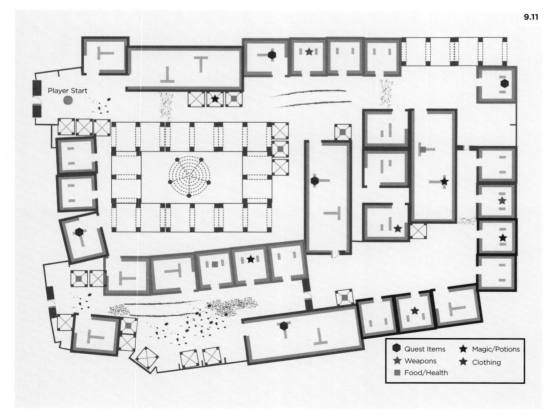

Quest Items · Magic/Potions
Weapons · Clothing
Food/Health

9.11
The marketplace with some placeholder art that suggests where areas of variance could fit. These could be cartwheel ruts, ditches, dirt, or brickwork. The lower left area is going to be the less desirable part of town, so it is already looking more unkempt.

CONNECTING
AESTHETICS
AND PLAYER
NAVIGATION

SIZING AND
FIELD OF
VIEW

WAYFINDING
SYSTEMS

**MODULAR
MODELS AND
TEXTURES**

SILHOUETTE
ENVIRONMENT
DESIGN

CHOKE POINTS
AND STRONG
POINTS

INTERVIEW:
MEDIA
MOLECULE

CHAPTER
SUMMARY AND
DISCUSSION
POINTS

Texture Sheets

When designing efficiently by reusing textures for buildings, furniture, and other art assets, the textures need to be planned out using what is known as a texture sheet. A texture sheet can be as simple as some solid colors that are placeholders for real textures that will be added later. Thus, if a light brown was the texture map placeholder for a specific plaster texture you wanted to use, as you built the 3D model all assets of that plaster texture would be colored that shade of light brown.

The sheet can be a simple Photoshop document that uses rectangular tiles to do a "quilt" map of the textures you will need in the level. For example, there could be a map for walls, paving, plaster, stone, wood, cloth, and metal. This is a more efficient approach to creating an overview of where textures need to be so that these can be changed or moved if there is too much repetition or if the flow doesn't work visually. When working in-game on an early prototype, it makes little sense to map

proper textures until you know that the level is working; it will also slow down the game engine if your model is too complex and this makes iteration a more painful process.

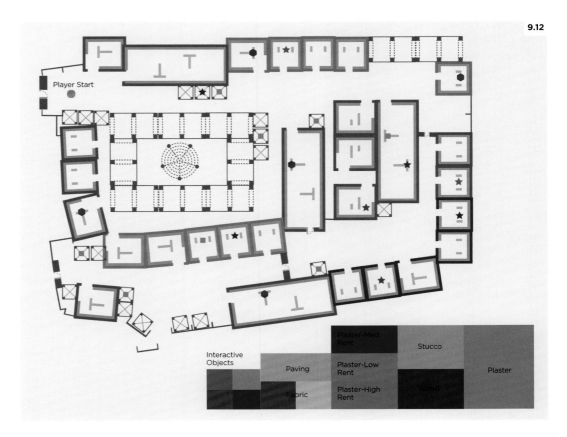

9.12

9.12
The texture sheet for the marketplace with key that associates color with proposed texture.

The Texture Atlas

Once the textures are mapped to the level's models, the next step is to create what are known as texture atlases. These are similar to a texture sheet, but they contain all the actual textures you will use in the level. The atlas will have the stone, wood, metal, and fabrics all in one, or more likely in several, large bitmap files. These are then assigned against a coordinate remapping table, which is built and loaded into the game engine. The coordinates are used to scale and map texture coordinates against each object in the level (for example, the texture "ancient stone" needs to be mapped to walls in coordinates X and Y and Z and then scaled to A of a castle's keep model). Loading one texture atlas into a game and then having the game engine match coordinates and scale reduces the cost on the graphics processor (GPU) and, of course, means that the same textures can be applied multiple times.

In general, you would have between 16 and 256 textures in each atlas. In the marketplace level, textures for the walls could be 512 × 512 pixels, which are then tiled (repeated) across the whole area. More detailed objects or elements, such as quest items, weapons, or water features could be 256 × 256 pixels because they are physically smaller objects. Architectural elements, such as roof tile or slate, can also be small bitmaps of 256 × 256 pixels, which can be tiled and offset to reflect human workmanship.

This chapter cannot cover in depth the approach of creating an atlas and how a game engine would map the coordinates, nor the intricate and complicated nature of aspects such as UV mapping. It is very useful to have some knowledge of these principles that can be taken further with additional research and practice. Texture compression and implementation are complex and math-heavy subjects. There are several texture atlas creator tools that can be used with game engines, such as Unity. They're also known as texture packers.

TIP | **DECALS: ONE-OFF TEXTURES FOR THE GAME**

Decals are unique (non-repeating) textures, such as in-game posters or signs that are applied to the surface of an object with a fixed projection (i.e., viewed from a single angle). Decals are easy to use and add to models that bypass the complexity of the texture mapping process.

9.13
This game prototype shows how one texture can be mapped to a variety of meshes (models) which are from the Unity game engine. The green areas are mesh and the top left shows the texture that will be applied to them (in this case repeatedly mapped rusted metal sheets).

One wood texture map (.tga file) can be mapped and applied to surfaces across the entire environment in different ways (green shaded areas).

CONNECTING
AESTHETICS
AND PLAYER
NAVIGATION

SIZING AND
FIELD OF
VIEW

WAYFINDING
SYSTEMS

**MODULAR
MODELS AND
TEXTURES**

SILHOUETTE
ENVIRONMENT
DESIGN

CHOKE POINTS
AND STRONG
POINTS

INTERVIEW:
MEDIA
MOLECULE

CHAPTER
SUMMARY AND
DISCUSSION
POINTS

9.13

SILHOUETTE ENVIRONMENT DESIGN

Silhouette design is a practical way of communicating the fundamental form of your character or object through an outline, but its importance is in gauging how well distinguished a significant building or character is from the less significant. From an architectural point of view, the question for the level designer is how easily can players focus on, or reorient themselves towards, a geographical goal in an environment? There is a reason players tend to have to go towards towers, high castles, or radio towers; it is because their outlines are so easily distinguished from other architecture.

The Principles of Silhouette Design

- Outline must be discernable from other environmental assets. (For example, in *Fallout 3* the mutants look like X, Bandits look like Y. Even from a distance, it is easy to discern which faction is coming the player's way.)

- Must have memorable shapes. These can be tall imposing structures, chasms that look like ambush areas, or a sense of scale that imparts a sensation of wonder or tension in the player. Those will be areas players remember. (The "Ravenholm" level in *Half Life 2* is often remembered because it leans more towards a horror environment than the rest of the game.)

- Original or unique. The aircraft carrier (home to a friendly faction) in *Fallout 3* does not look like any of the surrounding environment and stands out as a focal point for the player.

Utilizing these principles, even an inexperienced player is more likely to be curious about an area, building, or object that stands out from its environment. It has become part of the vocabulary of video games, and a large part of navigation design, to encourage the player to move towards the designated object or pathway using subtle signifiers.

9.14

9.14
This is a silhouette design for characters in a student project RPG, *Tendagi*. The characters are both humanoid bipedal, but in silhouette you can easily discern enemy (on the left) versus friend (on the right) with limited detail. This is how silhouette design works.

9.15
A real-world architectural example, the Hungarian Parliament building in Budapest. If this building were a focal point in a level for a player, it would work very well. As the image progression shows, in silhouette it stands out well against the rest of the city. It also translates well at a distance, so players could orient themselves to it as a landmark. Using real-world examples or variations from the world helps the player make visual connections.

9.16a
In *Fallout 3* an old aircraft carrier was used as a base and living quarters; from a silhouette design point of view it is exceptional in standing out from the other parts of the map. It becomes a focal point for the player.

9.16b
Churches and unusual architecture serve as navigational points as well as unique areas or objectives. In this scene from *Dead Island*, the framing of the church as different from the surrounding buildings means it becomes a focal point for the player.

CHOKE POINTS AND STRONG POINTS

Choke points are usually smaller or restrictive areas in a level (for example, ravines, small rooms with locked doors at both ends) that can be used as a pacing element or focus for the player. These areas in a level are designed to trigger a pre-scripted event or focus the player on a puzzle or trap. They can also be used as a technical way of enabling other areas of the map to load or more enemies to be animated while the player is contained within a smaller part of the level. In an open world or large level, a player can easily miss or traverse past a major story point or important object, but setting waypoints that navigate towards well-crafted choke points gets around that, without seeming to be out of context of the level. Choke points can also be used to "bookend" levels. The player leaves the openness of the level to clear an ambush in a ravine and is then rewarded with a cut-scene (narrative exposition) and the next part of the level opens up seamlessly.

Strong points are usually reached after a choke point, at the end of a level or in a specifically designated area (the end of a quest, beginning of a boss battle, and so on). They are defined as areas that are more difficult to traverse or that contain very specific objectives or actions (such as that ravine ambush). For example, strong points could be a puzzle on a door that the player has to solve to move to the next quest area, or a battle arena the player enters to begin combat. A choke point could be a narrow hallway or entrance that opens on to a larger area where a "strong point" awaits and a pre-designated action occurs.

Strong points take on a variety of forms, and the level designer needs to plan and map out where they happen and how the player will approach them—especially if the scripted event deforms the level (areas or parts of it are destroyed or changed) or reveals a previously unseen part of the level (for example, an explosion opens up a blocked entrance to a mine).

9.17a

9.17a
A strong point such as this one in *Fable III* is akin to an arena. There is an obvious entrance and exit—the door in front of them. Usually this exit is barred until the player has defeated enemies in this area or figured out a puzzle to open the door.

9.17b

9.17b
An example of an in-game choke point in *Dead Island*. Tight level design can bring an increased level of tension and excitement for the player without having to create any new mechanics.

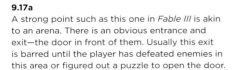

CONNECTING
AESTHETICS
AND PLAYER
NAVIGATION

SIZING AND
FIELD OF
VIEW

WAYFINDING
SYSTEMS

MODULAR
MODELS AND
TEXTURES

SILHOUETTE
ENVIRONMENT
DESIGN

**CHOKE POINTS
AND STRONG
POINTS**

INTERVIEW:
MEDIA
MOLECULE

CHAPTER
SUMMARY AND
DISCUSSION
POINTS

TIP | DISTINCTIVE AREAS

Unique or distinct areas can provide a navigational aid or a focal point in a level. Examples would be ornate fountains, artworks, and places of worship, such as churches or mosques. Distinct areas can also tell more stories and relay background to the player; a sculpture could be of a ruler or hero that tells a tale of the city or the culture. Distinct areas should be used sparingly to be effective.

9.18
In *Gears of War 3*, the "Mercy Courtyard" strong point has a prominent central feature that acts as cover and also orients the player. It can also be used as a landmark in multiplayer mode to make issuing directions and commands easier.

TIP | LOOKING BACK IS IMPORTANT

In the previous chapter, we looked at the potential of level design to foreshadow an event, location, or goal (priming). It is also worth noting that this works in reverse, as well. Players should be able to look back on a level they have traversed and relate it to their journey through the game. This is not always possible, in the same way that foreshadowing is not always possible, but players being able to escape from an area and then see the effect of their presence (something on fire, dead zombies, explosions, or a more peaceful landscape) is important in reinforcing their own sense of a being players on a journey.

9.19
Allowing players to look back reinforces their feeling of progressing through the game. It can also be used to "close" the level out for the player. Allowing players to look back reinforces their feeling of progression. It can also be used to "close" the level out for the player, here Lara Croft looks back over her own trail of destruction.

MEDIA MOLECULE

Video Game Company

Media Molecule (MM) is a video game development studio based in Guildford in the UK. They are the creators of *LittleBigPlanet* (2008), *LittleBigPlanet 2* (2011), and *Tearaway* (2013).

How quickly do you usually go from concept to working prototype for a game? How important is a rough, playable prototype at Media Molecule to get designers and stakeholders on board?

Rex Crowle, Creative Lead:
"It depends on the project, but as our process is very iterative we all try and get something up and running almost immediately, so we can really feel the ideas. Those prototypes may be a functional game, or they may be just a tiny element of the interaction. At the start of development on *LittleBigPlanet*, David Smith (MM co-founder) had a playable platform game operational and running in a couple of weeks, and then we gradually built around that to form the game. The important thing was that players would have a reaction while playing, they'd be laughing, or screaming in terror, as they tried to swing through the level."

"Without a prototype like this, it's very hard to experience what's interesting about the game, and get everyone on board to either continue its funding, or to start contributing further ideas and improving on it."

9.20

9.20
LittleBigPlanet characters.

How does the art and design team go from initial game concept to establishing an aesthetic for a game?

Kareem Ettouney, Art Director:
"To reach an aesthetic that is both original and integral to the game experience is pretty hard but it comes from the fusion of different elements:

The design vision: This is the integration of form and function. For example, if the game is a racing game then it's all about speed, so how can the visuals help emphasize that? In our case, our games encourage creativity, so how can our aesthetic contribute to disarming and inviting the user to have a go at being creative? In *LittleBigPlanet* the familiar 'art and craft' aesthetic went well with the physics-driven platform game.

The art direction: Which visual combinations suit the project from an emotional point of view? Which visuals express the team's unique styles and would stand out in the big tapestry of wonderful competition? What would be a statement and what elements could transcend being of its time and enter the arena of timelessness?

The engine technology: Everything we see on the screen is made possible by the rendering capabilities of the engine, which is then exposed to the users to express with, so the engine programmers are big players in achieving the aesthetic, and they need to be inspired and believe in the vision.

Serendipity: These are the happy accidents that happen while we are all collaborating to reach a dream. A surprising combination of things happens and we like it—that contributes a lot to the styles."

How do you go about establishing rules and boundaries while balancing for openness and creativity?

Rex Crowle, Creative Lead:
"We like showing how we've built our worlds right there inside the games. In *LittleBigPlanet*, you can see the nuts and bolts that are rotating the platforms or animating the characters. In *Tearaway*, you can look at the paper construction of the scenery—and both share our interest in creative materials and the interesting limitations they provide. If we tasked our players with building 'anything with everything,' they would be staring at a blank canvas, with nothing to build out from or be inspired by. Furthermore, by having no limitations, there would be no interesting puzzles to solve, or fun attempts to subvert the framework they've been given."

"I think games need to allow the players to experiment and through that experimentation they learn more about the game. But that can only happen if the rules of the game are easy to understand and connect with our own world and experience."

"Physics-based gameplay is endlessly entertaining, and playfully experimental because we know the properties of various materials and how they react, but we've not always been able to try out all the combinations in the real world."

"By using real-world rules, a player is able to access the content more easily. If a feature can only be partially implemented and will start to deviate from its real-world equivalent, then it may be better to remove that feature entirely, as it will need to have its limitations explained in the game, and that will remove the magic and openness of the system."

"In other words, the less on-screen interface the better; if the interactions make sense then the player should be left to explore them. After all, games are supposed to be playful systems, so we need to let our players play in them."

CHAPTER SUMMARY

Over the last two chapters, we have laid out some of the principles and practices of basic level design. These can give you a solid head start when approaching your own level design. It is at this stage that the final game begins to take shape. Level design allows you to put into practice your concepts, aesthetic, and mechanic ideas and apply them to a prototype that players can interact with. The use of color signatures (signage, NPC costuming, levels of decay or newness, etc.) create the feeling of a "lived in" world, and this color key can be used to create an emotion curve across the levels (the color palette could get darker or lighter dependent on the quests the player is undertaking). Color, texture, movement, weather (an autonomous system), and lighting inform the overall narrative of the video game. Even if the game has no explicit narrative "storyline," the level design informs the world as a system for the player to be immersed in.

9.21
Media Molecule's concept art in various stages, from very early on (top) to more refined (above). These artworks might not be included in the final game, but the concept art establishes tone, feeling, and context for the level design.

CONNECTING
AESTHETICS
AND PLAYER
NAVIGATION

SIZING AND
FIELD OF
VIEW

WAYFINDING
SYSTEMS

MODULAR
MODELS AND
TEXTURES

SILHOUETTE
ENVIRONMENT
DESIGN

CHOKE POINTS
AND STRONG
POINTS

INTERVIEW:
MEDIA
MOLECULE

CHAPTER
SUMMARY AND
DISCUSSION
POINTS

DISCUSSION POINTS

1. Examining any game from any period, how does the level design inform the player about the world without using explicit exposition? What story is the level design telling you as a player about the world you inhabit?

2. In any game level, look for and map out any choke points, strong points, and other subtle pacing elements. How do they relate to the overall flow of the level? Do they interfere and break immersion or do they create a sense of purpose and focus?

3. How could level designs from one genre map onto level designs of other genres? Could you take the level design elements from an RPG or action game and map them onto a real-time strategy (RTS) or other form of game? How would you approach succeeding in this?

PART 3: SYSTEMS AND DESIGNING WORLDS

CHAPTER TEN
KEEPING THEM PLAYING

10.1
Super Mario 3D World
developed by © Nintendo (2013).

Chapter Objectives:

- **Understand and develop rewards systems to keep the player engaged.**

- **Design motivation into the game.**

- **Use tutorials to get the player on-board with the game.**

REWARDING THE PLAYER

Rewards are a large part of why video games are so engaging. We are conditioned early on as children to respond very positively to any form of reward, and this carries over into adulthood. It becomes hardwired into our psyches and so we collect, buy, play, and interact because our brains dish out small amounts of dopamine in response to rewards, and that makes us feel good. Game systems reward players in many ways, from loot drops in *World of Warcraft* to experience points (XPs) that can be used to attain more skills in *Middle-earth: Shadow of Mordor* (Monolith Productions, 2014). These rewards are gained through challenge and are a part of the game progression process.

The balance is in delivering rewards that are not just about playing the game. Rewards in games should be nuanced; the rewards could come from solving a puzzle in a mentally challenging game (e.g., *Portal*, *Portal 2*, Valve, 2007, 2011) or from knowing your reactions are quick (e.g., *Bayonetta*) or if the story is mysterious or compelling, the reward of discovering and uncovering a narrative (e.g., *Mass Effect*, *BioShock*). These rewards are not as obvious as more experience or a bigger sword but are just as important. If you then add to these psychological, emotional rewards the ability to collect and upgrade items or characters, you have an even more compelling reason for the player to stay in your game.

10.2a
In simulation games such as *Gran Turismo 5* (Polyphony Digital, 2010), players can compete in races with the bonus reward system of being able to use the in-game currency to buy or upgrade cars. Players can go into minute detail with the upgrades and modifications to their cars, all of which are a form of reward for the player.

10.2b
Rewards systems can include upgrading of items gained in a game—in this case, being able to "craft" better weaponry in *Tomb Raider*. This form of reward system has been in use since the earliest days of video games.

REWARDING | DESIGNING
THE PLAYER | REWARDS

INTRINSIC
AND
EXTRINSIC
REWARDS

MOTIVATING
BY DESIGN

TUTORIALS
AND
REWARDS

ON-BOARDING

SMART
PLAYERS AND
COMFORT
LEVELS

INTERVIEW:
KENNETH
YOUNG

CHAPTER
SUMMARY AND
DISCUSSION
POINTS

DESIGNING REWARDS

Curiously, rewards are difficult to design well. In 1973 there was an experiment by Mark Lepper, David Greene, and Richard E. Nisbett that involved rewarding children for drawing. The unforeseen results were that as the children received rewards for their drawing, they began to draw less. Those students who were not given rewards continued to draw at the same pace. The conclusion was that giving children a reward led them to see the act of drawing as a *job*. The quality of the children's work also declined as they found that they could draw a minimal amount and still get a reward. Drawing for fun was sidelined, and the reward became the focus. Those students who were not given rewards carried on freely enjoying the act of drawing because it was still fun for them. The original motivation to "draw for fun" was changed to "draw for reward," and this ended up demotivating the children.

We like to play; we like to be rewarded. However, there's a fine line between the two that, if crossed, alters the experience and our motivations for playing. In games such as *World of Warcraft*, players usually have to "grind" up levels by performing simple tasks to get experience points, sometimes for hours. The players put up with it because they know that the reward of being able to get deeper into the game is worth the time spent on the mundane tasks. We play for fun and escape; when it becomes work, we stop playing. If the perceived reward is worth it, we can put up with an amount of "work" to get to the positive payoff.

The Skinner Box

The psychological study of the effects of rewards on humans has been underway for decades. An experiment devised by Burrhus F. Skinner in the 1930s looked at developing subject conditioning in a more nuanced way than had ever been done before. Skinner (1966) built on the work of Pavlov and his dog and was curious to see if conditioning could be applied to rational human beings. Pavlov conditioned his dog by ringing a bell and giving the dog a treat; thus, his dog would expect a treat and salivate every time he heard the bell, regardless of whether a treat was present. Skinner created a machine or box (the operant conditioning chamber, better known as a "Skinner box") and placed a pigeon inside it with a button to push or not push. If the pigeon pushed the button, it received a food reward. Pavlov's dog was conditioned to expect food when it heard the bell, and salivating became an automatic response. However, in Skinner's experiment, the pigeon was making an active decision. Skinner found that his process of making active decisions for a reward (which he called "operant conditioning") worked on humans as well as pigeons.

Skinner found that people were willing to hit the button for a reward, but only for a short time. The subject (or player) became bored (or full, if given food) and would stop pushing the button. Skinner found that if he randomized the reward, the subject became far more engaged. Skinner had found the rationale most people use when justifying gambling as opposed to working. Random rewards that seem to be part of discernible patterns are incredibly engaging. A gambler may willingly spend hours in a casino pushing slot machine buttons for very little reward, but if asked to repeat the same action in a factory for a steady paycheck, will find the action boring (even if the paycheck was larger than the casino winnings). It is the unpredictability and "win-state" that triggers the dopamine release and this "high" keeps gamblers (and gamers) playing.

Skinner found that primary reinforcers as rewards (food, biological needs) dropped off in effectiveness once the subject was no longer hungry or in biological need for that reward. However, secondary rewards, such as money or social status, never dropped off, and subjects would continue on much further with those than with primary reinforcement. Humans are psychologically complex, but manipulating them through rewards is surprisingly easy (if you do not think so, look at how people go crazy for a free T-shirt or "swag" at a sports game or conference).

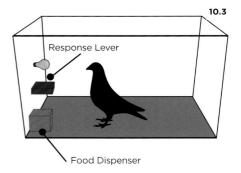

10.3

10.3
A version of the Skinner box operant conditioning experiment. In this Skinner box, the button would not always deliver a treat; it became a "surprise" when it did work and so was much more engaging for the subject because the reward was not automatic.

A Model for Rewards

There is no one "best" reward system for any one game or genre, but there are similarities across games that allow us to think about definitions of rewards systems. They can generally be categorized into four main types: success/glory, provisions, access, and progression.

These models can be merged, manipulated, and included into the design of almost any video game, or even reversed. For example, the game *Demon's Souls* (FromSoftware, 2009) is notorious for being hard on the player to the point of almost punishing them (punishments can be seen as a reward too because losing against a hard enemy several times sweetens the eventual reward). The game offers very little in the sustenance category (players die a lot) but then offers far more in the access, facility, and glory categories. The game is hard, but the developers have employed access in an interesting way

and it becomes an integral part of the gameplay. Players find different routes through the space to avoid being killed, and can leave hints for other players about upcoming trials. Access is used so differently that players will sometimes kill their character in order to restart at a certain point so they can access a different area of the level that was previously locked.

Part of the psychological reward is in finding out that the game does not play in the normal linear fashion of most RPG games; in fact, it's quite the opposite. Exploration and discovery are what have made that game engaging for some and completely frustrating for others. Playing the game well leads to a form of mastery, which is part of the glory category, and the level of difficulty rewards the player because so many do not suffer through the game. It becomes a gamer badge of honor, in many ways.

These models can be merged, manipulated, and included into the design of almost any video game, or even reversed. For example, the game *Demon's Souls* is notorious for being hard on the player to the point of almost punishing them (punishments can be seen as a reward too because losing against a hard enemy several times sweetens the eventual reward). The game offers very little in the sustenance category (players die a lot) but then offers far more in the access, facility, and glory categories. The game is hard, but the developers have employed access in an interesting way and it becomes an integral part of the gameplay. Players find different routes through the space to avoid being killed, and can leave hints for other players about upcoming trials. Access is used so differently that players will sometimes kill their character in order to restart at a certain point so they can access a different area of the level that was previously locked.

10.4
Four main types of reward systems.

10.4

Success/Glory
High scores, achievements/ trophies, and mastery.

Provisions
Extra lives, health packs, building materials in simulation games.

Access
Unlocking levels, areas, or special game content on completion of in-game tasks.

Progression
Experience points that enable players to progress in skills based on their preferred way of playing.

REWARDING
THE PLAYER

DESIGNING
REWARDS

INTRINSIC
AND
EXTRINSIC
REWARDS

MOTIVATING
BY DESIGN

TUTORIALS
AND
REWARDS

ON-BOARDING

SMART
PLAYERS AND
COMFORT
LEVELS

INTERVIEW:
KENNETH
YOUNG

CHAPTER
SUMMARY AND
DISCUSSION
POINTS

INTRINSIC AND
EXTRINSIC REWARDS

Play itself is its own reward; fun and happiness are rewards for playing a game. As a pursuit, video games can make you feel happy and closer to your friends or other players. Reward systems in schoolyard games and other forms of activities start simple (fun, happiness, feeling part of a group as a reward) and become complex when you add the concepts of winning, competing, and bragging. These are internal hierarchies established by the rules of play and the mechanic. Video games have turned the concept of the "reward" into an art form and a lot of planning and time is spent on implementation and balancing of rewards.

The four types of rewards can be further categorized into two sets, intrinsic and extrinsic.

Intrinsic rewards: These are rewards within the game, such as new levels, new challenges, new story arcs, and so on. For example, in a puzzle-based game, such as *Portal 2*, player satisfaction comes from solving the puzzle in each room and in moving on to the next one.

Extrinsic rewards: These occur outside of the game. For example, slot machines paying out in a casino or friendships and bonds that are formed in *World of Warcraft* guilds. Other forms of extrinsic rewards are trophies, achievements, high scores, and bragging rights (highest kill ratio, quickest completion time—any form of feedback other players can see).

The expectation of reward, intrinsically or extrinsically motivated, is a large part of our psychological mechanism when playing a video game. Motivation is at the heart of designing rewards for the player. It is the motivation-as-reward application that releases dopamine in our brains, which makes us feel good and want more. Games, unlike other media, ask that the player be disappointed fairly often (e.g., *Demon's Souls*) and design rewards around *anticipation*. The reward system can signal dopamine releases in the brain of the player by motivating the player with the anticipation of reward; to put it another way, it is often the wait for the opening of the present that is far more enjoyable than the present itself. The promise of beating the boss eventually or figuring out how to escape from the cell is an expectation of an intrinsic or extrinsic reward. This is also why rewards are given early in the game; this sets the player up with a model of expectation of the next reward.

MOTIVATING BY DESIGN

So if the reward itself is not the important factor, but instead the anticipation of the reward is, then the way that the rewards are issued has to be balanced. They can be further defined as *fixed ratio* and *interval* rewards.

Fixed ratio rewards are ones that always occur at specific times, such as loot drops when you defeat an enemy or an extra life upon collecting X number of mushrooms. Or the reward ratios could be varied. For example, when fighting a boss there is a percentile chance that on defeating an enemy you may receive a rare item. Fixed ratios by themselves can be problematic because when there is no expectation of a reward, the player may give up. By varying the item/reward, the player is much more likely to be motivated to continue in the game (and this gets us further away from the Skinner Box).

Interval rewards can be time based and tend to occur in multiplayer games where a piece of armor, ammunition, weapons, or health packs return to the game once they have been picked up by another player. Much like the variable reward system, the interval can be randomized too; this can increase the feeling of "luck" within the game and excitement levels as special items may seem to appear just when the player needed them.

10.5

Examples of rewards systems are numerous, from leaderboards to high score boards to achievements and trophies. As a designer you need to map out a reward system for the player by listing which actions are rewarded and by how much. This can become unwieldy quickly, which is why games use shorthand. For example, your game may have awarded the player 15,000 experience points; that is a good reward, but also meaningless. If that is shorthand for "Level 9," it has meaning and is understood more easily. Another option is a visual indicator of progress; for example, points are collected and there is a visual analogue (usually in the character screen) where the player can see that they are X% closer to the next level or towards unlocking a useful skill.

10.5
Skills games such as *Dance Dance Revolution* (Konami, 1998) motivate players with positive reinforcement as well as a scoring system (which is a form of reward) that builds motivation in players because mastery of the game reflects their own physical ability.

Thoughtfully designed reward systems can make a game all the more compelling and engaging. As a designer, you are going to plan out a schema of ratio or interval rewards as well as extrinsic and intrinsic approaches. Once these reward systems have been designed, it is important to consider their relationship to the new or experienced player. Rewards can begin to work immediately when a player begins the game, but for those new to the genre or mechanic, rewards are not enough by themselves. You are going to have to create a way of making sure the player can understand how to play your game.

TIP

REWARDS AS META-GAMES

Reward systems can themselves become part of the game. As we've already seen, one example is "grinding" in *World of Warcraft*, which is a game within the game. The term "meta-game" is used because the reward systems inform the player of the wider game itself. Grinding by killing lower level enemies is rewarded with leveling up but the meta-game is about collecting points and being a better fighter, which aids the player throughout the larger game. The meta-game could be viewed as layering a reward onto an activity in the game to make it more engaging, such as collecting in the world of *Skyrim*. There is no reward for collecting all the skulls or cheeses in *Skyrim* other than the intrinsic reward in the satisfaction of being able to do this. Other games, such as *Pokemon Red and Blue* (Nintendo, 1996), have collecting at their heart and although the game is seen as a battle arena, it is also very much about collecting as a meta-game that signifies progress-as-reward in the game. A real world analogue could be the "game" of being awarded color belts in karate along with the subset of working for the colored stripes that signify progress towards the next belt.

TUTORIALS AND REWARDS

The first level of a video game is usually some form of a tutorial level. It's where the player learns how to play the game, but what the tutorial is actually doing is revealing the entirety of the game mechanic. Level 1 establishes game tone, story arc, play mechanic, and the environment. Everything else evolves from that first level and gets the player on-board with the game. There are different approaches dependent on the game genre and on the audience. Mobile and social media games have wide audiences that are perhaps not used to playing video games (or do not see themselves as even playing a video game) and so the approach to those has to be different from, for example, *Call of Duty Modern Warfare 3* or *Far Cry 4* (Ubisoft Montreal). No matter what the audience or platform, every game requires some form of learning mode that enables the player to be successful quickly in your game (for example, by employing a tutorial and a First Order Optimal Strategy—see Chapter 3).

Tutorial Design

In Chapter 6, we examined the planning process and focused on creating a playable version of the game concept as soon as possible. One way to approach a playable prototype is with a tutorial of the game. You are going to need a tutorial level anyway, and a solid tutorial level can also be used for marketing purposes months before the final game is ready to go public. Tutorial levels should also be rigorously play-tested by "Kleenex" testers to ensure that the beginner or experienced player can understand the intention of the game. In-game tutorials have become far more elegant over the years and have made long-form printed manuals completely obsolete. The player is invited to learn about the gameplay through the act of playing. There are two popular approaches to tutorials: step by step and positive reinforcement.

Step by Step and Positive Reinforcement

These tutorials guide the player in learning the controls of the game and interacting with the system. This format is popular because players generally do not want to read a long manual or sit through instructional videos. Players just want to get on with it and assume that they will be able to figure it out as they go along. The step-by-step approach introduces gameplay elements over time; this could be as simple as asking the player to look up, down, left, and right just to "calibrate the visor" (as the *Halo* franchise does), which shows the player how the movement controls work. There are often on-screen visual elements or non-player-character (NPC) audio expressing positive feedback such as, "OK thanks, we got that, nice work." This simple feedback system may seem pointless to an experienced player, but it's important to support the player in the game's early levels through positive feedback. The player will feel more competent and even happy to be told by the game they've accomplished a task successfully.

REWARDING
THE PLAYER

DESIGNING
REWARDS

INTRINSIC
AND
EXTRINSIC
REWARDS

MOTIVATING
BY DESIGN

**TUTORIALS
AND
REWARDS**

ON-BOARDING

SMART
PLAYERS AND
COMFORT
LEVELS

INTERVIEW:
KENNETH
YOUNG

CHAPTER
SUMMARY AND
DISCUSSION
POINTS

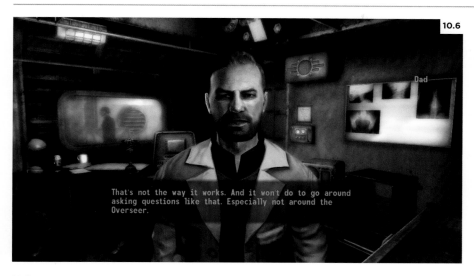

10.6

Dad

That's not the way it works. And it won't do to go around asking questions like that. Especially not around the Overseer.

The purpose of positive feedback is to get players in a positive "win-state" that they then carry on into the next areas of the game. As the game gets harder, this "win-state" emotion carries over and goes a long way in assuring players that they can accomplish the new goals because they have a model that tells them they managed to accomplish tasks earlier on. It's simple but effective psychology that gets the players into the right mindset to take on the whole game.

10.6
As shown here in *Fallout 3*, non-player characters can be used for narrative and exposition as well as to provide feedback to the player. A character who is pleased or displeased with a player's actions nudges them towards a deeper game experience.

10.7
Positive win-states are implemented early on in tutorial levels and the player refers back to the win-state when they reach a point that is harder than a previous encounter. They know that the goal is achievable because the game has established this mindset in the player early on.

10.7

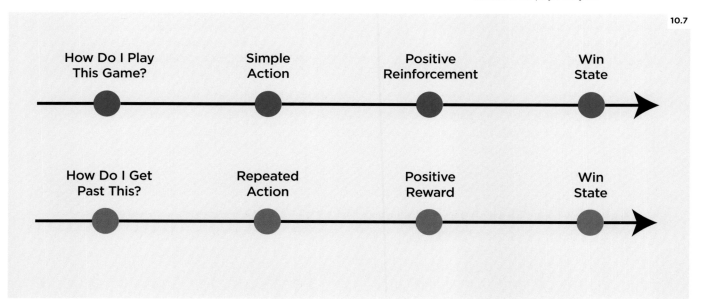

How Do I Play This Game?   Simple Action   Positive Reinforcement   Win State

How Do I Get Past This?   Repeated Action   Positive Reward   Win State

On-screen Prompts or Hints

Sometimes known as the "Glowing Choice" technique, on-screen prompts and hints are used in large open-world games to guide the player towards actions, on quests, or as a wayfinding (mapping) system. By their nature, open-world games are large and the player is encouraged to explore, but the downside is that the player can wander and not be able to find quests or tasks, especially early on in the game. One approach is to include prompts in the environment such as a glowing area (well-lit areas that look different from the area the player is in) or non-player characters that differentiate themselves from others in the world (by glowing, gesturing, etc.). Difference can be used to guide the player; the convention is for characters that are highlighted when in the field of view of the player to be quest givers (for example, *Assassin's Creed* uses this method, as does the *Fable* franchise). On-screen prompts and in-game hints have the advantage of enabling a feeling of choice for the player, their use (or disuse) is dependent on the player and their style of playing. On-screen prompts can also instruct or remind a player how they can better achieve a task. For example, in a fighting tutorial, a prompt could be: "Hold down the X button as you swing your sword for a more powerful attack."

Win Early, Win Often

When designing a game, it has become the convention to reward the player far more frequently early in the game than later on (once again, this brings us back to the First Order Optimal Strategy and similar mechanisms; see Chapter 3). Early wins (XBox achievements, Sony's trophies, points, or experience) in a game's first tutorial level are exciting for a player, even an experienced one, because it is always exciting to win. A "win-state" reinforces a level of mastery in a game even if the player has only just begun. It's a powerful tool but one that has to be balanced. The simple "wins" cannot continue into the main game; the mechanic has to become incrementally more difficult to provide engaging challenges for players as they gain mastery over the game.

If the ramp up in difficulty is gradual enough, players should feel accomplished but also nervous about their ability to complete the next challenge. This balance is important; getting it right enables players to bask in a sense of victory over seemingly much harder odds, as well as reflect on their progress in the game. This is often accomplished with a boss battle or quest item reward that is seen as a rite of passage for the player—proof that they have reached a level of expertise in the game.

REWARDING THE PLAYER

DESIGNING REWARDS

INTRINSIC AND EXTRINSIC REWARDS

MOTIVATING BY DESIGN

TUTORIALS AND REWARDS

ON-BOARDING

SMART PLAYERS AND COMFORT LEVELS

INTERVIEW: KENNETH YOUNG

CHAPTER SUMMARY AND DISCUSSION POINTS

ON-BOARDING

On-boarding is literally "getting the player on board"; it occurs during the first play of the game and is a subset of the tutorial process. Tutorials focus mostly on the mechanic, answering questions like: "How do I punch?" "How can I pick up these for more XP?", and so on. On-boarding is a subtle set of tools that create the most positive experience for the player and maintain that sense within them until they feel confident enough to go it alone. Most players do not even notice the "training wheels" coming off if the designers implement the on-boarding process well. The more positive players feel about the game, the more likely they are to continue with it.

As we've already seen, one method to increase the success of the on-boarding phase is to ensure the player has a conscious sense of reward. This can be achieved via progression (player walks around the space and is given narrative rewards), accomplishment (player shoots a target and is told "well done"), and interaction (simple controller instructions such as "use button to look up, look down"). The introduction to the game has to be designed so that the player feels they have learned something, even if it's as simple as "Button X is jump; try jumping." There's a sense of accomplishment that goes along with the player completing even the simplest of tasks and games (our brain rewards us with small amounts of dopamine for even the simplest accomplishments, such as backing out of a driveway without hitting anything). When building an on-boarding process, you should look for opportunities to positively reward the player through feedback.

As always, do some research; *Call of Duty Modern Warfare 3*, *Halo*, and *Assassin's Creed* all have on-boarding built into their first levels, from the target-based training level in *CoD's Modern Warfare 3* to the "virtual reality" training in the first level of the original *Assassin's Creed*. On-boarding ends when a level of mastery or familiarity of play has been achieved; this can be as early as the completion of the first level, but can also be metered out over multiple levels as new accomplishments enable new skills or abilities. Games such as *Gears of War* have limited tutorial and on-boarding systems because although the weapons may increase in power, the controls do not change sufficiently. A game such as *Shadow of Mordor* constantly rewards the player with new abilities that the player needs to learn— almost up to the end of the game.

10.8

10.8
This example of on-screen prompts instructs the player in how to place an item in the multiplayer levels of *Gears of War 3*. The instruction also has information for the advanced player, informing them of the condition of an item or what it is used for.

On-boarding Methods

There are several approaches to on-boarding and they have to be contextualized within your game.

The tutorial room: This approach is used in *Assassin's Creed*, *Metal Gear*, and *Batman: Arkham City* (Rocksteady Studios, 2011). Although the player has learned some simple controls in the on-boarding part of the game, these "training rooms" give the player the opportunity to practice or learn combat moves without penalty. The designer has to anticipate the unwillingness of the player to drop out of the main game to follow tutorials and make sure that all the game interactions are introduced within the main game too. The understanding is that if a player spends time in these tutorial rooms, they will gain a level of mastery faster than those who do not.

Contextual: This is the player learning the ropes in-game as the action unfolds. It is essentially one long tutorial split up into smaller chunks throughout the level. For example, in the game *Sleeping Dogs*, the player's character meets a group of thugs and must fight them. As the action unfolds, the player is told which buttons to press to activate certain punches or kicks. In games such as *Uncharted 3*, the game is actually paused with an overlay, which shows the player what to do next, and then the game restarts. This works well in relatively fixed, linear games but would be harder to implement in a more open game framework. *Sleeping Dogs* also has a training room (a dojo) where the player can learn new skills as a reward for completing simple fetch quests. The on-screen contextual prompts slowly go away in the main game but can be revisited through the training room, reinforcing the acquisition of skills and mastery.

Relevant contextual: This is a subset of contextual, but instead of being an overlay with an instruction such as "press X," the relevant contextual information is supplied through signs that are embedded into the game space itself. For example, when a player character gets to the edge of a platform in a side-scrolling game, there is a sign that points upwards with a corresponding button-map so that the player knows to press "up" rather than jump or move right.

There are ways in which to blend these tutorial types with on-boarding methods, but they work most effectively with inexperienced players. Players who have played previous games in a series or who play the genre often are less likely to spend time in tutorials. The balance is in being able to offer levels of introduction to different kinds of players, and tutorials therefore need to be tested by experienced and inexperienced players.

10.9

10.9
The training room (dojo) in *Sleeping Dogs* where players learn new skills as rewards for completing simple fetch quests.

REWARDING THE PLAYER

DESIGNING REWARDS

INTRINSIC AND EXTRINSIC REWARDS

MOTIVATING BY DESIGN

TUTORIALS AND REWARDS

ON-BOARDING

SMART PLAYERS AND COMFORT LEVELS

INTERVIEW: KENNETH YOUNG

CHAPTER SUMMARY AND DISCUSSION POINTS

SMART PLAYERS AND COMFORT LEVELS

When designing the on-boarding process, the most important rule is to never make the player feel stupid or make the process too hard. The first few minutes of any video game is a critical juncture for many players and unless they are on board with the game early on, they may never get further into it. Common practice is to create levels of on-boarding, starting with the first level being easy for players, so they have time to learn the controls via on-screen prompts. Over the years, video game designers have evolved a range of solid on-boarding levels and tutorials, and you should examine these processes across many genres.

On-boarding is achieved in many ways; one route is to make it as clear as possible for players to know their mission objectives and destination. Getting lost in a large map isn't a great experience when you're new to the movement mechanic. Another on-boarding method is to enable levels of difficulty within the gameplay. Games such as *Call of Duty: Modern Warfare 3* and the *Gears of War* franchise have explicit levels of difficulty, from "I rarely play these sorts of games" to "I play these a lot, let me get on with it." These difficulty levels also encourage players to replay the game; once they have mastered the "rookie" difficulty, they can play again at a higher level.

KENNETH YOUNG

Head of Audio, Media Molecule

One powerful way designers can keep players immersed and engaged with a game is through effective and responsive soundtracks and sound design. Kenneth Young is head of audio at the award-winning UK-based game studio Media Molecule. They have designed *LittleBigPlanet*, *LittleBigPlanet 2*, and *Tearaway*, and are currently working on *Tearaway Unfolded*.

Audio is important in setting tone and driving immersion in a game. How do you approach scoring tracks/audio when so much of what is seen or visited is driven by the player?
"The truth is that in most games, you have a pretty good idea of the general flow of things and what the player will be doing. So you build systems which respond to these known locations, events, and entities, and the interactions that happen between them. And even in games that are much more open and allow the player to go where they like, you develop strategies for dealing with this. It's very rare that it's a genuine free-for-all. The player has to accept the rules of the game or game world and play within those limitations, and we as audio designers design the audio experience to work within and take advantage of those limitations too."

"Perhaps there's no better example of this than music. It has the wonderful ability to inform and influence what the player is feeling, and so we take advantage of that to reinforce the wider game experience and to act as one of the primary methods of communicating what is going on in the game. We are always conscious of how the player might be able to react and so we design our music playback systems to be dynamic and respond to the player's actions when appropriate."

"As a designer, when playing the game you always have to consider the wider experience. For example, music isn't always appropriate, and you can overuse it. You need to be able to evaluate the experience you are creating for people and make decisions about what is appropriate, and that doesn't just mean evaluating the thing that is right in front of you but also considering every other aspect of the game."

What do you feel are the most overlooked aspects of audio in game development?
"Sound and music are weird; you really need to go out of your way to understand them which, inevitably, people do not tend to do. So the biggest challenge is fighting against a lot of ignorance, common misunderstandings, and assumptions."

"In my experience the biggest issue is when people have no understanding or experience of sound and music beyond their personal consumption of it. People get confused between their feelings (which are for the most part genuine and true) and their attempts to ascribe meaning to those feelings (which are often false). That's not a failure of language in describing their feelings; it's a lack of understanding and experience. Whilst this is not a problem unique to audio, it is absolutely the number one challenge for audio personnel or, at least, it is at the root of a wide range of issues in the development process."

CHAPTER SUMMARY

This chapter examines ways to persuade gamers to take a leap and play your game, and then how to keep them engaged. In-game tutorials are becoming more and more ingenious, with the ultimate goal of players (of any level of expertise) not feeling that they are being "taught" but instead that they are already playing the game. Learning by doing is an important part of the on-boarding process; it gets players hands-on into the game, and reward systems, such as positive reinforcement, aid that process. Knowing when to give players rewards, balancing abundance with scarcity, is part of what will make your game engaging.

Players are constantly given new items or opportunities to progress, and this pushes the operant-conditioning, dopamine-response buttons in players. Few aspects of our everyday lives combine fantasy and wish fulfillment with positive rewards and the opportunity to feel emotionally fulfilled by the choices we make—this is a major reason for the popularity of video games.

REWARDING
THE PLAYER

DESIGNING
REWARDS

INTRINSIC
AND
EXTRINSIC
REWARDS

MOTIVATING
BY DESIGN

TUTORIALS
AND
REWARDS

ON-BOARDING

SMART
PLAYERS AND
COMFORT
LEVELS

INTERVIEW:
KENNETH
YOUNG

CHAPTER
SUMMARY AND
DISCUSSION
POINTS

DISCUSSION POINTS

1. How would you innovate on an existing reward system? Are there rewards that could have more meaning to the player in any given game (social, sharing, peer-based, etc.)?

2. If you were to sketch out a reward system for a new game (or one you have played recently), how would the rewards be communicated to the player and when? How do you map the "What, Where, When" aspect of the reward schema?

3. How would you approach balancing the scarcity or abundance of rewards in a game? Could you increase or decrease rewards? What effect would this have on the player? What are the intrinsic and extrinsic rewards for the game?

References

Lepper, M. R., D. Greene, and R. E. Nisbett (1973), "Undermining Children's Intrinsic Interest with Extrinsic Reward: A Test of the 'Overjustification' Hypothesis," *Journal of Personality and Social Psychology*, 28 (1): 129–37. Available online: http://psycnet.apa.org

Skinner, B. F. (1966), *The Behavior of Organisms*, Englewood Cliffs, NJ: Prentice-Hall.

PART 3:
SYSTEMS AND
DESIGNING WORLDS

CHAPTER ELEVEN
INTERFACE DESIGN
AND AUDIO DESIGN

11.1
Fallout: New Vegas, developed by Obsidian Entertainment, 2010.

Chapter Objectives:

- **Apply principles of interface design.**

- **Design robust feedback for the player.**

- **Understand applications of audio in the game.**

CONSTRAINED CHOICES

Pick a Path, Designing Constraints

In the previous chapters, we examined the wish fulfillment and experience-driven nature of video games. On top of this, there is yet another layer: indirect control. This is the practice of giving the player the feeling of freedom and choice, but then being able to constrain their options without being too obvious about it. Open world games and "on-rails" video games are built around mechanics, rules, world physics, and player objectives. To facilitate a positive experience, video games suggest the idea of players being able to "do whatever they want to," but that would be an impossible game to make.

There is "total freedom" and then there is "freedom to choose from a limited set of options." For example, there is a difference between the statements "Choose any fruit" and "Pick one of these fruits: orange, apple, pear." Asking someone to pick from a list suggests there is freedom of choice, but asking the person to choose any fruit would range into thousands of possibilities. That overwhelming range of choices would usually overwhelm a person into picking the most obvious fruit anyway (such as orange, apple, or pear) as those are at the top of most people's minds. By constraining the possibilities, a game designer can convey the illusion of freedom because the player is able to operate within the parameters that make most sense.

If a player is in an empty room and is given two identical doors to look at, chances are good that they will pick one and go through it. The door is a metaphor—what is known as a "call to action" for the player because we know doors to be interactive; they can be opened or closed. This example gives players very little choice, but it is a choice; they can choose the left door or the right door, or simply do nothing. Because this is an interactive game, and players have entered the "field of play," they are going to feel that they have the freedom to make a decision and will activate a door based mostly on wanting to progress in the game and out of curiosity to see what will happen next. This is still a constraint; there are not infinite doors with infinite possibilities behind each one, but giving players that one simple choice makes them feel in control of their destiny in the world.

Building on the concept of freedom to choose in games, designers can further constrain choices without negatively impacting players by using objectives. If the objective is to find a particular item, players are going to engage in activities (looking, opening, exploring) that lead towards that conclusion. If players are looking for gold and there are a lot of identical boxes in the room, it will be hard to predict which they'll look in first. But if three of the chests have locks on them, you have a better prediction of where the player is likely to go first. The locks immediately suggest special contents; this is a simple but effective method of narrowing focus for the player.

Although video games may also put in a lot of *flavor* items (coffee cups or trays that can be picked up for no real purpose), these items connect the player to the world and serve to enrich the experience. Even so, it is a conscious choice by the designer to decide what the player can or cannot interact with, which is a sensible constraint. Another subtle approach to narrowing options and choices is through the virtual and physical interface the player has with the game. Animated cut-scenes are also a form of narrative constraint; they prevent the player from having agency and move the story arc forward without input (usually) from the player.

CONSTRAINED
CHOICES

INTERFACE
DESIGN

INVISIBILITY
AND
FEEDBACK

INTERFACES
ARE COMMU-
NICATION

INTERFACE
TYPES

MAPPING AND
MODES

INTERFACE
OVERLOAD

AUDIO
DESIGN

INTERVIEW:
TYSON STEELE

CHAPTER
SUMMARY AND
DISCUSSION
POINTS

11.2

11.2
This may not be much of a choice, but it does
offer up possibilities for the player.

INTERFACE DESIGN

Interface design for video games is not really about interfaces as you may normally think of them; instead, it is about player control. The more intuitive an interface, the easier it is to master and the more in control the player will feel. This will translate to a more positive experience. When designing a game interface, it is important that the player should fight bosses, puzzles, or enemies, not the interface.

When we think about interfaces, we will most often think of menu screens and options that can be selected. In addition, in video games we may add the concept of button mapping of the control system ("A" button to attack, "Square" button to

pick up items, etc.) as well as interfaces such as menus and inventory screens. These are all the methods in which your player interacts with the game from the outside world, but the biggest interface is the one between the player in their world and the game world on their screen. Interfaces split into two categories, the *physical interface* and the *virtual interface*. For purposes of efficiency, I will use the game console model as the primary example. In this case, the *physical input* is the game controller that the player holds and uses to facilitate agency in the game world and the *virtual interface* is what the player sees on-screen.

Virtual Interfaces

The virtual interface contains all the information a player can see while playing or starting a game. This could be an icon that tells the player how much health or ammunition remains. It could be what spell they have ready to cast and how much "mana" they are going to use up. Alongside this, players are also conscious of where they are in the level, and where they need to go next in the larger world (perhaps a directional overlay or a mini-map is providing information). These are all parts of the information that is channeled from the game into the player.

Virtual interfaces can be described as the information the player receives that is not obvious just by looking at the game world. There are layers of information (also known as channels) that are separate from each other, but which coalesce in the consciousness of the player as the player shifts focus around a screen. There is a *what*, *when*, and *how* facet to these information channels:

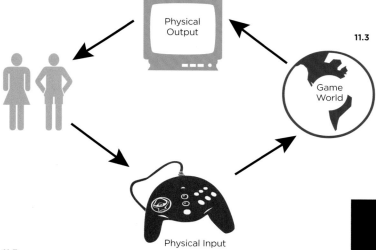

11.3

11.3
Physical and virtual interfaces.

11.4
Menus (such as this one from *Mass Effect*) also need to be designed as sparingly as possible because few players intend to spend much time in these interfaces. Charts, bars, and easy-to-understand stats (e.g., this gun is more powerful than that one but has less range) enable the player to make clear decisions and get back to the game.

11.4

CONSTRAINED
CHOICES

INTERFACE
DESIGN

INVISIBILITY
AND
FEEDBACK

INTERFACES
ARE COMMU-
NICATION

INTERFACE
TYPES

MAPPING AND
MODES

INTERFACE
OVERLOAD

AUDIO
DESIGN

INTERVIEW:
TYSON STEELE

CHAPTER
SUMMARY AND
DISCUSSION
POINTS

What: If the players can see they are in a dense forest, the interface does not need to say "You are standing in a forest," but it may need to tell them where they are in relation to other players or the level. The interface may be consistent in showing how much ammo or health the character has because these factors are always important to the player.

When: Does the player need this information constantly? If it's ammo or health—then the answer is probably "yes." But players may not need a constant reminder of which items they've picked up to use later. When do you give the player specific information, such as the position of enemies or items that are nearby?

How: The information must be delivered to players without interfering with their interactions in the game world. Do they need to pause the action to open the inventory? How much or how little information is the player comfortable with visually digesting? Are there elements that require overlaid interfaces (such as other screens) or can the player interact with parts of the environment directly?

The virtual interface is not just focused on what the player can see, but also what they can hear. If players are digging through their inventory system while another NPC is giving them important information that will impact their progress, the interface is getting in the way of the game. The best interface is one that feels natural to the player and one that is effectively "invisible" as an interface.

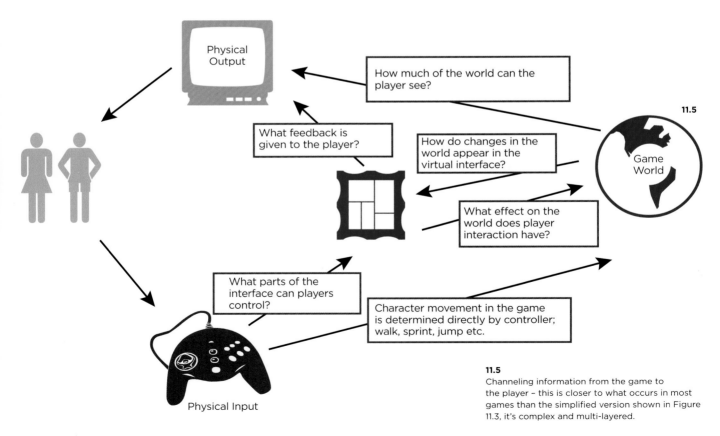

11.5
Channeling information from the game to the player – this is closer to what occurs in most games than the simplified version shown in Figure 11.3, it's complex and multi-layered.

223

INVISIBILITY AND FEEDBACK

The best interfaces go unnoticed. This is hard for designers, because you want players to marvel at every aspect of your game. The point is there are parts that should just work and not get in the way of the gameplay, and this is particularly true for interface design. This is where feedback communicated to the player is used. As outlined above, it is important to know what information to give the player and when. An example of limited feedback is an elevator button. When pressed you usually get some feedback, the little arrow lights up and then you have to wait, but you have no idea how long it will be before the elevator will arrive. There are numbers indicating what floor the elevator car is on, but essentially this is meaningless because the car may stall on a floor for what seems like an eternity. Other guests, even when they see the lit button arrow, will inevitably press the button again, even though we know this has absolutely no effect on the speed of the elevator. This is because the guests are given insufficient feedback on the progress of their elevator car. They will become frustrated when their actions are not responded to quickly, and then go on to believe there is something wrong with the equipment. A more useful interface is exemplified with pedestrian crossings in Europe and in North America. Some will light up with a "wait" sign as soon as you push the button and display the length of time until you can cross. A simple countdown prevents the frustration of multiple button pushes and impatience because the pedestrian is getting useful, updated feedback.

The general rule is you have 1/10 of a second to give the player feedback before they assume the game is in some way broken. Solid interfaces give players feedback all the time. As soon as they hit any key on the controller, something happens. The controllers are designed with sticks that can be pushed forward and back, so that even if players have no idea what the buttons do, if they waggle the sticks *something* will occur on screen. New players will tend to try the thumbsticks because they are analogous to levers in the real world. Levers are pushed and pulled and action occurs, and in a video game the character or spaceship will immediately move.

Interface Design Schemes

Getting the correct balance right is difficult. Games have specialized designers—called interface designers, or user interface (UI) designers—whose job it is to understand the problems inherent in interface displays, button customization, and control systems. Talking with students in my video game design courses, what has put many of them off playing a game is "anything that looks too complex" (this includes the controllers themselves; many consider the Super Nintendo Entertainment System to have had the ultimate controller because it was so simple). Players want to get into the game and start playing and then learn as they go, and because of this interfaces and controls have to feel intuitive and natural to players based on experiences they have had with other games or in the real world (buttons are pushed, handles are turned, etc.).

INTERFACES ARE COMMUNICATION

Metaphors are really useful when thinking about interfaces. If you have played more than one FPS in your life and see a small glowing green vial or white box with a red cross on it (itself a metaphor for health taken from the red cross or medical world), you are immediately going to know that this is a health pack. This is a video game convention and does not make any sense in the real world; instead, it is a visual metaphor. It is the same with character design: Men with pointy beards and arched eyebrows (like Jafar from Disney's *Aladdin*, 1992) are perceived as evil because we have been conditioned within the genre; see Chapter 4 for more on stereotypes.

The problem with video game metaphors as interfaces is they only exist within video games, so players who are new to the medium could struggle with the conventions (this

is what on-boarding and tutorials try to prevent). Metaphors are useful shortcuts for players to help them learn the conventions of the medium. So, for example, an inventory system that looks like a backpack the character wears helps the player understand the connection between an inventory screen of items collected and the world of the video game (for example, Joel's backpack in *The Last of Us*). The metaphor is not the same as a real-world backpack— the character may be able to carry a ridiculous array of items, unlike in the real world—but players understand the connection.

Metaphors are also used to convey complex systems simply. A visual metaphor may be used to convey information to a player; for example, a wall that has a crack in it that seems overly large or can only be viewed with switching to infra-red or "bat-vision"

(e.g., in the *Batman Arkham* series) suggests difference and therefore interaction. Interface metaphors of difference can also be used to denote climbable areas as opposed to ones that are inaccessible (e.g., *Tomb Raider*'s white scuffed climbable walls). These examples are all metaphors that eventually become learned behavior and conventions within not just one video game but many.

Menu and interface systems provide feedback for the player in other ways; no in-game character (or real life person) is going to talk to you about how close to the next level you are or how far through a level you have come. Instead, these tasks are provided in other areas of the game's interface and are accessible on demand so that the information does not get in the way of the gameplay.

11.6

11.7

11.6
In the parkour-inspired game *Mirror's Edge*™, players navigate an environment with areas inexplicably painted yellow. The yellow becomes the visual shortcut for "run here, it will enable a special ability," which would make no sense in the real world but is consistent and part of the rule set and mechanic of the game.

11.7
This is an example, from *The Last of Us*, of a clearly defined accessible area in a game that acts as contextual interface. The "caution" tape works in the context of the world—it would usually be employed to prevent falls—and in this case, it is used to mark out an area of difference that signifies interaction.

INTERFACE TYPES

Thematically, the interface needs to match with your game aesthetic, especially in menus and other information screens. This may seem obvious, but too generic an interface can break the player out of the game.

Diegetic Interfaces

Designers are always looking for more intuitive and embedded interface options; for example, the interface in the *Metro 2033* (4A Games, 2010) series is projected into the game's level and seen from the point of view of the character. This is known as a diegetic interface. Diegetic interfaces are incorporated within the game world. These forms of interface keep the player in the game and can add to narrative and immersion experiences. An example would be the "dark vision" power from *Dishonored*, which players use to highlight enemies and track them in the level. They are not a solution that will work with very complex inventory systems, such as leveling up and crafting. Dead space separates out those forms of interface into unique areas in a level, from suit to crafting/upgrading to inventory.

11.8
Metro 2033 uses a diegetic interface: The watch on the character's wrist measures how much oxygen the player has left.

11.8

Non-Diegetic Interfaces

These are what most people would call interfaces in the traditional sense. They are often overlaid onto the screen in games such as *World of Warcraft* where many options overlay the main action area. They are also used in games such as the *Mass Effect* franchise where the player exits out of gameplay completely to perform certain tasks, such as weapon load outs, leveling up, and so on.

Meta Interfaces

Meta interfaces overlay the world aesthetic to convey information to the player. A good example is the strawberry jam metaphor of blood splattering onto the player's screen as the main character takes damage. In a first person game, there is no body in view that can be used to visualize damage. So in games such as *Call of Duty: Modern Warfare 3* or the *Gears of War* franchise, red "blood" is splattered on the screen or red fades in from the sides to limit the field of view as a visual metaphor for taking a hit, bleeding out, and dying. Other forms of meta interface are informational graphics overlaid onto a scene, a mission objective, or titles.

Spatial Interfaces

Spatial interfaces break out of the game aesthetic but provide detail to players when they need it. An example is wayfinding systems, such as animated arrows that provide players with directional information based on their current objective (*BioShock: Infinite*, *Fable 3*, and *Tom Clancy's Splinter Cell: Conviction* [Ubisoft Montreal] all use these).

11.9a

11.9c

11.9b

11.9a
The Pip-boy interface in *Fallout 3* fills the entire screen and takes the player out of the active game. It has been designed to appear as a pseudo-diegetic interface, because it includes a blurred in-game background and the player character is modeled to be wearing the device.

11.9b
Another form of meta interface is information projected into the game space, such as in *Fallout 3*. This is an aesthetic choice as well as an interface design decision.

11.9c
This interface from *Mass Effect* is designed for a specific task and to convey specific information. While it takes the player completely out of the game, it is still aesthetically consistent with the game's design.

MAPPING AND MODES

Interface design involves mapping and modes. Mapping interfaces involves literally drawing or designing a sequence of events attached to every input and output of the player. Simply put, the map answers the question, "What happens when the player hits the 'A' button in this circumstance, or in that circumstance?" The simpler the interface and actions the player can do, the easier the map becomes. For example, multi-touch controls on smartphones or mobile devices have necessarily simple controls due to the nature of the hardware. They also use gestural controls in a way that console and PC games do not (for example, swiping across the screen to "cut" in *Fruit Ninja* [Halfbrick Studios, 2010]).

On top of the one-to-one mapping of buttons to in-game actions, there are modes. A mode is a contextual user interface that will change dependent on what the player is doing in the game. For example, the "B" button might usually make characters run faster, but when they go close to ladders, it allows characters to climb. If applied clumsily, modes can be confusing for the player because they have to reassess their relationship with the control scheme of the game when they come across one. Changing learned use behavior is tricky, but consoles have a limited set of buttons to use for a complex variety of actions.

Context is a useful and more elegant method of introducing mode changes. For example, when a player transitions from being a pedestrian to driving a car in an open-world game, the button map for *punch* could be remapped to *change gear*. Once outside of the car, the mode returns to its original use. This makes sense to players because the mode changes in response to their actions, and there is also a visual switch within the context of the game (walking versus being in a car).

11.10

11.11

11.10
Console controllers have a limited array of buttons, often with context-sensitive actions (one button does multiple in-game tasks). In-game tutorials and on-screen prompts ease the player into familiarity with the control system until the interface between player and game feels intuitive.

11.11
In *Skyrim*, the control system changes completely depending on the in-game context. For example, the buttons used for talking or fighting are remapped to perform tasks such as cooking when the player has entered the cooking mini-game context.

CONSTRAINED
CHOICES

INTERFACE
DESIGN

INVISIBILITY
AND
FEEDBACK

INTERFACES
ARE COMMU-
NICATION

INTERFACE
TYPES

MAPPING AND
MODES

INTERFACE
OVERLOAD

AUDIO
DESIGN

INTERVIEW:
TYSON STEELE

CHAPTER
SUMMARY AND
DISCUSSION
POINTS

INTERFACE OVERLOAD

When designing interfaces, designers have to be wary of giving the player too much or too little information. We can accept a certain number of information channels before becoming overwhelmed. This is the point at which the "signal to noise ratio" is high and we are forced to prioritize information. Designers avoid this kind of overload because it gets in the way of the gameplay.

Contrary to popular belief, we do not multi-task, we attention switch. We decide what is the most important and relevant information at any one point and absorb it. For example, when playing *Mass Effect 3* (Bioware, 2013), if an enemy is coming at the player, the player will focus less on the environment, cool level design, and what items are in the room and more on the threat, levels of ammunition, and health/protective shield level. If there is a lull in combat, the player can switch to looking for more health packs and ammunition and taking in the surroundings.

11.12
Codemasters' racing game *GRID 2* (2013) simplifies the interface elegantly, while still providing essential feedback such as speed and a map. The focal point of the car being a low-profile object helps in freeing up valuable screen space.

11.13
The quantity of information displayed in this interface for Paradox Interactive's *Crusader Kings 2* (2012) could be confusing to the uninitiated player.

TIP | VISUAL HIERARCHY

Designers are aware of visual overload and the attention-switching problem because they are taught about visual hierarchy. Visual hierarchy is a common tendency, when people are visually overwhelmed, to ignore the least visible in favor of the most visible. Thus, a person looking at a poster is going to notice the bright bold text and the good-looking model, but will probably not notice the smaller print or tagline. This is why level designers who have richly modeled environments have to make interactive or useful objects stand out. For example, there are a lot of crates and boxes in the *Assassin's Creed* games, but some have a cone of light over them. This difference draws players towards the object because it stands out in their visual hierarchy. Once a player has encountered this form of interface—the "glowing object"—they will seek it out in other areas of the levels because they now understand that metaphor of interaction. Any item that the player needs or should interact with must be at the top of the visual hierarchy. This can be done in an obvious way, as in *Assassin's Creed*, or more subtly, in games such as *Dishonored* in which interactive and non-interactive items are only differentiated when under the direct gaze of the character.

As with every aspect of video game design, the interface has to be thought out, planned, and iterated upon as soon as a prototype is up and running. Generic interfaces can be used in early versions to test the mechanics, but interface design needs to be thought out in all stages of planning and implementation. Video game designers tend to be very visually focused, which makes sense; however, another indirect form of interface and control system is audio design.

AUDIO DESIGN

Sound effects and uplifting musical scores create atmosphere and pathos to direct players' emotional states as well as to inform them of nearby objectives. The glowing *Assassin's Creed* treasure chests also have a light, yet discernible, audio attached to them. It is akin to an aural "twinkling," and it helps players home in on the location of the chest. Audio increases immersion when it works with the visuals and mechanics. Audio can also become iconic and live outside of the game world (for example, Mario's jump sound, or *Metal Gear Solid*'s detection exclamation point sound).

Sound designers add culture and psychology to their arsenal in the same way that visual designers do. In a horror game, it is a fair assumption that sounds of human suffering, particularly the crying of children, are going to affect the player emotionally. As with visual design, audio can be overused and, once the player becomes too aware of it or begins to expect a certain sound, the emotional resonance is lost. This is less true for positive sounds or music (such as the audio in *Mario* games), but an endless loop of even the most uplifting of sounds will grate after a while.

Sound as Manipulation

Manipulation has a negative connotation, but as we explored in level design and other aspects of game design, trying to create the best possible experience for a player involves coercion and manipulation. Games such as *Uncharted* or *Mass Effect*, which draw from action and science fiction tropes, use orchestral music to punctuate emotional or energetic peaks into a scene or cut-scene. Independent games may rely more on ambient music and sound effects to communicate a sense of place. This can be as simple as communicating the emptiness of an area by amplifying and echoing footsteps, as in *LIMBO* (Playdead, 2010), or using sound to subtly inform the player they are backtracking (previously visited rooms may sound different from new ones).

Audio can operate on several levels at once; for example, in a car chase or racing simulation, the audio designer may use high-paced music to encourage the player to drive faster. The more frenetic the music, the more intense the experience feels for the player. Audio cues can also steer players towards or away from areas in a level. Happier, upbeat sounds are going to establish friendly, "come stay a while" areas, whereas darker sounds may make players more apprehensive about going deeper into an area until they feel more powerful or have better equipment. Audio can change the mood of players without them even noticing. In *Fable III*, each city has a distinct soundtrack or *leitmotif*, a short loop of music that is associated with one character or scene (an example of *leitmotif* is the imperial march theme that is always played when Darth Vader makes an appearance in *Star Wars*). In the city of Bowerstone in *Fable II* and *III*, there is ambient music that has an upbeat, pleasant background, which is markedly different from other areas in the world. The music may go consciously unnoticed by players, but subconsciously they will be listening to this audio cue and react emotionally to it.

11.14
As well as being visually different, the towns of Bloodstone and Bowerstone in *Fable II* have very different audio aesthetics. The ambient noises and music exemplify the characters of these areas.

11.14

Sounds Design

We all know what a lightsaber sounds like; reams of *Star Wars* films and animations have given us the exact sound of this made-up weapon. It is the same for phasers in *Star Trek* or blasters in other science fiction films. Sound effects made by sound engineers make inanimate objects or fantasy items real.

Experimentation is important when designing sounds. It may be that the best sounds come from odd places in the outside world. For example, the iconic sound of Darth Vader's breathing is from sound designer Ben Burtt using scuba breathing equipment and putting the results through some filters. The sound of the lightsabers came originally from film projector motors. Creating a sound library is useful, as is having portable sound recording equipment.

Sound designers will record everything: firing guns, engine noises at different speeds, the countryside at different times of the year. In the same way that people know when a visual is off—if it does not look or feel quite right—so it is with audio too. Even if the player has never heard a Ferrari engine or fired a ray gun, there is an expectation for the sound to feel right within the context of the game world. Recording live allows for sounds to have their own distinct "voice" in the game. In film, you have real actors on real sets; in video games, all of the sounds have to be created for the game.

TIP | **FOLEY**

Traditionally, foley is the art of adding recorded sound effects to a movie after filming. It is also used in video game design, and the sound effects can come from the most unusual sources. Foley artists record sounds, usually in studios in order to get the cleanest possible sounds, and the sounds are then dubbed into games and films. Foley is most commonly used to create sound effects, such as closing doors, clinking plates, and footsteps. In a video game, foley can produce sounds that would be hard to capture in the real world. For example, a bone-breaking sound can be achieved by recording fresh celery being snapped, and "squishy" brains being mushed can be achieved by moving hands around inside a ripe watermelon.

Audio for Atmosphere

Ambient sounds in video games flesh out the world and make it complete. They extend the imagined world beyond what can be seen. Players do not need to know where the engines on a spaceship are, but if they can hear them, they know that they exist.

Ambient audio can prepare or prompt player action. It can forewarn players through distant but ever-closer sirens or helicopter rotor blades advancing on the player's position. What differentiates film and video game audio is that game audio can be interactive. Some players may never get to the scenario where sirens blare; the context of the game informs what the players may or may not hear. Sounds in the world outside of the immediate viewpoint of the player reflect the audio environment of the world and add immeasurably to the immersion. Interactive or responsive audio is used across many game genres, from sports crowds that cheer when the player scores to music changing when the player approaches a boss battle scenario. Creating an appropriate atmosphere for your game requires knowing your game intimately. Only you can know the sounds the world you have created will make, and getting them right requires time and iteration alongside the development of the game itself.

11.15

11.15
Every aspect of sound design works toward selling the game to the player. This is especially difficult when there is a real-world analogue, such as a human voice. Here we see Phil Simms and Jim Nantz incorporated into the *Madden NFL 13* game they voiced. The actors or commentators embody the on-screen characters to make them feel real to the player. Voice, sound effects, and music all align to create an immersive virtual reality that a player can get lost in.

INTERVIEW

PART 3:
SYSTEMS AND DESIGNING WORLDS

**CHAPTER ELEVEN
INTERFACE DESIGN AND
AUDIO DESIGN**

TYSON STEELE

User Interface Artist, Epic Games

Tyson is a developer, designer, and artist with experience in print and interactive media creation. His work is informed by a focus on the user experience and the elegance of procedural artwork.

You're a User Interface (UI) and User Experience (UX) designer at Epic Games. Can you explain what UI and UX design are in relation to video games?

"UI doesn't have the same cool factor as other parts of game development, such as animation or gameplay design, but it is a vital component of most titles and is often neglected for lack of staff, time, or recognition. UI can make or break a game, so the majority of my career has been devoted to fulfilling that role."

"In video game development, UI is just one component of a much larger field of user experience design. While UI is, in literal terms, just the set of menus and display elements that the player uses to navigate your game and understand vital information, UX considers the huge amount of secondary factors that affect usability, accessibility, motivation, and ergonomics. At Epic, our UX team is headed by Celia Hodent, who has a PhD in cognitive psychology. We employ extensive, in-house testing and iteration to refine our interface design."

What differentiates good UI design from bad UI design?

"In my interview at Epic, I was asked to describe the ideal UI with one word. My answer was 'invisible.' Good UI should serve the player when they look for it, but in most cases should not draw attention to itself for risk of breaking flow. How effectively your interface displays information and navigation without distracting from the core loop of gameplay should be the primary concern of design. 'Bad' UIs are typically difficult or tedious to use, distracting, or confusing."

As a UX designer, what are the most important aspects of the design to get right? How do you approach each project when thinking about UX design?

"Messaging to the player is usually the most difficult component of a successful UX design. Often the best place to start is in understanding your audience, their intentions, and experience level. Operations that a player performs repeatedly and in multiple contexts should be separated early on from more user-friendly, guided paths. Even if the core game loop contains mechanics of 'irreducible complexity,' crafting what is known in the social/mobile industry as a FTUE (First Time User Experience) may be the difference between a player staying around long enough to discover the depth of your game or giving up."

What advice would you give a new designer wanting to create positive, fun, or engaging experiences in the games they're working on?

"Drop the player into your world quickly. The idea of an 'elevator pitch' in game design is the expression of your core game loop and premise compressed into a few sentences. If we stepped into an elevator together and in that 20 to 30 second ride, you needed to convince me your project should, or better yet, MUST be made, what do you say?"

"Take that message and figure out how to deliver it to the player within a few minutes of gameplay. If the mechanics of your game are complex and engaging, tease at the depth without going all in. If your game is all about action, put the player right in the middle of it. If it's a sandbox experience, leave room for the player to craft their own narrative."

CHAPTER SUMMARY

Interfaces and sound complete the game design process. Get them wrong and the game is likely to fail. Designing the look and mechanic of the game and fixing them early on is a good idea, but when you ask how the player lives in your world, you also need to ask how your world sounds to the player. This could be the qualities of a character's voice or the way that sound informs players that they have achieved a new level in your game. Interfaces are a level of communication on top of the visual layer of the game and, like sound, need to be somewhat invisible and nuanced so that the player can use them without being taken out of the game space.

You now have a world with a mechanic, levels, audio, interfaces, and interaction. In Chapter 12, we will explore what is next for the game designer. What options do you have for marketing your game or using it to get noticed by others in the industry?

CONSTRAINED
CHOICES

INTERFACE
DESIGN

INVISIBILITY
AND
FEEDBACK

INTERFACES
ARE COMMU-
NICATION

INTERFACE
TYPES

MAPPING AND
MODES

INTERFACE
OVERLOAD

AUDIO
DESIGN

INTERVIEW:
TYSON STEELE

CHAPTER
SUMMARY AND
DISCUSSION
POINTS

DISCUSSION POINTS

1. Interfaces are one area of game design that many players overlook. Which game interfaces have worked the best for you, and which ones have not?

2. Taking a cursory inventory of a few recent games, or of very old arcade games, how does the interface go from being visible to invisible? How does the game designer achieve this?

3. How does audio affect your game experience positively or negatively? Examine and list some games that have well-crafted audio and some in which the audio (for whatever reason) gets in the way of the experience.

PART 3:
SYSTEMS AND
DESIGNING WORLDS

CHAPTER TWELVE
MONETIZATION,
COPYRIGHT, AND
INTELLECTUAL PROPERTY

12.1
The Last of Us Remastered, developed
by Naughty Dog (2014).

Chapter Objectives:

- **Understand funding models.**

- **Debate the pros and cons of working with publishers.**

- **Consider copyright and intellectual property issues.**

GETTING DOWN TO BUSINESS

In this final chapter, we will cover some of the business-oriented aspects of video game design. Whether you are interested in the crowd-funding model and digital distribution of your independent title, or planning to work for a game design studio that already has a publisher, this chapter covers some of what you need to know. The caveat is that this is not an exhaustive review: There are new financial models popping up almost every year (e.g., "freemium" and "free-to-play" business models are newer as successful models). The title you are working on may have multiple levels of stakeholders dependent on the property and no one business model will fit all titles. It may be that you are working on a licensed video game (for example, a video game based on the *Hunger Games* franchise) and, if so, there are going to be outside influences that exert control over your creative process. The licensed game may be part of a much larger marketing rollout, so deadlines may be tight, control over the actors' voices and portrayal may be restricted, and so on. The point is, whoever has input into the game and makes financial decisions can have a marked impact on the game itself, right down to the mechanic and aesthetic (for example, a publisher or marketing department may push the game to follow popular trends instead of allowing the game to evolve as the design team has planned).

Like any creative medium, video games follow trends and so do financial models. As of 2014–15, the free-to-play model is very popular; in 2011–12, there was a gold rush towards Zynga-style *Farmville* games (2009), with many industry experts calling Facebook and other social media platforms a viable gaming platform. Before that, the PC game format had been declared well and truly dead until its reanimation over the last eight years. Some companies have made a lot of money innovating on financial models (Riot Games, which created *League of Legends*, for example) but this can also create a "gold rush" mentality, with many other publishers and developers eyeing this trend as a sure-fire avenue for profitability. As with any creative endeavor, there is no one way of making money. There are risks involved on all sides, and as a designer you have to decide which model works best for your game.

When developing any video game (on any platform) there are two rules:

Rule 1: Make sure that what is best for your content stays ahead of what is best for your monetization model. Bad content is not going to sell well, no matter what financial model you use. Good content is likely to sell well regardless of the monetary model.

Rule 2: Make sure you have a financial model in place as soon as possible. Adding an in-game store or suddenly making the game free-to-play is as huge a change in development as changing the mechanic from first person shooter to platformer.

12.2

Licensed works such as *Back to the Future: The Game* from Telltale Games (2010) (on IOS platform) comes with obvious creative restrictions (or freedoms, depending on how you look at it). The characters have to sound and act like the movie characters and the world has to be consistent with the original. Players and fans alike will expect this. From a designer point of view, the financial risk is much lower because of the existing fan base and cultural attachment to the franchise.

12.2

UNDERSTANDING MONETIZATION AND FUNDING

Choosing the best business model for your game (how you are going to sell your game and hopefully make money) is not a straightforward enterprise. There is a distinction between what monetization is (how you are going to make money) and funding (what allows you develop your game). An example of a relatively new funding model is the recent raft of successful Kickstarter crowd-sourced video game projects. The game *Broken Age* by Double Fine Productions (2014) made history by raising the $3.3 million to fund their episodic game title through Kickstarter crowd-funding. This allowed the game development to get underway but created another issue for the studio—having to then figure out how much creating a video game costs. In the publisher-developer model, the publisher will fund a game's development up front until release, then recoup a large percentage of the game's eventual profits (usually around 30%). This means that the publisher is taking a large financial risk with the developer and is unlikely to fund anything "risky"—which is one reason for the many sequels to popular games.

What Double Fine did was become their own publisher—because publishers can have a significant impact on the creative process. The issue with publishers is that they are primarily focused on making money, not on the creative process. Understanding the finances of any business is difficult, so even though Double Fine is a studio with many years of experience in video game creation, they ran out of their Kickstarter funding money halfway through the development cycle.

TIP | THE DESIGN DOCUMENT

Chapter 2 covered design documents from the planning perspective; their other function is financial. If you seek a publisher for your game, you will need a very detailed design document. There are internal and external design documents (sometimes the external documents are called *technical* or *pitch* documents) and they go into detail not just about the game itself but also about the business plan, which includes market research, market analysis, financial costs, budgets, and timelines.

Once you have a document, you are going to have to pitch your game to the publisher; this means having a playable demo and working on a pitch presentation that focuses on persuading the publisher that your game is awesome, that you can really make it, and that it will sell. Design document and pitching is outlined further on this book's website **(www.bloomsbury.com/Salmond-Video-Game)**.

PUBLISHERS: A CATCH-22

Publishers are a divisive topic in the video game industry. At any game developer's conference, you will hear as many people deride publishers as praise them. The role of the publisher is to finance the development of the game, usually in two ways: funding a video game developer (known to the publisher as *external development*; for example, Sony Computer Entertainment publishing Naughty Dog's *Uncharted* series) or funding an internal developer (referred to as a studio; for example, Ubisoft developing and publishing *Assassin's Creed*). Publishers are also useful because they take on aspects of the game's distribution and marketing. They also deal with issues related to licensing (of an existing property or franchise) and console licensing (the amount you have to pay the console manufacturer just to have the game run on their hardware) as well as advertising costs.

Publishers do have input: They will manage and oversee the game's development as producers or project managers (these are not usually external people, but the project manager is going to liaise with the publisher). It is these people's job to monitor the progress of the game and to ensure milestones and deadlines are met. They will also give input on the development process, which may involve cutting or adding features based on financial decisions.

Publishers will usually advance money to external video game developers periodically when the developer reaches certain stages of development (milestones). The advantage of working with a publisher is that the designers will get paid regardless of whether the game does well or bombs. The disadvantages are in the input (when it is unwanted by the designers) and the percentage that the publisher takes of the profits from the external or internal studio (which are significant compared to self-publishing).

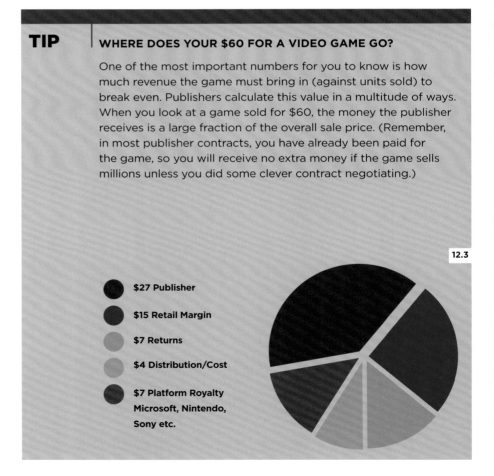

TIP | **WHERE DOES YOUR $60 FOR A VIDEO GAME GO?**

One of the most important numbers for you to know is how much revenue the game must bring in (against units sold) to break even. Publishers calculate this value in a multitude of ways. When you look at a game sold for $60, the money the publisher receives is a large fraction of the overall sale price. (Remember, in most publisher contracts, you have already been paid for the game, so you will receive no extra money if the game sells millions unless you did some clever contract negotiating.)

12.3

- $27 Publisher
- $15 Retail Margin
- $7 Returns
- $4 Distribution/Cost
- $7 Platform Royalty Microsoft, Nintendo, Sony etc.

12.3
Where the money goes.

GETTING
DOWN TO
BUSINESS

UNDERSTAND-
ING MONETI-
ZATION AND
FUNDING

PUBLISHERS:
A CATCH-22

GOING IT
ALONE: SELF-
FUNDING
AND CROWD-
FUNDING

MONETIZA-
TION MODELS

COPYRIGHT
AND
INTELLECTUAL
PROPERTY

CONCLUSION:
THANKS FOR
PLAYING

Before contacting publishers and pitching your game to them (If you get that lucky) know that there are some caveats to what you could be giving up:

1) *IP (intellectual property) rights.* As explained in the second part of this chapter, these are your ownership over your creative works. Sometimes a publisher will want full or part ownership over your IP. This makes sense for the publisher, because if the game is a break-out hit, the publisher can then control sequels, media translations (TV shows, novels, films, etc.), and merchandising. If you sign this over, you lose these potential income streams (sometimes referred to as residuals).

2) *Multi-game deals.* This sounds great; in these deals, the publisher is asking you to stay with them and make multiple games. However, if your game is a break-out hit and does really well, you cannot re-negotiate your terms for the next X number of games. So, essentially, if you get paid very little to make a game that does really well, you'll get paid the same to do the next two or three. Conversely, if your game does not do well, there is usually a get-out clause that allows the publisher to drop you, but not you to drop the publisher.

3) *Transparency.* Publishers are in the business to make money and are often very good at it. They also have contracts and lawyers and many tiers of producers and accountants. When you go into a contract with a publisher, you are always going to be on the back foot; they have all the advantage because they are going to fund your game.

If you get publishers to invite you to present (pitch) your game to them, be aware that they want to be excited and wowed by your game idea and professionalism. You need to prepare slick trailers and a playable demo as well as have all the costs and timelines worked out. The demo must look and play as close to a finished product as possible, even if it is only a few minutes of gameplay. Publishers are looking for something they can invest in and sell, and they do tend to be risk averse. Showing them a half-developed game with placeholder art assets, no sound, and no core gameplay is not going to bowl them over. This assumes that you get that far: The reality is that around 90% of games submitted to publishers (outside of the studios they already represent) get turned down.

This may sound overly negative, and not all publishers work this way. There has been much discussion in the industry to persuade publishers to change, and some certainly have. Good publishers build relationships with their developers and consumers as well as ensuring that all parties get along. As with any endeavor, being forewarned means that if you do enter into a negotiation with a publisher, you are doing so on a more even footing.

GOING IT ALONE: SELF-FUNDING AND CROWD-FUNDING

If you are a small team or a solo developer, getting a publisher to fund you is probably out of the question (although it worked out fine for Hello Games, creators of *Joe Danger* (2010) and *No Man's Sky*, (2015) and Thatgamecompany, who created *Flower* and *Journey*). Today, there are many potential routes towards getting your game funded by other people. The more popular methods are currently Steam Greenlight, Kickstarter, Indie Fund, and Steam Early Access.

Given how popular these funding models now are, your game idea really needs to rise above the noise to be seen by others. All these sites have a similar approach to getting you started. You'll make a video of your game (the prototype being played or a trailer) to get people interested, and you'll provide other materials, such as developer diaries, artwork, and so on. You are effectively pitching your game to the site's population. As a complete unknown, it is going to be harder to get noticed, but you are also pitching to a huge population of people who really, really love games and innovation.

Crowd-funding

For many independent developers, crowd-funding options have proved to be the best method to secure funding for their games. That is not to say that most indie developers give up their full-time jobs to create their games. Crowd-funding of an unknown (that is you) may not even reach its intended goal, and you, as the developer, need to keep pushing people with new content to make sure they get on board with your game. Because of the nature of video game development, Kickstarter has detailed guidelines for setting expectations among users, backers, and project creators. They have instigated a basic set of criteria for project goals and delivery. Creators are expected to explain the development process and where the backers' money is going but, as with publishing, the risk is still in the hands of the backers. If you do go the route of crowd-funding, realize that you are asking people to give their hard-earned money to you up front, based on your promise to deliver your game.

This means creating backer rewards and delivering them to deadline. From posters to T-shirts to naming rights—whatever the backers seem to be enthusiastic about. There is a very real responsibility to deliver on the promise of creating a deliverable video game. You have to be (and be seen to be) innovative, passionate, and dedicated in order to raise money and keep the backers on board with your game.

TIP | VENTURE CAPITAL FIRMS

Although usually associated with Silicon Valley startups, venture capital firms do take on video game studios in their funding portfolios. For example, Benchmark has funded the likes of Riot Games, Hammer & Chisel, and Gaikai.

Venture capital firms effectively "buy" their way into your company and will expect returns of 30% to 40%, depending on their investment (how much funding you received). The venture capital firm, like a publisher, will soak up a lot of costs by funding you, but unlike a publisher, it will rarely get involved in creative decisions. These firms also understand that there is risk involved and that your game may not sell well enough to recoup their investment.

GETTING
DOWN TO
BUSINESS

UNDERSTAND-
ING MONETI-
ZATION AND
FUNDING

PUBLISHERS:
A CATCH-22

**GOING IT
ALONE: SELF-
FUNDING
AND CROWD-
FUNDING**

MONETIZA-
TION MODELS

COPYRIGHT
AND
INTELLECTUAL
PROPERTY

CONCLUSION:
THANKS FOR
PLAYING

Self-funding

Self-funding is another option. This might come from savings, loans (be *very*, *very* wary of this option), or the "bank of mom and dad." If the game is a labor of love and you do not have to pay anyone to do it (assuming your team agrees) then, obviously, your costs will be minimal. Equally, the chances are good that your development time is going to be years, not months (Tom Francis, interviewed in Chapter 8, took two years to develop *Gunpoint* while working full-time as a video game journalist). All of the crowd-funding sites have detailed information on how to submit; some (like Steam Greenlight) charge a fee to submit while others take a cut from funded projects (Kickstarter takes 5% from the final funding amount). To get

more information on these processes, the documentary *Indie Game: The Movie* (2012), directed by Lisanne Pajot and James Swirsky, is a crash course in the struggle to launch a successful video game. You can also read developer diaries from Double Fine that take you through the trials and tribulations of their Kickstarter campaign.

Even if you have a fully funded game, that funding will only cover creating the title; you also have to think about making money once the game is sold. Currently, the arguably most open platform for independent developers is the PC and the Steam or GOG online stores. The advantage of PC is that no one company owns the hardware to

insist on QA technical requirements or to demand licensing rights just for having the game run on its platform. The PC can be easier to develop for and there are far more tools, free and paid, available from which games can be created. In the last few years, the PC platform has become the *de facto* independent game developer choice.

MONETIZATION MODELS

The main issue with making money from your game is that there are many other factors outside of just how much it costs that can affect the game's performance. Best-selling games combine marketing, game press interest, visual appeal, launch date, sound technical mechanics, and easy-to-use monetization options. Even so, there is no formula for success, as Kate Flack (EA) said in an interview with *Gamasutra* (Rose, 2013):

"Everyone seems to be looking for an off-the-peg solution to monetization – a one size fits all silver bullet that will lead them to profitabilityville. This idea that there is one 'right way to do things' is a fantasy."

Just because game X has made a fortune through the free-to-play model, doesn't necessarily mean that's the right option for your game. Also, giving away a first game to "build the brand" can sometimes be successful, but then there is the problem of consumer expectation in reaction to that: "Your last game was free, I don't want to pay for your games." Most games on the Android and Apple app stores make very little money on average (approximately 1.5% of people who download free games put money into them). So what are the options? There are many, and below I have explored some of the more recent innovations in monetization models.

12.4

12.4
The MMO *Guild Wars 2®* (ArenaNet®, 2012) is purchased in the traditional way (disk or download) and also contains in-game purchases or micro-transactions that are available to players. *Guild Wars®* also has a player marketplace for trading in-game items. This hybrid model is contentious but has proven popular among developers because they are able to recoup their development costs with the sale of the game and then cover ongoing costs through micro-transactions.

GETTING
DOWN TO
BUSINESS

UNDERSTAND-
ING MONETI-
ZATION AND
FUNDING

PUBLISHERS:
A CATCH-22

GOING IT
ALONE: SELF-
FUNDING
AND CROWD-
FUNDING

MONETIZA-
TION MODELS

COPYRIGHT
AND
INTELLECTUAL
PROPERTY

CONCLUSION:
THANKS FOR
PLAYING

Free-to-play (F2P) and Freemium

Free-to-play works just as you would expect; there is no "entrance fee." Instead, you offer in-game purchases for players to finance the game and pay for its continued development or update. Free-to-play is not an entirely new model, but it is very popular, especially in the genre of MoBA (multiplayer online battle arena), with titles such as *Dota 2* and *League of Legends*. The issue with F2P is that although it has proven to be an incredibly successful revenue stream for some games, fans have tended to attach themselves to one game and do not seem to move around much.

The issue for developers is that the revenue stream has to be planned out and built into the entire design process. With a retail game, you put the finished title up for sale on a platform such as Valve's Steam, and then people (ideally) give you money to cover your costs and expenses. F2P creates another level of work in creating items for players to buy through some form of in-game store; you also need analytics to track which player has which item and who has paid for what. You will probably need some form of player exchange hub, too; players like to trade or sell items in-game or in external stores, and so on.

This makes the game creation process much more complex and requires additional planning and testing. The upside is the F2P audience is far more likely to play your game simply because it is free and people like free stuff. Once you have them playing your game, you need to make sure they also buy into it and purchase items to cover the development and ongoing costs. Because of this, as a developer you have no end-of-game. The game has to last as long as it can to maximize profits, as well as be updated regularly so it does not become stale for the player base. Many F2P games have short play times to increase player buy-in. Games created for mobile devices have play times of a few minutes whereas most *Dota 2* or *League of Legends* matches are around 40 minutes to an hour. With F2P, it's not about length of play; it is all about the player coming back on a regular basis until playing becomes a habit.

F2P games do tend to have a broader audience than console- or PC-based solo games. Although the examples I gave of the MoBAs are very popular, so too are the multitude of F2P mobile games and web-based games. These games can come under the wing of so-called casual games (a contentious term because it draws a line between game players based on the types of games they play). The casual audience is incredibly broad, with younger, older, and more female players who you, as a designer, have to learn to engage with. This factor alone could influence your interfaces, the aesthetic, and the mechanic of the game. F2P games tend to be social. That is how they are marketed: Players are actively encouraged to invite others to play via a socially connected device such as a smartphone. This recruitment strategy is made that much easier because the game is free, so there is no costly barrier to entry for the invitee. Many mobile and online-only games take advantage of the social graph (players connected to players) to increase the numbers of converted customers. This is as true for *DayZ* as it is for *Candy Crush Saga* (King, 2012).

12.5a

12.5b

12.5a

Hearthstone (Blizzard Entertainment, 2014) is
a F2P virtual card game that also has micro-
transactions as its monetization. It is seen as a
casual game because most games last less than
an hour, but players can also play for much longer
to really master the game. The micro-transactions
are used to buy different card decks and entry
into arenas. The card game taps firmly into the
collector mentality that many players may have
experienced as younger baseball card collectors.

12.5b

In the F2P game *League of Legends*, player skins
cost a few real-world dollars to purchase. Some
of the skins bring special abilities, while others
are primarily cosmetic. The character Fiddlesticks
was given a birthday skin conceived by the
player community. F2P games need continued
community support to thrive because players
become ambassadors for the product.

GETTING
DOWN TO
BUSINESS

UNDERSTAND-
ING MONETI-
ZATION AND
FUNDING

PUBLISHERS:
A CATCH-22

GOING IT
ALONE: SELF-
FUNDING
AND CROWD-
FUNDING

**MONETIZA-
TION MODELS**

COPYRIGHT
AND
INTELLECTUAL
PROPERTY

CONCLUSION:
THANKS FOR
PLAYING

The F2P genre has several different monetization considerations:

Co-marketing: An example of co-marketing would be asking players to register on another website, which then pays you for the traffic you drive to it.

In-game advertising. Advertisers pay you to have their ads in your game or on your website for the game. This is tricky because advertisers are most likely to give you money if you can prove a base of players exists for them to advertise to. Therefore, this does not work as a development stream, but once the game is up and running it can be worth it to seek it out—that is, as long as the ads are not too intrusive and do not interfere with the gameplay.

Freemium. Although similar to F2P, there is a model of Freemium that encourages subscribers. Once players have subscribed (monthly, weekly, etc.), they receive access to more content or a more complete version of the game than what is available free.

Restricted access. This is not a very popular option, and it could be said to have started as long ago as 1992, with *Wolfenstein 3D* (id Software, 1992), whose first level was available on a floppy disk. You could play this first "teaser" level as much as you wanted to, but to get the full game, you needed to purchase it. Restricted access can also apply to paying to get into multiplayer, higher level attainment, and so on.

F2P is a viable model for some, but there is a lot of upfront expense that goes into creating a 'free' game. There is a lot of effort that goes into creating layered enticements, in-game monetary systems, and rewards (hats are apparently a big thing), so you need to be fairly certain of being able to recoup your game development costs when giving away a game for "free." Even the big publishers get F2P wrong (for example, Mythic Entertainments' *Dungeon Keeper* for iOS, 2013) and fickle players who are getting content for free have arguably less buy-in to a franchise when something new comes along.

12.6
There are different approaches to in-game advertising; some mobile games can be intrusive while other games use product placement as a revenue source. In this example, T-Mobile is placed well on screen in *Tony Hawk: Ride* from Robomodo (2009).

12.7

12.7
The free-to-play, browser-based game *Fallen
London* (Failbetter Games, 2009) can be
played completely for free. Players can speed
up elements of gameplay by using real-world
currency and buying upgrades if they wish. *Fallen
London* is a very community-based game that
balances the freemium model and making money
against annoying or alienating its player-base
(many games annoy the player continuously with
micro-payment options).

GETTING DOWN TO BUSINESS

UNDERSTANDING MONETIZATION AND FUNDING

PUBLISHERS: A CATCH-22

GOING IT ALONE: SELF-FUNDING AND CROWD-FUNDING

MONETIZATION MODELS

COPYRIGHT AND INTELLECTUAL PROPERTY

CONCLUSION: THANKS FOR PLAYING

Early Access

The early access model was essentially how Double Fine got out of their financial predicament after their Kickstarter funding for *Broken Age* ran out halfway through development. Rather than go to an outside publisher to finance *Broken Age* (and potentially lose control of their title), they released the first episode on the Steam store and used money from the sales of Part One to fund the development of Part Two.

Not all early access developers charge money for access to their game. It really depends on how much game they have to offer and how much more game there is to make. Early access as a proposition is seen by some as a "pay-for-a-demo" model. In effect, what used to be a free ad for a game to persuade you to buy it has now been labeled as "early access" and may incur a cost. This is not necessarily a problem; if the player who pays for the game is aware that they are playing an unfinished title that is still in development and needs more funding, then it is a case of caveat emptor (buyer beware). For some titles, such as *DayZ*, early access has proved to be incredibly successful as a funding model for development. Players have two roles: they fund an early version of a game they find interesting and they also provide incredibly useful feedback, finding bugs and all forms of emergent gameplay, which is passed on to the developers to improve the game.

Due to the success of early access, Steam have updated their rules and guidelines in an attempt to balance the expectations between a player paying for early access and a developer who is trying to build a game. Essentially, Steam wants to ensure the game's designers understand that early access must blossom into a final, finished game and dissuade designers from making promises to players that may never come to fruition, such as multiplayer or co-op features that are unlikely to be implemented. There are also some telling warnings from Valve's experiences, such as not relying on early access as a funding model, being consistent in how you talk about your game across media, and making sure the game is actually playable.

Once you have a funding model and financial model in place, you must think clearly about protecting your creative intellectual property. One of the most pressing issues in the mobile games market is that of "clone" games. Although you may have created the next innovation in gaming, you need to be aware of how to protect your game from those who would copy it. This is not a simple process, and copyright law has become increasingly complex because of the Internet and the ease of "cut and paste" game creation.

12.8
DayZ was released in Alpha stage in December of 2013 as early access, and it has proven incredibly popular for a game that was essentially unfinished. Open "sandbox" style games in which gameplay is emergent seem to do well using the early access model. Players can find their own paths, exploring the game's rules as well as being able to make their own.

12.8

COPYRIGHT AND INTELLECTUAL PROPERTY

Copyrights, patents, trademarks, intellectual property (IP), and other important legal issues are a book in themselves. Based on my years of teaching game design to undergraduate and graduate students, the one area I will focus on is copyright and IP. When a student gives me a new game to play, one question I ask is, "How much of this game is yours?" None of my students would ever knowingly rip off someone else's work and present it as their own; instead, my question is nuanced in asking them to think about how much of the game is their creation in totality. Did they borrow some code from a website or art from an asset store? Perhaps they used a few icons or textures from a Google image search. If so, did they get the correct licensing agreements or permissions to use these assets in their game if they decide to sell it? This might seem a small detail, but if they have ignored this, the student is operating in a gray copyright area (even down to the fonts they have used in the interfaces).

What Is "Original"?

An extreme example of copyright infringement is taking an existing game, swapping out some art assets, and then pushing it as a new game (known as *rebadging*). If you have created a platformer video game in the style of a *Mario* or *Super Meat Boy* (Team Boy, 2010), but with its own mechanics and art assets to bring something new or different to the genre, that is original. You are building on what has gone before. That game would be a *derivative*, a game within a genre with original content and execution. No one owns exclusive rights to the platformer mechanic or the FPS mechanic. There is no copyright on genres like action or assassination-based gameplay— but there are copyrights on the games *Hitman* (IO Interactive) and *Assassin's Creed*.

There Was No © , So Can I Use It?

When creating assets for your game, do not assume that because code or artwork is online and there is no © next to it, it is not in copyright. Laws on how copyright is established vary from country to country. In the USA, as soon as any idea/creation is fixed in some medium (i.e., not just in the creator's head), it is held in copyright. So if someone has written code on a website and has not given you specific permission to use it, and you use it, you could be subject to copyright infringement. There are plenty of gray areas in copyright law, and the law is finding it hard to keep up with the changes in digital technologies.

If you are at all unsure about elements of your game, then the surefire answer is to seek some form of legal counsel, which may be expensive up front but will save a lot of money should you get into legal wrangling further down the line. By the same extension, when you have created a legitimately new intellectual property (your new video game), you also want to be able to defend it from being cloned by others. To do this, you need to make yourself aware of the copyright laws in your country as well as any country the game is going to be distributed to (in essence there is no international copyright law, but many countries, such as the UK and US, have legally binding agreements on how to deal with infringers across borders).

GETTING DOWN TO BUSINESS

UNDERSTANDING MONETIZATION AND FUNDING

PUBLISHERS: A CATCH-22

GOING IT ALONE: SELF-FUNDING AND CROWD-FUNDING

MONETIZATION MODELS

COPYRIGHT AND INTELLECTUAL PROPERTY

CONCLUSION: THANKS FOR PLAYING

If in doubt of the legality of any assets in your game, ask the original owner for permission. Even if this means parting with some money, it could save headaches later. There are people who have created Creative Commons and open source works that you can use under certain (very open) permissions.

You may even want to talk with members of your team about ownership of aspects of your game. If, for example, the lead artist wants to sell merchandise containing drawings from your game, would that be acceptable? As always, it depends. It is very hard to write up contracts among friends, but on the other hand, there are many friendships and businesses that have fractured because of a lack of legal contracts. Video game design is a business. As in any design practice, you do not have to be aggressive or offensive; a professional approach will prevent heartache and unwelcome scenarios from the outset.

Another way to think about copyright and permission issues is that you, too, are creating a video game, which others may want to blatantly rip off (or politely borrow from) one day. That should make you think about how you approach your creative process.

12.9
An overview of the US copyright system and your rights to your work. This is a very simplified version, and the copyright system has not kept up with the digital world very well. As always, it is well worth looking deeper into intellectual property rights for yourself.

12.9

Copyright ©

The exclusive rights given to an author or creator of an original work 📖

The author/creator has the right to:

 Reproduce the work in any manner or form.

 Publish the work.

 Include the work in other media formats.

 Adapt the work.

Original works fall under copyright protection for 50 years.

Works are protected from the date first made public or published.

If not published or made public, from the end of the year of the death of the author.

Copyright is an automatic right; there is not a requirement to register for copyright.

CONCLUSION: THANKS FOR PLAYING

Thank you for reading to the end. You now have all of the knowledge and conceptual background you need to start making your first video game. Learning how to play as a designer—analyzing what games are and how they are built—empowers you to see past the entertainment factor and study the building blocks of video games. You now better understand industry methodologies, approaches to thinking about video games, and how to implement those processes. From here on out you can get to grips with creating worlds, levels, characters, and interfaces and know to avoid clichés and negative stereotypes. You will also be better informed when making decisions regarding funding models and monetization. As with any design practice, you have to begin the process by thinking and acting professionally. Knowing how to protect your game and build relationships with other team members is an important part of that. As you move towards a prototype game that is ready to launch, you also need to focus on your own community, getting the word out, and making sure other people are as excited about your game's development as you are.

GETTING
DOWN TO
BUSINESS

UNDERSTAND-
ING MONETI-
ZATION AND
FUNDING

PUBLISHERS:
A CATCH-22

GOING IT
ALONE: SELF-
FUNDING
AND CROWD-
FUNDING

MONETIZA-
TION MODELS

COPYRIGHT
AND
INTELLECTUAL
PROPERTY

CONCLUSION:
THANKS FOR
PLAYING

Remember, these days anyone can make video games—in the same way that anyone can make music. The problem is that there are a lot of bad songs and bad video games out there. What makes a difference is having the passion and drive to create a really good game. Your passion also needs to be balanced by a willingness to work hard, put hours into research and revision, and establish critical thinking methods. Most importantly, you need to acquire the ability to listen to others. As a designer, the ability to listen to others—your mentors and your peers—will serve to elevate your creative output. Seek input and feedback all the time, and remember that ultimately the game is yours to discover and make.

So, go make your first game, which will be terrible. Then make your second one, which will be much better. And then your third, which will be great. Good luck!

References

Rose, M. (2013), "Understanding the Realities of Video Game Monetization." *Gamasutra*, December 22. Available online: http://www.gamasutra.com/view/news/205412/Understanding_the_realities_of_video_game_monetization.php

FURTHER RESOURCES

Industry Standard Software for Non-programmers

Adobe Gaming SDK (Adobe Software): Adobe Gaming software development kit (SDK) brings together Adobe Flash, Flash Builder, and Adobe Scout to enable the creation of multi-platform games from desktop to browser or mobile. Flash was the industry leader for many years as a platform for creating browser-based games and still has a huge community with a plethora of online resources. Some of the most-played games in the world were created using Adobe's gaming SDK, most notably *Farmville* 2 from Zynga.

Game Maker Studio (www.yoyogames.com/studio): Game Maker Studio was developed specifically with the non-programmer in mind. It has a "drag and drop" programming interface that enables users to create simple games easily and then build more complex games as they become more proficient and get "under the hood." Tom Francis used Game Maker Studio to create *Gunpoint* and he is using it to create his new game, *Heat Signature*. Tom has also created a YouTube series of tutorials on Game Maker Studio (http://goo.gl/E0wnHR).

Game Salad (www.gamesalad.com): Game Salad runs on Mac OS and Windows OS and is designed to make creating games for the web and mobile easy and fun. The application focuses primarily on mobile and web-based games but can output to a variety of platforms. It has a drag-and-drop "programming" for real-time physics and game behavior systems. Arguably the biggest game to come out of Game Salad is *The Secret of Grisly Manor* (Fire Maple Games, for iOS & Android).

RPGMaker (Enterbrain Inc.): As the name implies, this is a development toolkit specifically focused on making role playing adventure games (RPGs). It offers a tile-based engine usually associated with game styles such as the *Dragon Quest* series (Armor Project) or *Final Fantasy*, but the software can be used to make a variety of different RPGs or narrative-based games. A notable game from RPG Maker is *To the Moon*, from Freebird Games (2011).

Unity Game Engine (unity3d.com):
Unity is a cross-platform game development system that has free and paid versions. The free version enables developers to output games to Mac, PC, and the web. It is a robust and affordable game engine for all levels of developer. (*Gone Home* was created in this engine.)

UnReal SDK (Epic Games; www.unrealengine.com): The UnReal engine is an industry standard game engine used to create games such as *Gears of War* and *Batman: Arkham City*. The game development software is available free. The UnReal engine is not as immediately easy to use as Unity, but it is a game engine that AAA title developers use. UnReal does offer some tutorials, although they tend to be technical (https://udn.epicgames.com/Three/VideoTutorials.html).

Open Source (Free) Tools and Communities

3DS Max, Autodesk Software: 3DS Max is an industry standard 3D modeling, animation, and programming application. It is widely used in the video game and film industry. It has been used on *Halo 2*, *Rock Band* (Harmonix, 2007), *Fallout 3*, and *Far Cry 2* (Ubisoft Montreal, 2008). As with Maya, is it free to students for non-commercial use.

Cinema4D, Maxon Computer; Blender 3D (www.blender.org): Blender 3D is a free 3D modeling and animation tool (used by Cardboard Computer to create the game *Kentucky Route Zero*). Cinema 4D is arguably an easier tool to use for those getting started in 3D modeling and animation. It has a free version for students and educators (for non-commercial purposes) and is a bridge between basic modeling software such as SketchUp and the more high-end and daunting applications such as Maya. Cinema4D was used to create assets for *Viva Pinata* (Rare, 2006) and cinematics for *Syndicate* (Starbreeze Studios, 2012).

Google SketchUp (and Pro), www.sketchup.com: A free and easy-to-use 3D modeling application. For video games, its most common use is in creating quick prototypes of environments or levels. Robh Ruppel, art director at Naughty Dog, used Sketchup to conceptualize the look and feel of the game *Uncharted 2* (see http://www.sketchup.com/case-study/uncharted-2).

Maya, Autodesk Software,
www.autodesk.com/products/maya
Much like 3DS Max, Maya is an industry
standard 3D modeling and animation
package used in the video game, film,
television, and architecture industries.
It has been used to create assets
for series such as *Grand Theft Auto*,
Madden, and *Halo* (among many others).
It is available free to students and for
non-commercial use.

Unity3D offers an in-application store
where you can download (some free,
some not) models, characters, textures,
and materials to use in your game.

There are a huge number of websites
offering similar assets for all budget
levels (for example, archive3d.net, and
Unity's own community, http://goo.gl/
KlJJjX).

There are also communities and forums
such as Blender's (http://www.blender
.org/support/).

Further Reading

A Casual Revolution: Reinventing Video Games and Their Players. Jesper Juul. 2012

Better Game Characters by Design: A Psychological Approach. Katherine Isbister. 2005

Character Development and Storytelling for Games. Lee Sheldon. 2013

Chris Crawford on Game Design. Chris Crawford. 2003

Game Feel: A Game Designer's Guide to Virtual Sensation. Steve Swink. 2008

Game Usability: Advancing the Player Experience. Katherine Isbister & Noah Schaffer. 2008

Get in the Game: Careers in the Game Industry. Marc Mencher. 2002

Half-Real: Video Games between Real Rules and Fictional Worlds. Jesper Juul. 2011

Interactive Storytelling: Techniques for 21st Century Fiction. Andrew Glassner. 2004

Morphology of the Folktale. V. Propp & Laurence Scott. 1968

Pause & Effect: The Art of Interactive Narrative. Mark Stephen Meadows. 2002

Reality Is Broken: Why Games Make Us Better and How They Can Change the World. Jane McGonigal. 2011

Sex in Video Games. Brenda Brathwaite. 2013

Sketching User Experiences: Getting the Design Right and the Right Design. Bill Buxton. 2007

The Imagineering Workout Paperback. The Disney Imagineers. 2005

Theory of Fun for Game Design. Raph Koster. 2013

Understanding Comics: The Invisible Art. Scott McCloud. 1994

Websites You Should Know

D.I.C.E. (Design, Innovate, Communicate, Entertain): dicesummit.org

Eurogamer.net

Extra-credits.net

Feministfrequency.com

Gamasutra.com

Game Developers Association, Conference Video Vault: gdcvault.com

Gamepolitics.com

Gamestudies.org

International Game Developers Association (IGDA): www.igda.org

Polygon.com

Rockpapershotgun.com

COMMON INDUSTRY TERMS

80/20 rule (aka Pareto principle): 80% of the work goes into 20% of the game (Pareto principle states that 80% of the effects come from 20% of the causes).

Agile development: Solutions to design problems evolve through collaborations, cross-disciplinary teams, and self-organization.

Alpha: Stage of the process where core functionality, art assets, and gameplay are implemented, often first milestone stage.

Beta: All features and assets of the game are complete, only final QA, bug testing, and code fixes remain.

Buttons and rainbows: Used often in games such as *Candy Crush*, insignificant interaction from the player produces large aesthetic and psychological reward.

Chopping wood: Melee/fighting combat that feels reductive and boring.

Code freeze: No new code is added to the game, only bug corrections are made; occurs close to final shipping date.

Code release: Code is fixed, quality assurance (QA) has released game as working, and game is sent for manufacturer review.

Core pillars: The mechanics and assets that are core to the game (jumping, sneaking, magic spells, etc.) and from which the game evolves.

Crazy quilt: An environment with far too many textures and/or art assets that is overwhelming. There is no unifying theme or tone.

Crunch time: All hands on deck working on meeting a milestone or other publisher deadline.

Data wrangler: Person who tunes the gameplay based on character types, items, or systems in the game.

Design grenade: A "solution" implemented by someone that, when implemented, causes ripples of destruction in the wider game build.

Down the rabbit hole: Pursuing all possible outcomes of a game scenario or change to the game and its implications.

Engine gremlins: When something that was working magically breaks for no apparent reason.

Failing upwards: High-profile individuals getting promotions over more deserving people just to get them out of the way of hurting the development process.

Fat finger: Breaking a game's build by accidentally deleting/mistyping code.

Feature creep: Unplanned (and unbudgeted) features are implemented in a game through subtle and mostly unofficial means (i.e., programmer just decides the game needs X and implements it).

First playable: Prototype game version that contains assets, mechanic, and gameplay that represent the overall game.

Flavor (in-game art): Posters, graffiti, interactive items that add depth or "realism" and back-story to the game environment (posters in *BioShock*, graffiti in *Portal*, etc.).

Flavor text: Background text inside or outside of game (e.g., *Skyrim*'s books, text on the box art for the game describing game's scenario).

Frankenbuild: Parts of a game, its code, or assets that were never supposed to be put together that kind of work yet are pretty ugly to look at.

Going gold/Gold master: Testing is completed and the game is ready to go out for general release.

Grinding: Describes the tedious aspects of game development (also tedious actions in a game).

Grok/grokking: To understand a problem or scenario thoroughly.

Hello, Monster moment: The encountering of bad design decisions, like marketing people who want the game to copy trends. ("Can we put in multiplayer? That's hot right now," is a Hello, Monster moment.)

High level: An idea that is too conceptual and usually unspecific.

Idea guy: Person who buys into the myth of ideas being more important than working on the game itself.

Ivory tower: Usually derogatory term for academics; in the video game industry, refers to those higher-ups and decision makers who hand down decrees from on high.

Janky: When something (art or mechanic) does not look or work correctly.

Localization: Translation of the game for foreign markets (voice acting, subtitles, or cultural tropes).

Milestones: Usually set by the publisher, these are major events during the development process used to track progress.

Nerfing: Reducing power of in-game assets or characters in an attempt to balance a game quickly.

Palate cleansing: Used in pacing the game, breaking the player out of the main gameplay to do something else before coming back to the core game (for example, exploring the landscape or hunting in *Far Cry 4* before going back to the main mission quests).

Quacking duck/Misdirection: Adding something obviously aesthetically displeasing to a game build to give execs/marketing something to focus on and have an opinion about, distracting them from focusing on the actual game.

ROI: Return on investment.

Sacrificial lamb: Developers add something to a game deliberately knowing management/marketing/executives want to feel powerful by taking at least one element from a game.

SCRUM: Project management, a flexible all-encompassing development strategy where the development team works as a whole towards a common goal (programmers, script-writers, sound, art direction, etc.—all together).

Shelving point: Knowing the game might have a point at which the player stops playing and never returns to the game.

Showstopper: Major bug that comes to light when a game is ready to move to gold status.

Tardis effect: When artists design an interior space that is bigger than the exterior.

Tech pimping: Making the game and mechanic look good for a demo even though the game itself may barely work.

Trade show demo: Readying a playable demo of the game (as well as other marketing materials, such as posters and video trailers for a major tradeshow such as E3 or PAX).

More industry terminology can be found in *A Game Studio Culture Dictionary* compiled by Kain Shin, 2011. http://www.gamasutra.com/view/feature/134872/a_game_studio_culture_dictionary.php.

INDEX

INDEX

INDEX

McLees, Rob, 132

Mechanic-Dynamic-Aesthetic (MDA) model, 82, 86, 92

Mechanics, 13, 49

Media Molecule, 9, 135, 196–197, 198, 214

Menus, 52

Meretzky, Steve, 137

Meta-games, 207

Meta interfaces, 227

Metal Gear, 212

Metal Gear Solid, 19

Microsoft Flight Simulator, 36

Middle-earth: Shadow of Mordor, 202

Milestones, 117

Minecraft, 96

Mirror's Edge, 7, 224

"Modding," 48

Modes, 228

Modular models, 188–190

Mojang, 96

MolyJam game jam, 81

Monetization, 241

Monetization models, 240, 246–251

Monolith Productions, 202

Monopoly, 112

Mood boards, 146–147

Motivations of character, 134

Movie genres, 86

Multi-game deals, 243

Multi-User Dungeons (MUDs), 67, 68

Multilateral competition interaction pattern, 112

Multiplayer games, 15, 19

Multiplayer online battle arenas (MOBAs), 66

Multiple individual players versus game interaction pattern, 112

Murray, Jill, 132

N

Namco, 25, 129

Names, 138

Narrative emotional event trigger, 89, 92

Narrative video games, 97

Naughty Dog, 34, 96, 98, 167, 179, 183, 239

Necrosoft Games, 80

Negative stereotypes, 76, 77

Neuroticism trait, 70–73, 89

Nintendo 64, 56

Nintendo Entertainment System (NES), 33, 56, 60, 76, 78, 107

Non-diegetic interfaces, 227

Non-player characters (NPCs), 32, 53, 88, 145, 146, 168, 209, 223

Non-violent games, 76

Nordhagen, Johnnemann, 102

Novelty domain, 71–73

O

Objectives of play, 29, 37

Occlusion culling, 184

OCEAN model, 70–74, 83

OCEAN Personality Test, 73

Oh, Deer!, 81

On-boarding, 105, 172, 211–212

On-screen prompts/hints, 210

Open world "sandbox" games, 32

Openness trait, 70–73

Outcomes of play, 29, 36

Overdraw, 184

P

Pac-Man, 25, 129

Pacing, 59, 91, 97–101

Pajot, Lisanne, 245

Paradox Interactive, 229

Personality, 134

Personification, 134

Pikmin, 78

Pimentel, Victoria, 114

Planning, 111, 128

Platform-based games, 33, 49

Play

    Bartle's taxonomy of, 67–69

    definition of, 16

    importance of, 14

    new models for new forms of, 66

    rhetorics of, 17

    rules of, 29, 32–35

Player archetypes, 74–75

Player engagement

    aesthetics and player navigation, 178–181

    arc, scene, and action, 100–101

    designing into games, 96–101

    engagement curves, 100–101

    First Order Optimal Strategies, 54–55

    interest curves, 96–97

    modular models and textures, 188–190

    pacing, 91, 98–99

    silhouette design, 192–193

    sizing and field of view, 182–185

    wayfinding systems, 186–187

Player interaction patterns, 112

Player motivation, 71–73

Player numbers, 112–113

Player path, 166–169

Player resources, 29, 38–39

Player types, 67–69

Player versus player interaction pattern, 112

PlayStation controllers, 50

PlayStation Mobile games, 81

PlayStation Mobile platform, 81

"Point and click" games, 48

Polygon budget, 118

Polyphony Digital, 202

Pong, 25, 45

Portal, 111, 202

Portal 2, 202

Portnow, James, 54, 60–61

Positive feedback, 209

Positive reinforcement, 208

Post-production, 117

Powerups, 39

Pre-planning, 110

Preparation phase, 110–111

Priming, 36, 53, 168, 195

Production, 41, 117

Production testing

    focus groups, 122

    game testing, 21

    initial feedback, 121–122

    practical approaches to, 124–125

INDEX

PICTURE CREDITS

Cover image: *Kentucky Route Zero* courtesy Cardboard Computer

0.1 Courtesy Electronic Arts Inc. *Mirror's Edge*™ is a trademark of Electronic Arts Inc. and its subsidiaries

1.1 *LittleBigPlanet*™ ©2008 Sony Computer Entertainment Europe. "LittleBigPlanet," "LittleBigPlanet logo," "Sackboy," and "Sackgirl" are trademarks or registered trademarks of Sony Computer Entertainment Europe. All rights reserved

1.3 *WipEout HD*, Sony Computer Entertainment

1.4 *Viva Piñata*, Microsoft Studios

1.5 *Call of Duty*®: *Modern Warfare*® *3*, Activision Publishing, Inc.

1.6 *Halo 2*, Microsoft Studios

1.10 *Metal Gear Solid 4* ©Konami Digital Entertainment B.V.

1.11–1.13 *Canabalt* screenshots and photos by Finji, Copyright 2009

1.14 *Gravity Hook* screenshots and photos by Finji, Copyright 2009

2.1 *Kentucky Route Zero*, Cardboard Computer

2.2 *Mass Effect*™ *3* Courtesy Electronic Arts Inc. *Mass Effect* is a trademark of Electronic Arts Inc. and its subsidiaries

2.4 *Call of Duty*®: *Black Ops II*, Activision Publishing, Inc.

2.5 *Gears of War 2*, Microsoft Studios

2.6 *Resident Evil 5* ©Capcom Co., Ltd. All Rights Reserved.

2.7 *Gone Home*, Fullbright

2.8 *Forza Motorsport 5*, Microsoft Studios

2.10 *Resident Evil 4* HD, ©Capcom Co., Ltd. All Rights Reserved.

2.11–2.14 *Kentucky Route Zero*, Cardboard Computer

3.1 *Gone Home*, Fullbright

3.2 *Madden NFL 25*. Courtesy Electronic Arts Inc. The mark "John Madden" and the name, likeness and other attributes of John Madden reproduced on this product are trademarks or other intellectual property of Red Bear, Inc. or John Madden, are subject to license to Electronic Arts Inc., and may not be otherwise used in whole or in part without the prior written consent of Red Bear or John Madden. All rights reserved.

3.4 *Forza Motorsport 3*, Microsoft Studios

3.5 *Sleeping Dogs*, Courtesy Square Enix

3.6a *Batman: Arkham Origins* image used courtesy of Warner Bros. Entertainment Inc.

3.6b *Call of Duty*®: *Modern Warfare*® *3*, Activision Publishing, Inc.

3.7a *Dead Space*™ Courtesy Electronic Arts Inc. Dead Space is a trademark of Electronic Arts Inc. and its subsidiaries

3.7b *Resident Evil 4* HD ©Capcom Co., Ltd. All Rights Reserved.

3.9 *Mass Effect*™ Trilogy and *Mass Effect 3* Courtesy Electronic Arts Inc. Mass Effect is a trademark of Electronic Arts Inc. and its subsidiaries.

3.10 *Extra Credits* YouTube Channel, James Portnow/Rainmaker Games LLC

4.1 *flOw*, Sony Computer Entertainment

4.8 Getty/James Braund/D. Sharon Pruitt, Pink Sherbet Photography

4.9a *Grand Theft Auto V* screenshot Courtesy of Rockstar Games, Inc. All Rights Reserved. No part of this work may be reproduced in any form or by any means—graphic, electronic, or mechanical, including photocopying, recording, online distribution, or information storage and retrieval systems—without the written permission of the publisher or the designated rightsholder, as applicable.

4.9b *Journey*, Sony Computer Entertainment

4.10 *Shadow of the Colossus*, Sony Computer Entertainment

4.11 *The Elder Scrolls V: Skyrim*® ©2011 Bethesda Softworks LLC, a ZeniMax Media company. All Rights Reserved.

4.12 *Fallout*® *3* ©2008 Bethesda Softworks LLC, a ZeniMax Media company. All Rights Reserved.

4.13 *Gunhouse*, Necrosoft Games

5.1 *Final Fantasy XIV: A Realm Reborn*, courtesy Square Enix

5.3a *Dishonored*® ©2011 ZeniMax Media Inc. All Rights Reserved.

5.3b *Tomb Raider*, courtesy Square Enix

5.6 *Geometry Wars: Retro Evolved 2*, Activision Publishing, Inc. *Everyday Shooter*, Sony Computer Entertainment

5.7 *Fallout*® *3* © 2008 Bethesda Softworks LLC, a ZeniMax Media company. All Rights Reserved.

5.9 *The Elder Scrolls V: Skyrim*® ©2011 Bethesda Softworks LLC, a ZeniMax Media company. All Rights Reserved.

5.12 *Uncharted 2: Among Thieves*, Sony Computer Entertainment

5.13 *God of War II*, Sony Computer Entertainment

PICTURE CREDITS

5.14 *Kentucky Route Zero*, Cardboard Computer

5.15–5.17 *Gone Home*, Fullbright

6.1 *GoldenEye 007: Reloaded*, Activision Publishing, Inc.

6.2-3 *Resident Evil* 5 © Capcom Co., Ltd. All rights reserved.

6.4 *Titanfall*™, courtesy Electronic Arts Inc. Titanfall is a trademark of Respawn Entertainment LLC. Courtesy Electronic Arts Inc.

6.5 Multi-path narrative sketch, Victoria Pimentel

6.6 *Halo 3*, Microsoft Studios

6.8 Draft art assets, Victoria Pimentel

6.9 *The Diaries of Professor Angell; Deceased*, Michael Salmond

6.10 *The Walking Dead*, Telltale Games

6.11 *Diablo 3* ©2014 Blizzard Entertainment, Inc. All rights reserved. Diablo, Blizzard, Battle.net and Blizzard Entertainment are trademarks or registered trademarks of Blizzard Entertainment, Inc. in the U.S. and/or other countries.

6.12 This screenshot is from DayZ game and was used with the permission of Bohemia Interactive a.s. DayZ mod is created by Dean Hall. ©Copyright Bohemia Interactive a.s. All rights reserved

6.13 *Gone Home*, Fullbright

7.1 *Tomb Raider*, courtesy Square Enix

7.2 *Halo 3*, Microsoft Studios

7.3 *Batman: Arkham Origins* image used courtesy of Warner Bros. Entertainment

Inc.

7.4 *Gomo*, courtesy Daedalic Entertainment GmbH

7.5a *Fallout: New Vegas*® ©2010 Bethesda Softworks LLC, a ZeniMax Media company. All Rights Reserved.

7.5b *LittleBigPlanet*, Sony Computer Entertainment

7.6 *Tomb Raider,* courtesy Square Enix

7.7 *Gomo*, courtesy Daedalic Entertainment GmbH

7.8 *The Elder Scrolls IV: Oblivion*® © 2006 Bethesda Softworks LLC, a ZeniMax Media company. All Rights Reserved.

7.9 *Rumble Roses XX* ©Konami Digital Entertainment B.V.

7.10 *Dead Island*, Koch Media

7.11a *The Walking Dead*, Telltale Games

7.11b *The Last of Us*, Sony Computer Entertainment

7.12 *Gomo*, courtesy Daedalic Entertainment GmbH

7.15 *The Elder Scrolls V: Skyrim*® ©2011 Bethesda Softworks LLC, a ZeniMax Media company. All Rights Reserved.

7.16 Moodboard images courtesy Getty Images, Hinterhaus Productions, Jeffrey Coolidge, Andrew Kornylak, Maria Luisa Corapi, Buena Vista Images, Science Photo Library, Mike Harrington, Willie B. Thomas

7.17a *Army of Two* Courtesy Electronic Arts Inc. Army of Two is a trademark of Electronic Arts Inc. and its subsidiaries.

7.17b *Tomb Raider*, courtesy Square

Enix

7.18 *The Lighthouse and the Lock*, courtesy James Fox

8.1 *Gears of War 3*, Microsoft Studios

8.2 *The Elder Scrolls V: Skyrim*® ©2011 Bethesda Softworks LLC, a ZeniMax Media company. All Rights Reserved.

8.5–8.6 *Gomo*, courtesy Daedalic Entertainment GmbH

8.9 *Dead Space 2* courtesy Electronic Arts Inc. Dead Space is a trademark of Electronic Arts Inc. and its subsidiaries

8.12a *Gears of War 3*, Microsoft Studios

8.12b *Uncharted 3: Drake's Deception*, Sony Computer Entertainment

8.14 *Fallout*® *3* ©2008 Bethesda Softworks LLC, a ZeniMax Media company. All Rights Reserved.

8.15–8.17 *Gunpoint*, courtesy Tom Francis

9.1 *The Elder Scrolls V: Skyrim*® ©2011 Bethesda Softworks LLC, a ZeniMax Media company. All Rights Reserved.

9.2a *The Last of Us*, Sony Computer Entertainment

9.2b *God of War III*, Sony Computer Entertainment

9.5 *Uncharted 3: Drake's Deception*, Sony Computer Entertainment

9.8a *Fable II*, Microsoft Studios

9.8b–9.9 *The Elder Scrolls IV: Oblivion*® © 2006 Bethesda Softworks LLC, a ZeniMax Media company. All Rights Reserved.

9.16a *Fallout*® *3* © 2008 Bethesda

ACKNOWLEDGMENTS

A big thanks to all who participated in the making of this book.

My contributors:
Tom Francis, Adam Saltsman, Jake Elliott, Tamas Kemenczy, Ben Babbit, James Portnow, Brandon Sheffield, Steve Gaynor, Kate Craig, James Fox, Rex Crowle, Kareem Ettouney, Kenneth Young, Tyson Steele, and Victoria Pimentel.

A dedication:
This book is dedicated to the memory of Terrence W. Salmond, 1933–2014.

Much thanks to Jacqueline Salmond for so much support and proof reading, Georgia Kennedy for being an extraordinarily understanding editor, and Katie Greenwood for chasing down all those image permissions.

The publisher would like to thank:
Albert Chen, Arturo Sinclair, Tom Sloper, James Thompson, Chris Totten, and Simon Reed.